CLINTON

★ ★ ★ ★

YOUNG MAN IN A HURRY

CLINTON

★   ★   ★   ★   ★   ★

YOUNG MAN IN A HURRY

BY JIM MOORE
WITH RICK IHDE

THE SUMMIT GROUP
FORT WORTH, TEXAS

Published by The Summit Group
1227 West Magnolia
Fort Worth, Texas 76104

*Library of Congress Cataloging in
Publication Data*

Moore, Jim.
    Clinton, Young man in a hurry/
    Jim Moore, Rick Ihde.
    P. cm.
    ISBN 1-565-30-006-8

    1. Clinton, Bill, 1964—Biography.
2. Presidential candidates—United States—
Biography. 3. Presidents—United States—
Elections. I. Ihde, Rick. II. Title.

E840.8.C5M6 1992   937.927
                            QBI92-574

Jacket design by Rishi Seth
Jacket photograph by Cynthia Johnson/*TIME
MAGAZINE*
Photographs courtesy of the Arkansas
governor's office and Robert Mellhorn, the
Clinton for President Campaign, Virginia
Kelly, and the author.

Manufactured in the United States of America
First Printing 1992

To the memory of
N. O. Kenner, my great-grandfather
and the wisest man I ever met;

And to Ricky, Lori, and Julie Ihde

CONTENTS

★   ★   ★   ★   ★   ★

PREFACE

★　　　★　　　★　　　★　　　★　　　★

I first met Bill Clinton during my weeklong foray to Arkansas Boy's State on a hot summer morning in 1976. Clinton had been defeated two years before in an ambitious and overreaching bid to unseat Arkansas' lone Republican congressman, John Paul Hammerschmidt. Now, in the nation's Bicentennial year, without Republican opposition in November, he had just effectively won the post of Arkansas' attorney general.

Some of my best friends in high school had campaigned for Clinton during his battle to unseat Hammerschmidt, and I had been enraptured hearing them speak of this new sort of Democratic wunderkind. I had seen and heard him speak late in the '74 campaign and watched in blank amazement as—in three short minutes—he turned a tired and listless Russellville audience into an enthusiastic, cheering crowd. To say that I was anxious to meet Clinton in person was an understatement. During his speech to several hundred teen-aged boys gathered in the University of Central Arkansas' Old Main auditorium, Clinton stressed the value of a solid education and pointed to our own interests in political careers as a hopeful sign for the future.

During the question-and-answer session which followed Clinton's talk, someone in the crowd addressed a hot topic—whether the investigation of the assassination of President John F. Kennedy should be reopened. Of course, the issue was one of considerable importance to me, and I was gratified when Clinton responded that he felt that a new inquiry was justifiable and called for, given the inconsistencies which then surrounded the case.

After the questions from the audience had subsided, I seized the opportunity to rush to the stage to shake Clinton's hand and ask for his autograph. I was particularly struck by Clinton's ability to communicate effectively, whether in small groups or in front of a large gathering. He was—and is—a very personable young man, gifted with an extraordinary memory and a supreme appreciation of the adulation of those he serves.

Over the years, my contacts with Bill Clinton became almost regular. During the presidential campaign of 1976, I corresponded with him several times regarding my efforts to help elect Jimmy Carter. Clinton was the chairman of Arkansas' Carter campaign, and I recall being impressed by his warm response to my letters. In 1977, after he had been elected attorney general, I called Clinton to ask his advice about running for a vacant Russellville, Arkansas, school board seat. "Don't do it unless you really want it," I was told. Later that fall, as he launched his first campaign to become governor of Arkansas, I met Clinton at several whistle stops. A photo he inscribed to me at one of those meetings—in December 1977 at Arkansas Tech University, where I was a student—still hangs in my office today, a reminder of a time in my life when my interest in politics was more passion than passive.

In 1980, having felt betrayed by Jimmy Carter, I switched allegiance to the Reagan camp and aided the Republican cause as best I could despite a heavy class load and long hours working at a local radio station. My one political inconsistency, however, was in backing Democrat Bill Clinton in his bid for reelection as governor of Arkansas. Like most Arkansans, I expected that Clinton would have no difficulty beating his little-known Republican challenger, Little Rock businessman Frank White. Confidence turned to dismay on election night, when—despite my happiness over a Ronald Reagan victory—I watched White surge ahead to wrestle the governor's mansion away from Bill Clinton.

To those of us who were immersed in the Arkansas political scene, Clinton's loss was unbelievable. Today, having learned that Arkansas is nothing if not an unusual place, I can understand Frank White's victory much more easily . But in the fall of 1980, the shock took several days to wear off. When it had, I sat down and wrote the governor a long letter in which I maintained what the state's leading newspaper was saying— that Clinton's loss was Arkansas' loss as well.

The governor responded with a kind note. "Thanks for your fine letter," he wrote in his spidery handwriting. "Perhaps we'll have another day." Some days later, an invitation arrived to join the governor and his wife Hillary at a farewell reception at the mansion in Little Rock.

I put on my best suit—not much of one at the time—and with a stunning redhead named Jennifer DeFrancisco on my arm, drove to the state capital on the appointed Sunday afternoon. After wringing Bill's and Hillary's hands, gaping at the magnificence of the governor's residence, and jostling with hundreds of other guests for refreshments, there was little for Jennifer and me to do but drive the hour and a half back to Russellville. Before we left, the governor handed each of us a small card, and asked us to write down our names, addresses, and phone numbers. "Maybe next time," Clinton intoned, "we'll use the darned things."

To my surprise, I came to like Clinton's successor. Perhaps my growing affection for Frank White was due to encroaching maturity and a deep-set sense of conservatism. My new wife and I found ourselves spending a fair amount of time at Republican fund-raisers in 1982—and because I was news director for a pair of radio stations, Frank White cultivated my friendship. The "next time" Bill Clinton had spoken of two years before was happening around me—and I was on the other side of the political fence.

As nearly all Arkansans expected, Bill Clinton, contrite but purposeful, won his rematch with Frank White. Clinton's loss and subsequent triumph are topics for discussion in the body of this book. Suffice to say, however, Frank White's defeat in the fall of 1982 marked for me the first time I had sat on the wrong side of the political arena.

Ten months later I left Arkansas, embarking on a career with Texas-based Success Motivation Institute. Except for a year's leave of absence from SMI—during which I returned to Arkansas to manage the two radio stations I had worked for previously—I have been an outsider to Arkansas politics,though looking in with cultivated interest.

My contact with Bill Clinton has, over the past few years, been sporadic at best. Until I began this book, I had not spoken with him in more than five years. But, like most Southerners, I have watched his career from afar. To say that I have been impressed by Bill Clinton would be a vast understatement. I have not, however, been surprised by him.

That sense of awe—there is no other word for it—and my own innate curiosity propelled me to seek out this project and to write this book. I have never intended to create an industry out of my humble writing talent. That fact is borne out by the vexed attitude with which I approached my first work, a book on the Kennedy assassination. Convinced that the American public had not heard the other side of the story, I set out to tell it. When Conspiracy of One was being edited for publication, thoughts of writing another book were quite literally the furthest thing from my mind.

My second book, which deals with the Gene Simmons mass murders in Arkansas, was a product of an interest and curiosity I had held since the crimes were committed around Christmas 1987. Since my wife and I and so many of our closest friends lived in the epicenter of those events, it seemed to me that the subject lent itself to my style of writing. That book, incidentally, is scheduled to be published shortly after this work appears in print.

On the other hand, I was—and remain—awed by the necessity for a candid look at Bill Clinton. Given the continuing economic downturn and the fickle nature of the American voting populace, the man could well be our next president. Six months ago, that was an unthinkable prospect. But now, with the Democratic nomination appearing solidly within Clinton's grasp and the sliding popularity of the current president, we must at least address the possibility that come 1993 we might be led by a man most of us know little about.

Hence, this book. It is, to be sure, not an overly sensational or overly critical look at Bill Clinton. I freely admit my admiration, respect, and affection for the candidate. I am, on the other hand, a Republican. It is my hope that the overall tone of this book approaches something of a middle ground.

Bill Clinton is, like most of the rest of us, not perfect. Nonetheless, having lived in Arkansas, I have been a witness to the changes he has wrought in state and local government. I think it fair to say that if Clinton can do what he has done in as inhospitable a political climate as Arkansas, he can fairly work miracles in Washington, D.C.

And, in my estimation, we need a miracle worker. The problems which face us are numerous, pressing and exceedingly difficult. Bill Clinton, if elected, would bring to bear new ideas, a grand vision, and surprising energy. It seems to me that, Democrat or Republican, the person elected president in 1992 must possess those characteristics.

I am certain that my more vocal critics will charge that this book is an attempt to curry a political favor from Bill Clinton. Let me lay that thought to rest by presenting two considerations worthy of note. Rick Ihde and I, aided by Arkansas State Senator Lu Hardin, did present our credentials (and our friendship with the governor) to his staff and requested that the campaign authorize this book. Such an authorization was not forthcoming. Rick and I made the decision to proceed with the project without the tacit endorsement of the Clinton for President campaign. If this book is published bearing the campaign's endorsement, readers should note that approval was given after the manuscript was completed and not before. Neither the prospect of an endorsement nor the actual authorization itself changed the tone of the book.

Secondly, I am quite content to spend the rest of my life as a Texan. I daresay Kathy and I would be quite ill at ease in the nation's capital. Some post there would justifiably be considered a reward of sorts should Clinton be elected president. The governor can live there alone for all we care. Should he lose the race for the White House, our immediate return to Arkansas is equally out of the question. Candidly, neither of us, although we grew up in Arkansas, would consider moving back in the forseeable future. Rick Ihde can make his own decisions, but as for me, there's very little in the way of reward that Bill Clinton could bestow, even if he were so inclined.

Of course, there will always be those who will contend otherwise. To those individuals, I issue a challenge to wait and see for themselves. If they remain unsatisfied, bad cess to them.

This book is written in a half dozen parts, and the first chapter — which recounts my days traveling with the Clinton for President campaign — actually parallels the last, which focuses on what Bill Clinton might do if elected chief executive. The second and third chapters deal with Clinton's childhood, education, and early political career, as well as his first term as governor, his defeat by Frank White, and the rematch campaign that ensued.

The chapter "Years at the Helm" details month by month Clinton's continuous tenure as governor from January 1983 to the present day. Rick Ihde and I wanted to present a running account of Clinton's accomplishments in Arkansas. Along with the position statements and the appendix to this book, the governor's track record is, in reality, the only tool by which readers can judge Clinton's probable success or failure in Washington, D.C.

With a tumult of media attention circling around the governor's wife, I thought it prudent to include a brief chapter on Hillary Rodham Clinton. To be sure, this chapter is not the definitive Hillary biography, but I hope it serves as a quick primer on this impressive woman who, if current ecconomic conditions remain constant, may become our next first lady.

Bill Clinton's strongest commitment has always been to education, hence the chapter which focuses on his accomplishments in that arena. Of all the concerns which preoccupy this country today, most have their roots in problems with the educational system. There is, therefore, an intense need for a sense of how Clinton might improve our ailing national school systems.

The last chapter is a summary of Clinton's positions on vital issues and his attitude toward the presidency itself. As an appendix, I have reproduced the three speeches Clinton has given over a period of some months at his old alma mater, Georgetown University. As the appendix title indicates, careful study of those addresses will do much to show all of us how Bill Clinton has evolved as a politician.

A last note: In his inaugural address in January 1977, President Jimmy Carter—the last Democrat I supported, save for Bill Clinton—candidly told Americans that the time for racial discrimination was over. Fair enough. Today, 15 years later, it seems to me that the time for partisan politics must come to an end as well. The only way we as Americans can move from the shadows of our past and into the promise of our potential is to work together for the common good and to leave old political divisions behind us. It follows that Bill Clinton is one of the few politicians in modern times to attempt to do exactly that. In writing this book, I have chosen to follow his lead.

I cannot gaze into some magical crystal ball and determine to my own satisfaction whether Bill Clinton will win the Democratic Party's nomination and the White House. I do find it difficult to believe that, even as a Republican, I could work against his election in the fall. Whatever happens at the Democratic National Convention and in November, Bill Clinton will land on his feet, ready and willing to face the challenges that lie before him. If he and Hillary aren't packing for a move to Washington, D.C., a year from now, it won't be because he didn't try.

Jim Moore
Fort Worth, Texas
January 1992

ACKNOWLEDGMENTS

★   ★   ★   ★   ★   ★

For the authors, this book has been a whirlwind of deadlines, details, interviews, and research. The demanding schedule was necessitated by our desire to place the book on the market prior to the Democratic National Convention. We were, however, always mindful of the need for attention to detail. This biography is as accurate as we can make it.

For the simple fact of this book's existence, we have several individuals to thank. First is Arkansas State Senator Luthur B. "Lu" Hardin, who has been our friend for many years. Senator Hardin arranged our initial interview with Governor Clinton's trusted friend, Bill Bowen, who is serving as Clinton's Chief-of-Staff. During that meeting, we presented the idea for this book to Bowen. Our intent was to request that this work be authorized by the campaign. We communicated this desire to Mr. Bowen, who then transmitted it through the campaign organization. At the time these acknowledgments were written, that authorization was still in abeyance. Whether we eventually receive it will not affect either the content or the production of this book.

Mr. Bowen, a Little Rock banker of long standing, was certainly gracious and kind. We walked away from the governor's office convinced that, in Bill Clinton's absence, the state was in good hands.

The staff of the Clinton for President campaign office in Little Rock has been most helpful, responding to our requests for information and interviews with great rapidity and understanding. We especially want to thank Terry Wolf and Dave Bauxbaum for all they have done in our behalf. What the Clinton organization lacks in precision it more than makes up for in enthusiasm and dedication to a cause. We deeply and sincerely appreciate its help.

Thanks to Joyce McCain at the Tomlinson Library on the Arkansas Tech University campus for her help in locating and utilizing research materials. Our appreciation goes as well to Scott Morris, a former Arkansas Gazette reporter who worked the capital beat, and helped us with much of the legwork required in Little Rock. Much of this book was written via long distance. We are grateful for Scott's help and professionalism.

We are grateful to Mr. and Mrs. Clinton for their friendship over the years, and for their willingness to contribute to this book. Similarly, we appreciate the efforts of the governor's unsung biographer, Dr. Charles Allen, whose doctoral dissertation was an invaluable resource for us.

A special thanks to Jim Moore's publicist, Johnny Heard, who assisted in scheduling interviews, obtaining photos and source material, and managed Jim's talk show schedule to allow him time to research and write this book. Johnny is a true professional, and we appreciate his effort and willingness to help with this project.

Thanks to Mark Hulme and The Summit Group, without whom this book would not have been written. We are grateful for the support of an eager, enthusiastic publisher, who shares with us the sense of urgency and accuracy which has driven this effort.

Finally, thanks to our families—to Jim's wife Kathy and to Rick's three children—for their patience, understanding, acceptance, encouragement and love. In completing this book, we have both discovered that these five qualities are priceless and worth treasuring when they are offered.

Jim Moore & Rick Ihde
February 1992

1

STALKING THE WILD
NOMINATION

★   ★   ★   ★   ★   ★

As you lean closer to the airplane window, you suddenly realize that most of a presidential campaign — unless you are the candidate — is tedious waiting. Already today you have spent six hours strapped to this same first-class seat; its gray leather has molded itself to the contours of your body. You glance at your watch; the time is nearly 10 p.m. You know that before you can sleep tonight, you will spend another two hours in flight and an hour getting to your hotel room. Tomorrow, of course, you will begin again — another day just like today.

Beside you sits a man named R.G. Ratcliffe. R.G., as his friends call him, is a reporter for a major Texas newspaper. Across the aisle, two newsmen from the British Broadcasting Corporation sit side by side, talking quietly. Because they are not among the cameramen scattered near the airplane's ramp, their day is almost over — as close to over as it can be when you are a few thousand miles from home.

R.G. is talking state politics while you watch the dismal New Orleans night sky spraying more rain onto the tarmac. It has been raining all day, from this morning's fund raiser in

Jackson, Mississippi, through the fund raiser in Alexandria, Louisiana, during the trip to the State Capitol at Baton Rouge and all during your brief two-hour stay in New Orleans. You stare into the night and wonder if the rain will ever end.

It's not that you are trying to avoid a conversation with R.G.; rather, you are heartily fed up with the topic. Today has been nothing but politics, politics, politics. Yesterday was the same. Tomorrow will be just like them. You wish for ten minutes in which to savor the lack of a political thought.

Two rows back, you hear Gene Randall from Cable News Network calling his Washington bureau to let his employers know where he is, where he will be going, and when he will get there. This morning, in Jackson, Mississippi, Gene had the unfortunate experience that sooner or later befalls every network news reporter on the campaign trail. When his network came to him live for an interview with the candidate, the candidate was not there. The fact that CNN was broadcasting around the globe did not help Randall's situation. He bore the brunt of his employer's displeasure, and tonight it shows in his black mood.

Like you, most of the writers and reporters on this plane have been standing, running, walking, and wading through the rain all day long. Your clothes cling to you, but the forced ventilation system on board the aircraft is quickly drying them. The flight attendants and the pilots—this 50-passenger jet has two of each—are the only ones who are still relatively dry. As they pass through the cabin taking drink orders, they look as though they had just stepped out for some sort of parade drill. The reporters in the plane, on the other hand, look for all the world as if the parade has run over them.

But if you have it bad, the cameramen out on the tarmac have it worse, for they can do nothing but stand in the driving rain. Like you, they are waiting for the candidate to leave the warm, dry sanctuary of the airport terminal, walk briskly to the waiting ramp, and climb the stairs to board the aircraft. At each city—Jackson, Alexandria, Baton Rouge, and New Orleans today—the cameramen film the candidate each time he enters or leaves his aircraft. Each time he touches new ground or leaves it, the cameramen are there to record every hurried movement. Here, on the tarmac in New Orleans, they have been waiting about 20 minutes. They will wait another five minutes before the candidate emerges.

On the aircraft, you are listening to media consultant James Carville, who holds forth with a running commentary on the way in which the press has handled stories regarding the candidate's private life. "This guy is the best damned candidate I've ever seen," Carville tells you and the others alongside. "And you print this...stuff," he adds, obviously searching for the right word. He ends his diatribe by calling the recent news articles and reports "the 'crack' of journalism," pointing out the addictive power such pieces represent for both the press who produce them and the public who read them.. Although you agree with Carville, you are careful not to let your anger show. Many of the members of the fourth estate sitting alongside you will zealously defend what they do, and you do not want to broach an argument with any of them. It has been a long enough day already.

As you glance back out the airplane window, you see TV camera lights suddenly snap on. Because you are only four rows back from the forward bulkhead, it is difficult to see the candidate as he exits the airport terminal and heads up the ramp. But even though all you can see are the camera lights, you know what is going on. The same scene is repeated several times each day every time the candidate climbs down or up the ramp. When the airplane stops, the cameramen hop out quickly, setting up their equipment on the tarmac while the candidate remains in his seat, waiting until the photographers are ready. This is the sort of carefully-staged affair that seems somewhat humorous to the candidate. Knowing that every entrance and exit is an arranged affair often makes him smile at inappropriate times. Back in Arkansas, he drove his own car and traveled on commercial flights, while the press generally left him to do it without undue attention.

In the main cabin, everyone seems to sit up a little straighter as he enters the aircraft. It isn't that the reporters are seeking his approval; rather, you and everyone else aboard know that this man is at the center of boiling controversy, and his mere presence is quite an attention-getter. The only reporters who do not respond as Bill Clinton enters the first-class compartment are those who are already asleep or trying hard to get there.

Clinton is standing across from his seat four rows ahead of you, slowly removing his suit coat. He is folding it carefully when he looks down the aisle and the blue-gray eyes land on you. "Hey," he says, calling you by name. It is a casual greeting, rather than a beckoning, the kind of hello usually reserved for an old friend. "Hi, pal," you say quietly in reply. Around you, you notice the reporters pause in mid-conversation or sit up quietly. They want to know to whom Bill Clinton is speaking. The fact that they don't really know you seems to make the candidate's greeting all the more interesting to them.

The five-term governor of Arkansas bends to his right to chat for a minute with James Carville. You wonder for a moment if the candidate is getting a report on the reprimand Carville delivered to the assembled media a few minutes before, but you notice that the candidate, rather than Carville, seems to be the one doing most of the talking. Carville, you learn later, is a man who is confident of his ability, does his job, and bides his time. He does not seek the approval of his employer; he is confident that his abilities will create results which speak for themselves.

Bill Clinton slides down into his leather-bound chair four rows ahead and across the aisle from you. You are surprised that he does not sink into the seat with the same sort of bone-tired weariness that the press contingent exhibits, but you have known Bill Clinton long enough that his energy level does not surprise you. The only sign of fatigue the candidate displays is the dArkansasening shadow beneath his eyes. He pulls a newspaper into his lap as the flight attendant asks him for a drink order. Clinton asks for hot coffee.

The presence of the press—whom the governor distrusts—does little to dampen his spirits. He has just savored the finest of moments, a nearly half-hour conversation with his daughter. The 11-year-old, still in Little Rock, asked her father for help with her algebra. This sort of interlude does a great deal for the candidate's attitude. Despite the rain and dropping temperatures, and even though another two-hour flight and yet another motorcade remain before this day is finished, Clinton feels a surge of energy and optimism. If all is right with Chelsea's little world, all can be right with his—at least, for the moment.

Earlier in the day, you asked the candidate how often he talked with his wife and daughter. He told you what you already knew: He talked with Chelsea once a day and with Hillary twice. "I try to call her late at night," he told you quietly, "and we usually have a long talk then." Clearly, his telephone conversations with his wife and child are the highlights of each long day on the campaign trail.

In the cockpit, pilot Bobby Thomas is about to start the starboard jet engine. His captain has just returned from filing his fifth flight plan in a single day. This hop, from New Orleans to San Antonio, Texas, may be the longest so far. It will take nearly two hours, and after a few hours' sleep the professional aviators will be back in their chairs once again early tomorrow morning.

On your right, the engine comes to life with a low whine. The power it generates gently shakes the aircraft, and you notice a heightened level of activity on the part of the two female flight attendants. The last cameraman is aboard, struggling to stow his bulky gear and trailing rainwater through the cabin as he heads toward the aft end of the seating section. Many of his companions are shedding their wet jackets and coats and sinking gratefully into the cabin-class seats at the rear of the plane.

You hear the aircraft door slam shut as the candidate's press secretary, DeeDee Myers, walks into the cabin. She is wearing a black knee-length leather coat, which at once protects her from the inclement weather and gives her a certain formidable, menacing appearance.

As DeeDee settles into her seat two rows ahead of you, the port-side engine starts with a shrill grind, dropping down into a low moan. In the cockpit, pilot Thomas monitors the engine's progress, making sure its performance is "nominal." When he is certain that it is, he passes the word to his captain. Aided by ground personnel, the jet begins to back away from the terminal. You and everyone else in the cabin hear the engines protest as they thrust backwards to aid in the pullout.

A moment later the engines reverse and the aircraft slowly lurches forward. Once near the runway, the plane shudders to a halt, and the pilots wait for clearance. By now, you have been waiting for nearly 45 minutes for the moment of takeoff, and the additional delay seems almost impossible to tolerate. And R.G.'s continuing monologue on the Texas political scene does nothing but add to the five-minute wait. At any other time, talking with Ratcliffe would be an enjoyable experience. Right now, though, you are too tired to pay attention, and the effort seems to drain you of what little stamina and strength you have left.

Up ahead of you, the candidate has his coffee. He holds the cup in one hand while he combs his hair with the fingers of the other. This, while it sounds simple, is an involved process. First, Clinton runs his fingers through the hair which hangs over his forehead. The motion continues until the fingers reach the back of the crown of the head. Then, in an unusual gesture, the governor finger combs the back and sides of his hair as well. The result, carefully noted by those who pay attention to the candidate's appearance, is hair which appears to have been recently finger-combed by the candidate's wife. You cannot say whether Bill Clinton has successfully cultivated this effect, or if it was totally unanticipated.

Not that it matters now, because the jet is finally moving forward. The small aircraft, with its human cargo of 50 press and campaign staffers seat-belted into gray and blue seats, fairly leaps into the air. Climbing rapidly, it enters the clouds that hang only a few hundred feet above the deck. The ground seems to melt away from view. To those at the airport, watching the plane and their candidate take off, the aircraft simply disappears. They turn around and walk toward their cars while you turn away from the window and stare at the back of the candidate's head. You can't take notes on the scene without losing some of its immediacy in the process, so you sit back and stare, letting the cabin's dim interior burn its way into your memory.

Four rows ahead, Governor Clinton is working the crossword puzzle in this day's edition of the Arkansas Democrat-Gazette. This is a habit he has cultivated since childhood. The immersion of body, mind, and spirit into the challenge of a good crossword always serves to help him forget, albeit momentarily, the problems that have beset his presidential campaign. As a youngster, he and his next-door neighbor would have Saturday-morning crossword puzzle races. Tonight, there

7

is no opponent, no spare copy of the puzzle if there was an opponent, and no real challenge except to beat the puzzle itself. The candidate does the next best thing. He checks the time on his black plastic Casio wristwatch and goes to work.

The problems from which Bill Clinton is seeking to escape are both very real and very threatening. Indeed, some of the very reporters on board the aircraft with you are wondering aloud if his candidacy for the nation's highest office is still viable. Five days before, the nation's press—using a super-market-style tabloid newspaper for their source of information—broke the unsubstantiated story that the governor had for twelve years maintained an illicit relationship with a former cabaret singer named Gennifer Flowers. You know that, having grown up in Arkansas, such gossip always circulated around Clinton. Now, however, the gossip has a face and a name. The clamor for the candidate's reaction is so strong that he and his aides have difficulty focusing on the issues at hand. But you and Bill Clinton both know that there is only one way to survive a debacle such as this—you just keep on going.

Last night, you watched in your hotel room as Clinton and his wife, Hillary, appeared on a shortened edition of the popular news program, "60 Minutes." It was a solid enough interview, with both husband and wife reaffirming their commitment to each other and dismissing the Flowers allegations as outright lies. For the Clintons, the interview was probably the biggest roll of the political dice they had ever taken, since how they were perceived by some 40 million viewers would largely determine the future of their candidacy. The popular perception seems to be that Hillary Clinton won the day when she maintained that she wasn't "some little woman, standing by my man like Tammy Wynette." As an afterthought, Mrs. Clinton mentioned her belief that the voters in New Hampshire and across the country would judge her husband fairly. If they were unsure about Bill Clinton's moral fiber, Hillary offered a simple solution. "Heck," she said candidly, using a word you have never heard her use before, "don't vote for him."

But the appearance on the "60 Minutes" program hasn't succeeded in quelling the questions from the press. Today, at each stop, the candidate has been dogged by queries about his personal life. This morning, during a stop at a magnet school in Jackson, Mississippi, you heard a reporter ask Clinton if his promise to be a "pro-family president" rang "hollow" in the light of the infidelity accusations.

You heard the candidate respond, his voice tightening and becoming more strident than usual. "If you look at my record as governor," Clinton said, "it's entirely consistent with that. What you are saying is, if you want to be a politician, you ought to be perfect, and if you're not, you should be divorced. That's what you guys are saying. I think it's wrong. I've said all I've got to say."

As you reflect, you realize that the comment may have indeed represented all Clinton had to say on the subject, but it certainly wasn't the last time he had to say it. At the next stop, in Alexandria, Louisiana, the local press greeted him with the same sort of questions as he stepped from the plane onto the airport tarmac. This time, you noticed, the governor's temper flared a bit.

"Enough is enough is enough," you heard him say. "Hillary and I were absolutely right," Clinton continued. "The voters are ready to go back to the real issues. We've said all we need to say. I'm not going to talk about it anymore."

At a private Alexandria fund raiser, the candidate told the audience that he believed that the "country is in deep trouble." Clinton added that "if what passes for journalism is people paying to tell stories on sleazy scandals, I just think... we're in trouble." You can't help but hope that the "trouble" the governor referred to is directed toward the nation and not toward his pursuit of the presidency.

Flying to Baton Rouge that afternoon, you noticed that the candidate and his staff seemed to be sitting on edge. With good reason too, since at that moment, Gennifer Flowers was holding forth with a press conference of her own in the Waldorf-Astoria Hotel in New York City. No one, the press included, knew what she would say or how convincingly she would say it. You thought that if Gennifer had been carefully coached, this press conference almost two thousand miles away could signal the death knell for the candidate's presidential ambitions.

It all seems slightly absurd. You know that, without being critical, the candidate is too much in love with himself and his political ambitions to gamble everything he has and everything he can become on an illicit love affair with someone you think is only marginally attractive. You have difficulty as an investigative journalist with taking a supermarket tabloid at face value about anything. And you know that, by the tabloid's own admission, it has paid Gennifer Flowers for her story. There's still the question of how much, of course, but perhaps what you've heard is right—everyone has their price.

Your next stop was Baton Rouge, the state capital of Louisiana. Again, you left the airplane in the pouring rain and ran for the sanctuary of the press bus. The cameramen did not have the luxury of racing toward the coach, because their heavy equipment demanded both careful handling and protection from the rain. When the last of them had dragged aboard, the bus pulled out. The driver wasn't quite sure where he was going, and following the motorcade was essential to arriving at the capitol safely. Nonetheless, he yielded to a campaign staffer's demand that he slow down and stop long enough to allow one of the standing cameramen to safely stow his equipment. The delay cost the driver his place in the caravan, but it accommodated the media, and most of the members present appreciated the gesture. Meanwhile, the rest of the motorcade headed for the capitol without the press bus in tow. Fortunately, you made it to the right place at the right time. You left the bus and stepped carefully through the pouring rain, entering the capitol on the west side.

You followed the press, who were following the candidate. Clinton was scheduled to speak to supporters and Louisiana legislators in the crowded Senate Chamber. Along with two or three hundred other people, you stood there dripping wet, waiting for the governor to be introduced. The room soon became a wilting oven because each body present generated the heat of a 100-watt lightbulb. As more people pressed in behind you, the air seemed almost too hot to breathe. Outside, the rain continued to fall and the temperatures were dropping steadily. Even the downpour would have been welcome relief from the oppressive heat and the overcrowding of the Senate Chamber.

You managed to make it through his speech—the same one you'd heard him make twice today already. That's one thing you admire about the guy—he makes the same speech everywhere he goes. Whether it's in New Hampshire, Arkansas, or Florida, every crowd gets exactly the same thing from Bill Clinton.

And this crowd loved him. At the end of the speech, "Clinton for President" signs filled the air and the applause rang on and on and on. Fighting for their opportunity, the press then seized the moment to ask the candidate questions about his speech, about his message and about other things.

First out of the blocks was Cable News Network's Gene Randall, eager to acquit himself of this morning's fiasco in Jackson. "Governor," Randall began, knowing where he will head but eager to build suspense, "we saw your old friend

Gennifer at a press conference this afternoon... " and the question rolled on. You watched Clinton's face as he waited impatiently for the questioner to finish. Finally, he got his chance to reply. He responded with substantially the same thing he's said during two earlier press conferences, adding that he believes the issue is behind him. The crowd cheered in support. This group, you remember thinking, was in the mood to rip the press apart if the questions about the candidate's personal life continued.

By the time the press conference had ended and the governor had left the Senate Chamber, you were downstairs at a pay phone. Fifty feet away, Bill Clinton walked by, recognizing you among the strangers at the phone bank. He gave you a small wave. You gave him a wave back in response, and you remember hoping that it didn't look too wan. You actually felt sorry enough for the guy to try to avoid adding to his black mood.

On the flight to New Orleans—today's next stop—you noticed that the press contingent was strangely silent, as if they had been castigated for their performance at the past three events. In the row of seats behind you, Gene Randall was back on his cellular telephone, calling his bureau chief in Washington. The BBC crew alongside you managed to sleep through most of the flight, stuffed to their British gills with food provided at the state capital. R.G. was sitting in back of you, and you had the luxury of two first-class seats to yourself.

You noticed that the candidate had a book on his lap, and every now and then his efforts toward reading were interrupted by a flight attendant or a campaign staffer. No one among the press ventured forward. There would, in fact, be little use in making the effort, since press secretary Myers has already laid down the proverbial law: Everything said on the plane is off the record. It seemed odd to you that, traveling toward the next stop with the press corps literally at his heels, Clinton is immune for the moment from the kind of questioning he has had to endure for the past few days.

Tonight, as a friend, you decide to broach a bit of conversation with the governor. Cautiously, clearing your approach with DeeDee Myers, you creep forward the four rows of seats which separate you from the candidate. He sees you and begins to move papers and books aside, preparing the first-class chair next to his. A glance at his feet shows that he has still not finished today's crossword puzzle.

All of this does not happen by accident. Since Clinton is the only member of the campaign contingent who knows you, you have had to fight not only for the opportunity to be on this flight, but for some time to talk with the candidate himself. While in New Orleans, waiting for Clinton to finish speaking at a private fund raiser, you made a telephone call to an old friend in Arkansas who happens to wield a little power in the circles of state government. Even though the hour was very late, he knew which buttons to push to get you some interview time with his friend Bill Clinton. Word passed from him to Little Rock, and from Little Rock to the aircraft. While you aren't exactly being welcomed to the governor's inner circle with open arms, you aren't being turned away either.

That is as it should be. During the past week, Bill Clinton has learned to fear the power of the press and to measure his own interests against every word the press might want him to utter. The fact that you are his friend makes little difference, not as long as you—like the press corps sitting behind you—hold the power to make or break his political career. You think that he overestimates the power of the media and underestimates the ability of the American people to discern fact from fiction.

But the least you can do is respect the candidate's feelings. As you slide into the gray leather seat next to his, he asks you if you are having fun on the trip. You are moved to reply that, like the candidate himself, you are tired but content. And you move ahead to things which concern him.

The day before, you saw him make the best speech of his political career, using no notes and relating to the audience better than any other modern politician on the stump. The thing that impressed you most was the governor's new and forceful speaking style. Coupled with new and forceful gestures, he is now capable of delivering a passionate and convincing case for his New Covenant. You wonder what prompted the change.

The candidate scoffs at your thought that perhaps he has been watching videos of President Kennedy, since JFK's jabbing forefinger has somehow been transmuted into Bill Clinton's style. Before this weekend, the governor's gestures had been two-handed maneuvers which lacked both emphasis and meaning. Yesterday, however, you doubted that any speaker on the face of the globe could have done better. Something is responsible for the change, and you aren't sure what that something is. One thing is certain: Bill Clinton could not, with coaching, change his style so rapidly and with such dramatic results. He must have made the changes on his own.

But that question really doesn't matter just now. Clearly, the candidate and those around him are pleased with his speaking style. And Bill Clinton has always been at his best on the stump when his blood is up. The wrong sort of media attention has certainly succeeded where other causes have failed.

You mention to the governor that you notice his energy level has remained undiminished since his days as Arkansas' attorney general. You covered him then for a radio station, and you remain amazed that Clinton can be up jogging at five in the morning, work through lunch and dinner, and still be going strong late in the evening. He attributes it, he tells you, to clean living. You know, as he points out, that he exercises a good deal and that he watches what he eats and seldom drinks alcohol. "Once in a blue moon," he tells you, "I'll have a beer. But not very often." You recall that Gennifer Flowers mentioned that Bill Clinton had a favorite wine. Knowing the candidate as you do, you sincerely doubt that part of Flowers' story, because you know that, true to his word, Clinton just does not drink.

You feel prompted, because of your political curiosity, to ask the candidate if he's looked at anybody in particular as a potential running mate. You preface your question with your realization that the convention is a long time away, but you know that as front-runner, the thought of a vice presidential choice must have crossed Bill Clinton's mind once or twice. He denies it. He wants to make sure that his campaign survives the unsubstantiated charges of infidelity, he tells you, and then he'll start worrying about the convention. Tomorrow night, you know, he will be back in New Hampshire, where the first primary has yet to be decided and January snow still hugs the cold ground.

You ask the obligatory questions about his wife and daughter and receive assurances that both are well, and that 11-year-old Chelsea, in particular, is unperturbed by the tabloid assertions of her father's illicit relationships. In an intensely private moment, the candidate shares with you some insight into the Gennifer Flowers episode, which seems to confirm your suspicion that the entire scandal had been rather carefully staged. Before sitting down to talk with Clinton, you were unsure— despite your friendship—whether the governor's denial was actually the truth. These few moments alone with the candidate are enough to banish all doubt. Bill Clinton may not be as

15

pure as driven snow, you conclude, but you are certain that he didn't have a 12-year affair with Ms. Flowers. The contradictions in her story and your knowledge of the governor all make Clinton's firm denial ring true.

Of course, the candidate has his trump cards. He can rely on former Pulaski County Sheriff Tommy Robinson, who, as head of the Public Safety Department for more than a year, was responsible for security around the governor's mansion during the time in which the media alleges that the governor had been seeing Gennifer Flowers, and Clinton knows it. Robinson, though not a political friend of the governor, will in days ahead assert that Clinton had no affair with Flowers. The press, predictably, will give the account little attention. Robinson himself will say that he believes Arkansas GOP party co-chairman Sheffield Nelson, a one-time Bill Clinton opponent, played a major part in orchestrating the Flowers episode.

Tonight, good news from New Hampshire is brightening the candidate's mood. You have just seen his aides rejoicing at the latest polls which indicate that Clinton not only leads in the first critical primary state, but has actually gained ground. Considering the accusations bandied about by the press during the past few days, it is a real wonder that more voters have not been lured away from the Clinton camp. For a moment, you watch the candidate smile. For Bill Clinton, light has just appeared at the end of a long, dArkansas tunnel.

All of this relaxes the governor, and understandably so. For the past one hundred-odd hours, his political future has been on the line. Understandably, he could not—and cannot—predict how the voters will react to the accusations and his denial. Tonight, for the first time in several days, he has solid evidence that all may yet be well.

You've noticed the tie Clinton is wearing is festooned with dozens of small hot-air balloons. Multicolored, the balloon print makes for a most unusual piece of neckwear. You ask the candidate what the balloons signify. "Up, up, and away," he tells you, "just like this campaign." For a moment, at least, it is refreshing to see the man in such good spirits.

It is nearing midnight. You and the candidate share a single commonality—both of you have deep, dark circles under your eyes. Your skin being a bit more tannish than the governor's makes his fatigue less noticeable than yours. Nonetheless, his energy level is dropping. He leans toward you, saying that he wants to take a quick nap before the plane lands in San Antonio. You understand. Quietly you rise from your seat, clasp his hand in a quick handshake, and move back four rows to your usual berth. As you settle in, you notice that R.G. is fast asleep beside you.

Staring out the window, you cannot see the city lights come into view, but you feel the engines throttle back as pilot Thomas begins the slow descent into San Antonio, Texas. When you finally land, you notice the usual cavalcade of cars out on the tarmac waiting for the candidate and his staff. He is still sitting with his eyes closed as you file past him and off the aircraft, but you doubt that he is sleeping. For one thing, you notice that the crossword puzzle is back on his lap.

The press contingent is mostly silent as you board the waiting press bus. For the time being, the rain has stopped, although the temperature has dropped and the clouds hang unabated in the sky above. From the warm sanctuary of your bus seat, you watch the candidate and his San Antonio hosts pile into the four waiting cars. Unlike this morning in Jackson, Mississippi, there are no foreign cars in the motorcade. The governor, you feel sure, has seen to that.

It is a long 20-minute drive to the hotel you'll stay in tonight. The outskirts of San Antonio are dark and quiet. The motorcade moves silently through empty streets, drawing up to the front of the St. Anthony Hotel just after 12:45 a.m. Wearily, you and the press contingent pile out of the press bus, and you catch a glimpse of the candidate heading across the hotel lobby. The desk clerks are waiting for you. They hand you a key in an envelope and tell you that the formal check-in procedures can wait until morning. Many of the members of the press mutter their thanks and appreciation. Quite a few of them looked ready to drop, and the prospect of standing in a long hotel line was almost unbearable.

You take the elevator upstairs to the fifth floor. Once inside your room, you kick off your shoes, untie your tie, and toss your suit coat on the bed. You head to the bathroom to wash your face. You can't do more until your luggage arrives, so you content yourself with another familiar chore. Sitting beside the bed, you pick up the telephone and dial home.

Three floors above you, Bill Clinton is doing the same thing.

2

GROWING INTO THE PART

★   ★   ★   ★   ★   ★

Considerable controversy is bound to ensue over the circumstances in which Bill Clinton grew up. Arkansas Democrat-Gazette editor John Robert Starr recently accused the media of inventing a Lincolnesque background for the governor, adding that he would not be surprised to hear some investigative reporter contend that Clinton had studied by candlelight.

Clinton himself has told interviewers that he grew up in poverty. Charles Allen calls Clinton's first home—with his grandparents—lower middle class. Starr maintains that Clinton began life firmly ensconced in the middle class. Consequently, the debate over Clinton's childhood surroundings is bound to continue almost unabated. In this case, Clinton himself seems not to be the authority; rather, he has become a part of the question. As "U. S. News and World Report" casually noted, "Few politicians have had more reason to wonder about their own moorings than he has."

The governor's mother, Virginia Cassidy, was a native of Hope, Arkansas. She worked for more than 30 years in hospitals and clinics across central Arkansas in an effort to provide for her sons. Today, she presents a unique appearance for the mother of a presidential candidate — her deep voice, blue eyes and hearty laughter are set off by her use of heavy makeup and jewelry and by the fact that her once jet-black hair now sports streaks of white. She has survived three husbands and today is married to a retired real estate broker. The couple still lives in Hot Springs.

Clinton's father died three months before the future governor saw light. Bill Blythe, a Texas car-dealer-turned-traveling-heavy-equipment salesman, was heading home to Hope from Chicago to see his wife, who was more than five months pregnant with their first child, when he was killed in an automobile accident in Missouri. Years later, Governor Clinton told Donald Baer:

I once went to find the place where he died on Highway 61 near Sikeston, Missouri. He was thrown out of the car and knocked out. He didn't die. He fell into a ditch full of water face down and drowned. It was just a fluke.

In our society, the odds are surely stacked against single mothers and their children, especially in a state like Arkansas. This child, born on August 19, 1946, in Hope, Arkansas, certainly faced adversity. For young William Jefferson Blythe IV, affectionately called "Billy," the impact was doubly severe because his mother left her infant son in the care of her parents while she headed to New Orleans to complete training as a nurse anesthetist. Years later, during the speech announcing his candidacy for the presidency of the United States, Clinton would recall his early years:

For four years I lived with my grandparents. They didn't have much money. Nobody did in Arkansas at the end of World War II. I spent a lot of time in the country with my great-grandparents, who by any standard were very poor.

*But we really didn't know we were poor because we cared for
each other, we didn't make excuses, we believed in the American dream and were the backers of family and hard work...*

This was the family, according to the governor, that "taught
me to live with my failures and disappointments and get up
again and again and again." Certainly, his grandparents' love
and care made it easier for him to grow through infancy without either parent at hand. Clinton's grandfather, Eldridge
Cassidy, suffered from a moderate drinking problem. He made
up for that handicap, as far as Billy was concerned, by instilling
in his grandson the love of education and learning. Early in his
childhood, according to the governor, his grandparents had
taught him reading fundamentals and simple arithmetics. "I
was reading little books when I was three," Clinton told Charles
Allen.

The governor's maternal grandparents, like many rural
Arkansans in the early twentieth century, lacked a great deal of
formal education. But they apparently fostered in their grandson an insatiable appetite for knowledge. "They really helped
imbue in me a real sense of educational achievement," Clinton
stated in a recent interview. When grandfather Cassidy managed to purchase a small grocery and market in a predomi-
nately black neighborhood, young Billy learned not only the
meaning of financial responsibility, but equality of treatment
as well.

Clinton still speaks of his grandfather in glowing terms.
"He was the kindest person I ever knew," Clinton told the
Arkansas Gazette. Still, the grandson admits that his
grandfather's kind personality was also a fault when it came to
business. Speaking of his grandfather's store, Clinton noted,
"The people around there were so poor, and he sold so much
on credit that he finally went out of business, not because

anybody tried to bilk him out of anything but because they just didn't have any money. Of course, this was before food stamps or anything like that."

By the time her son was four years old, Virginia Cassidy Blythe had married again. The new husband, as Charles Allen noted dryly, was "another car dealer." Roger Clinton would later legally adopt young Billy Blythe. Indeed, by the time the youngster was midway through grade school in the family's new hometown of Hot Springs, he was already known as Billy Clinton. The change of last names did not legally occur until Bill was fifteen years old.

Virginia and Roger Clinton led a stormy married life. Repeated separations marred the interludes of domestic tranquility between Roger's bouts of heavy drinking. The frequent partings aside, the marriage held together. By the time Billy was ten years old, Virginia and Roger had another son, Roger, Jr.

But even as Roger grew up, Billy still held a special place in Virginia's heart. Her adoration of Bill was the subject of the jokes and jibes of friends. "You know, she had pictures of him on the wall," old friend Carolyn Staley mentioned to an Arkansas Gazette reporter, adding that "we used to joke that there ought to be candles around the pictures."

Clinton attended second and third grade at a private Catholic school, St. John's, in Hot Springs. The year was 1954. Virginia had thought that the private school environment might make a better transition for her son as he moved from the small elementary school in Hope to the much larger public school system in Hot Springs. Clinton impressed his mother and teachers alike by being exceptionally willing and eager to learn. "He started reading the newspaper in the first grade," Virginia told Arkansas Democrat writer Terry Lemons, "He's always been well-read."

By the time Billy was nine years old, his family had acquired a television. During the hot summer of 1956, the ten-year-old governor-to-be was spellbound by the Democratic and Republican National Conventions, then televised in all their black-and-white entirety. As John Kennedy and Estes Kefauver battled for the vice presidential spot in Adali Stevenson's doomed bid to unseat Dwight D. Eisenhower, the future presidential candidate watched open-mouthed. "I think it sort of came home to me in a way on television that it wouldn't have otherwise." Clinton told Charles Allen.

His interest in politics heightened by ninth-grade civics teacher Mary Marty, Clinton watched the 1960 presidential campaign with interest. Indeed, Mrs. Marty asked her students to debate the merits of each of the two candidates for the White House, Richard Nixon and John F. Kennedy. "She and I were the only ones for Kennedy," the Governor recalled recently, adding that in heavily Republican Garland County, "virtually everyone else was for Nixon."

Clinton's passion for learning carried him through his grade school years and into Central Junior High School and Hot Springs High. John Wilson, now the principal of the high school, taught Clinton English during a summer tenth grade course. He told Arkansas Democrat reporter Terry Lemons that the future governor "had a keen interest in his studies," adding that Clinton "was sharp." Wilson recalled to Lemons that he and his student often debated the political issues of the time. The year was 1961.

That fall, Clinton walked into the office of his high school's guidance counselor, a woman named Edith Irons. He asked her which college would be best if he planned to study international affairs. She answered that Georgetown University in Washington, D.C. would be the college of choice. It was the only school to which Clinton applied. Ms. Irons recently told the Arkansas Democrat that she had few sophomores ask her about pursuing a course in international studies.

Billy Clinton spread himself thin enough during his high school years. As Ms. Irons later observed, "I don't know how he could be on the band field at six a.m. and be back at school and go, go, go all day..." But Clinton did just that. At Hot Springs High, he was a noted musical talent. He served as the Trojans' band major during his senior year in 1963. Additionally, he won first chair honors as an all-state sax player.

Indeed, the future governor played tenor sax with a jazz trio during his high school years. Rusty Goodrum, now a songwriter in Nashville, was also a member of the band. At one point in his life, it is fair to say that Bill Clinton was considering a career in the music field.

The school's band director, Virgil Spurlin, says Clinton had "all kinds of techniques." He told Terry Lemons that Clinton "was a soloist. He could play jazz. He could read every piece of music I put in front of him, even orchestral." Almost a quarter of a century after his high school graduation, Bill Clinton would display his musical talent by playing a saxophone solo on Johnny Carson's "Tonight Show" and then joining Doc Severinsen and the NBC orchestra.

While Clinton was maturing in high school, he was being forced to grow up even more quickly at home. He was often a willing babysitter for his younger brother, Roger. And the marital tensions between his mother and Roger Clinton continued to grow steadily worse. By the time Bill was 14, he was bigger than his stepfather. He told "U.S. News and World Report" that "the manifest tensions between them (Roger Sr. and Virginia Clinton) abated a little bit just because I was kind of the force for peace." Many of Clinton's oldest friends recall his concern for the way in which his stepfather was treating his mother. The Clinton marriage appeared a shaky vehicle, and it was. The couple briefly divorced when Bill was 15, only to remarry shortly thereafter.

As Clinton told the magazine, the disruption of his family life—never normal to begin with—tended to push him into maturity, despite his early age. He became "40 at the age of 16," the governor maintains.

But the strife at home did not seem to greatly affect his performance at school. Clinton was the elected president of his junior class, and readily participated in organizations such as the National Honor Society, the Beta Club—where he served as president, as he did in the Key Club— and DeMolay, an organization specializing in leadership training. In 1988, Clinton was inducted into DeMolay's International Hall of Fame.

One of Billy Clinton's favorite pastimes, according to his childhood friend Patty Criner, was to cruise around Hot Springs doing impersonations of Elvis Presley. Criner told Charles Allen that Clinton did an especially good rendition of "Love Me Tender." He also liked to experiment with various foods, particularly sandwiches. Peanut butter and bananas constituted his favorite sandwich creation during his high school years.

During the summer between his junior and senior years, Clinton was selected to attend Arkansas Boy's State, then being held at Camp Robinson near Little Rock. There, Clinton's boyhood friend from Hope, Mack McLarty, won the election as governor. And Clinton himself was selected as an Arkansas delegate to Boy's Nation. That gathering—held later that summer in Washington, D.C.—would put him face-to-face with John F. Kennedy...and change his life.

"I'd never seen him get so excited about something," his mother told the Arkansas Democrat. "When he came back from Washington, holding this picture of himself with Jack Kennedy," she told an interviewer, "and the expression on his face...I knew right then that politics was the answer for him."

Clinton himself has told researchers that his trips to Boy's State and Boy's Nation were "very valuable" and "a wonderful thing."

Patty Criner told Allen that the future governor was deeply moved by his experiences at the nation's capitol. "Shaking hands with John Kennedy and sitting in the Senate dining room with Senator Fulbright, whom he admired," she said, "that moved him."

As a senior at Hot Springs High, Clinton found himself embroiled in a political contest of another kind—a bout for class secretary with friend and next-door-neighbor, Carolyn Staley. Asked to wait outside the auditorium while the voting took place, Staley recalls that Clinton vowed never to forgive her if she defeated him and won the election. Staley did win—handing Clinton his first real defeat of that sort—but the two are still friends today. In fact, Staley now heads up the governor's Commission on Adult Literacy.

Bill did not participate in organized high school athletics. Instead, he picked up games of tag football and basketball with his friends. His height, impressive for a teenager, did make him a formidable athlete. Later, in college, his prowess would help him win a Rhodes Scholarship. But his lack of participation in high school athletics, according to long-time friend Carolyn Staley, was due to an understanding of sorts between Clinton and his mother. "She (Virginia Clinton) had seen so many sports injuries come into the hospital," Staley told the Arkansas Democrat, "I think she just let it be known she wanted to see her kids grow up to live a normal life."

Boyhood friend and Boy's State companion Mack McLarty, now chairman of Arkansas' largest natural gas supplier, noted some years ago that his friend Clinton had a love for basketball. In a candid interview with the Arkansas Gazette, McLarty noted that Clinton "loved to play sports, though ... he was perhaps not as coordinated as he would like to remember."

Clinton's teachers and classmates all paint a picture of an exceptionally well-rounded young man—remarkably so, given the strife that marked his life at home. Nonetheless, he was also exceptionally well-behaved. Carolyn Wilson, who graduated with the future governor in 1964, told the Arkansas Democrat that she once yelled at Clinton for being too good. "Don't you ever do anything wrong?" Wilson says she screamed. "You're a teenager...you're supposed to do things wrong!" Wilson's claim to the contrary, she claims that those scouring Clinton's high school record for blemishes won't find material for the grist. "You won't find anything bad about him," she insists.

Clinton graduated from Hot Springs High in 1964, finishing fourth out of a class of more than three hundred. He was a National Merit Scholarship semifinalist as well.

During his days at Boy's Nation in Washington, D.C., Bill Clinton had seized the opportunity to visit at length with Arkansas Senator J. William Fulbright, who headed the Senate Foreign Relations Committee. Fulbright had become something of a role model for Clinton, who later told an interviewer that he was "always proud that we had somebody like that representing Arkansas." Later, in the middle of his years at Georgetown, Clinton sought—and got—a part-time job from Fulbright which would help pay part of his college expenses. Relocating from Hot Springs to Georgetown University, Clinton was setting up shop in one of the finest institutions of higher learning in the land.

Clinton knew what he was going after. He worked for a bachelor of arts degree, majoring in international government studies. During his freshman and sophomore years, he served as class president. In his freshman class campaign effort, Clinton promised to print and distribute a class newsletter. Additionally, he vowed to improve campus social life for incoming freshmen via work on the class homecoming float and the freshman dance. "The feasibility of every plank has been carefully examined," Clinton concluded in his platform brochure.

In the spring of 1946, John F. Kennedy had climbed three flights of stairs in a Boston tenament to knock on the door of one Dave Powers and inquire if he would help him run for Congress. Powers said yes and remained Kennedy's closest friend until the day the President was assassinated. In the fall of 1964, nearly a year after the president's death, Bill Clinton knocked on the door of a young man named Thomas Caplan. Caplan, now a writer, says that Clinton's first words were, "Hello, I'm Bill Clinton. Will you help me run for president of the class?" Caplan had known the Kennedy family well, spending time at the compound in Hyannis Port. No doubt, the eager young man at his door—his new roommate, as it turned out— reminded him of the slain President. He said yes; Clinton won the student election, and the two young men became fast friends.

At first, Caplan did not trust Bill Clinton. Apparently, Clinton remarked to his roommate that, despite Caplan's wealthy background and extensive social contacts, he did not possess anything Clinton wanted. In a conversation with Clinton's mother, Caplan said: "I'll just put it to you as plain as I know how...there ain't nobody anywhere in this world this good—nobody. Until I saw how genuine he is, I could not trust him."

Some of Clinton's other Georgetown contemporaries expressed the same sort of thought. "I don't know what you're running for," Maryland native Stefanie Weldon told the young Arkansan, "but I want to vote for you."

High school friend Carolyn Staley visited Clinton occasionally during his years at Georgetown. One such visit took place in early April 1968 just before Clinton was scheduled to graduate. Martin Luther King had just been assassinated in

Memphis, Tennessee, and widespread rioting had broken out in the nation's capital.

"I remember flying in and seeing the city on fire," Staley told Charles Allen. She and Clinton volunteered to work with the Red Cross and drove Clinton's white Buick — with a red cross plastered on the sides — as an emergency vehicle. The pair fairly raced about the capital that long weekend, carrying provisions to people who had lost their homes to riot fires. Clinton and Staley had been instructed to pull hats and scarves over their faces to hide the fact that they were white. "We got out and walked throughout the city and saw the burning, the looting, and were very much brought into face-to-face significance with what was going on," Staley continued. At one point, the pair of Arkansans turned a corner and saw a half-dozen black men walking toward them. Clinton and Staley turned around and began walking back to their car because, as Staley later put it, "although our hearts beat with the cause, nobody could know that by the color of our skin."

Clinton's friends from Georgetown were always welcomed in his parents' Hot Springs home. At one Easter vacation, their guest was Tom Caplan, the young easterner who had become Clinton's roommate. "He's been to Europe," Clinton told his mother over the phone, "but he's never been to Arkansas." Caplan, having been raised in a more formal social environment, had a tough time loosening up at the Clinton home. "When he did," Virginia Clinton said, "I had him reaching for the butter in the middle of the table just like everyone else."

One thing marred Bill Clinton's last years at Georgetown— the death of his stepfather, Roger. Indeed, it was only after Roger had developed terminal cancer that he and his stepson began to forge a real friendship. When Roger became ill, Bill told his mother to call him home to Arkansas "before it was too late."

"I'll never forget how wonderful Bill was to (Roger) before he died," Virginia Clinton told Charles Allen. "Roger had such pride...now, he was vain...and as much as he drank, he was (still) one of the cleanest individuals you ever saw—well dressed. And when he got so that he was not able to go to the bathroom, for example, Bill would bodily pick him up and take him to the bathroom so that he could maintain his dignity."

Roger Clinton died in 1968. Bill Clinton was not yet 22 years old.

His studies at Georgetown fascinated Bill Clinton. "I was not only in love with the (college) experience," he told the Arkansas Democrat newspaper, "I was consumed by it." His part-time job with the Senate Foreign Relations Committee, working under Senator Fulbright's wing, took up what little spare time Clinton had.

"They gave me the job when I was nobody from nowhere," Clinton said. "My family had no money, no political influence, nothing." Actually, Arkansas Supreme Court Chief Justice Jack Holt had recommended Clinton to Lee Williams, who was Senator Fulbright's administrative aide. Clinton had campaigned for the chief justice's uncle during a gubernatorial campaign.

The position with the Senate Foreign Relations Committee couldn't have come at a better time. Clinton, on summer vacation, lacked the funds to return to Georgetown. "I couldn't afford to pay for it anymore," he later maintained. The night Williams called Clinton to offer him the job, the offer was pretty specific. "You can have a part-time job for $3,500 a year or a full-time job for $5,000," Williams said. Clinton asked, "How about two part-time jobs?" Williams replied, "You're just the guy I'm looking for. Be here Monday." The call took place on Friday morning. Clinton packed his bags and left, driving back to the nation's capital over the weekend. He'd had no sleep, but he was there for work on Monday.

Although Virginia Clinton was supporting her son financially during his Georgetown years, Clinton relied on income from his part-time job to pay for such necessities as food and clothing. When Clinton's mother came to the school to see her son graduate, roommate Caplan told her that he didn't know if the three would be able to eat breakfast that morning. As Virginia related to Charles Allen, Caplan said that he had bought breakfast the last time he and Clinton ate together, and now it was Clinton's turn to pay. "He won't eat until he can afford to buy," Caplan said.

Clinton hoarded gas money so that he could drive his big white Buick home to Arkansas for holidays and breaks from classes. One photo survives from this period, showing Clinton and his mother in the kitchen of their Hot Springs home during the Christmas season of 1964, Bill's freshman year at Georgetown. In the photo, Clinton is sitting and his mother is standing beside him, right arm around her son, gazing down at him with a broad smile on her face. Clinton is smiling too, the characteristic grin which would later become a popular feature in his years as Governor. The black, curly hair is close-cropped, and he wears blue jeans and a turtleneck shirt.

Clinton arrived at the top of his undergraduate career when he was invited to apply for a Rhodes Scholarship, which offers a select group of scholastic achievers the opportunity to pursue postgraduate studies in England. Patty Criner recalls that Clinton was incredulous at the thought of applying for the honor. "You won't believe this," he wrote Criner, "but the professors want me to apply." Criner maintains that Clinton felt he didn't have "a chance in the world" of being selected for the scholarship, but that he was "really studying and working hard."

Rhodes Scholars follow an illustrious tradition. The scholarships were established just after the turn of the century, in

1902, at the death of Cecil John Rhodes. Rhodes, for his part, had made his fortune in South African diamonds. To date, Clinton is the only presidential candidate who can boast a Rhodes Scholarship. As a matter of interest, a half-dozen current members of the U.S, Congress—Oklahoma Senator David Boren, New Jersey's Bill Bradley, Richard Lugar from Indiana, South Dakota's Larry Pressler, Maryland's Paul Sarbanes, and one of that state's representatives, Thomas McMillen—are all former Rhodes Scholars. Lugar and Pressler, for what it's worth, are Republicans, while the balance are Democrats.

It's also worth noting that Clinton's idol, Senator Fulbright, had himself been selected a Rhodes Scholar. "That's one reason I wanted to try to get one," Clinton told an interviewer some years ago, "because I knew Senator Fulbright had been one as well."

Criner calls the Rhodes Scholarship "the most exciting thing in the world" for Bill Clinton. She was waiting alongside Clinton's mother for a telephone call from Bill on the day the scholarship was to be awarded. Clinton was undergoing a final interview, having concluded a rather lengthy and highly competitive selection process. He had to travel to New Orleans for the final interview, and one of the interview questions dealt with the first heart transplant. By chance, Clinton had stopped at the airport and bought a copy of Time magazine, which carried an article on that very subject. Picking up that magazine, he later admitted, was "the luckiest thing in the world."

Virginia Clinton recalls the tension as she sat waiting by the telephone for her son to call. She told Charles Allen that she "had never refused to do an anesthetic in my life. But this was on a Saturday. And they had an emergency, and the doctor called me, and I said, 'I'm sorry, you'll just have to call somebody else.' I did not leave the phone all day long. I gave him a London Fog raincoat for good luck for him to take to New

Orleans. And, it was around five o'clock in the afternoon, and he called and he said, "Well, Mother, how do you think I'll look in English tweed?"

Just as he quickly made an impression on his contemporaries upon his arrival at Georgetown, Clinton quickly became well known to his fellow Rhodes Scholars. The group set sail for England aboard the S.S. United States. One of Clinton's fellow passengers was Harvard University professor and writer Robert Reich. Reich told the Arkasnas Democrat that he suffered from bouts of seasickness and spent most of the six-day voyage in his cabin, lying on his bunk. "Bill knocked on my door twice a day to see how I was doing and bring me refreshments. I remember being struck at the time at what a kind man he was. He had just met me."

If Clinton today considers his years at Georgetown "an incredible experience...like a feast," then the trip to England must have awed him. Clinton and his fellow Rhodes Scholars were en route to Oxford University to study for two years. For the future governor, it was a time to be thankful. "He would write to his mother and tell her how grateful he was," Patty Criner recalls. "He took every bit of it to heart and was so grateful for every bit of it."

Bill Clinton arrived in an England at peace, in sharp and dramatic contrast to the United States he had left behind. Lyndon Johnson, responding to his cabinet advisers and members of the army-industrial community — even though he had declined to run for another term as president — continued to escalate the country's involvement in the conflict in Vietnam. As the vocal and violent opposition to the war continued to grow, America resembled nothing so much as a nation torn asunder by civil war. Even far away at Oxford, Clinton and his fellow Rhodes Scholars were hard-pressed to totally escape from the war and the conflict and turmoil it engendered back at home.

For one thing, each male student was still subject to the military draft. Indeed, all those students who were not already enlisted in the military with some sort of sanctioned delay from active duty were in danger of being called up. Like many of his fellow students, Clinton opposed the Vietnam conflict, although he did not actively protest.

Later on, some of Clinton's political opponents —Republican congressman John Paul Hammerschimdt, who barely defeated a Clinton challenge in 1974, was the first—would allege that Clinton was an anti-war protestor. Clinton climbed a venerable old cyprus tree on the campus of the University of Arkansas in Fayetteville during the spring of 1969. From that lofty vantage point, he supposedly engaged in a verbal protest against the war effort. In point of fact, Clinton was in England at the time, which would have made such a protest impossible. Interestingly enough, the same "demonstrator" story would arise again in 1978, during the heat of Clinton's first campaign for Governor. Even now, some students at the university still repeat the story as gospel fact.

Bill Clinton's class of students at Oxford scored a first of a negative sort—the cadre of Rhodes Scholars boasted the highest percentage of students not to receive a degree as a result of their sojourn to England. Obviously, the turmoil created by the war in Vietnam was a significant part of the problem. Clinton and many of his fellow students continually changed courses because they never knew when they would be called to active duty. Fortunately for Clinton, he drew a high draft number and was never summoned to active duty.

Rather than spend his time at Oxford protesting the war, Clinton used it to study. According to his contemporaries, he developed interests in virtually every subject imaginable. His years in England marked the only time when he did not have a part-time job to earn additional money for college expenses.

Instead, he devoted himself totally to learning all he could about everything around him. Clinton himself believes that he made the most of his experience and time in England. "Being there was incredible," he told Charles Allen, "I got to travel a lot. I got to spend a lot of personal time—learn things, go see things—I read about three hundred books both years I was there."

For two years, Bill Clinton was forced by virtue of his circumstances to abandon his practice of planning literally every minute of every day. Clinton describes himself as "almost compulsively overactive," adding that to be in Oxford for two years where he could not script out his daily routine was "a great deal."

While in England, Clinton's best friend was Time magazine senior correspondent Strobe Talbott. During his Oxford years, Talbott says, Clinton was "extremely competitive." Talbott maintained to Charles Allen that a large part of the governor's success lay in his ability to compete with great intensity "but without turning people off." Talbott noted that Clinton "doesn't come across as being vicious or mean and hungry, and as a result, he doesn't frighten people or antagonize people." Based on Clinton's political success, Talbott argues that Clinton's personality hasn't changed greatly since his days in England.

In Hot Springs, Virginia Clinton kept the home fires burning. Throughout Clinton's pair of years at Oxford, his mother kept in close contact. One day, while she was in Chicago attending a medical convention, the president of Rhodes House called her on the telephone. Virginia told Charles Allen that the man had said, "You know the only thing that keeps your son from being one of the great intellectuals of all time?" The surprised mother waited in bewilderment for the man to answer his own question. "No, what?" she finally asked. "His love and care for people."

At the end of Clinton's first year at Oxford, newly elected President Richard Nixon took the first tentative steps toward winding down the Vietnam conflict. Surprisingly, only a couple of Clinton's fellow Rhodes Scholars had been drafted into military service. But, of course, the students themselves had no way of knowing what tribulation the immediate future might hold. Hence, many of them received no degree from Oxford, opting to return to the United States instead. Today, Clinton insists that he regrets not bringing a diploma back from England, and, rather fancifully, says that he would not mind spending another year at Oxford.

In Clinton's case, he could have spent another year in England as a Rhodes Scholar. Still, the offer he received from his native shore was too tempting to resist. When Yale Law School offered him a scholarship, he leapt at the opportunity.

Clinton hated to leave England, but he apparently harbored a strong desire for a law degree. Even though he could not be a traditional law student — Clinton had to hold down part-time jobs to make ends meet, even with his scholarship and a personal loan — he could not pass up the opportunity to study at Yale.

In fact, Clinton kept busy with as many as three part-time jobs at a time. He worked for a lawyer in downtown New Haven, worked for a city alderman in Hartford, and even taught in a nearby community college. Additionally, he became involved in Connecticut's Democratic party.

Like any other young adult, Clinton went through his share of girlfriends. He had just broken up with one young woman when he met Hillary Rodham. The two shared a class where, according to Clinton, the professor had written the textbook and tested from that source. Both Clinton and Ms. Rodham decided that the instructor was a better writer than he was a teacher; consequently, they seldom attended that particular session. Clinton had spotted Hillary in class, followed her outside, but lacked the courage to speak to her. His next opportunity came a couple of days later in the law library. As he related to Allen:

> *This guy was trying to talk me into joining the Yale Law Review and telling me I could clerk for the U.S. Supreme Court if I were a member...which is probably true. And then I could go on to New York and make a ton of money...And I kept telling him I didn't want to do all of that. I wanted to go home to Arkansas. It didn't matter to anybody (in Arkansas) whether I was on the Yale Law Review or not. And they were trying to get southerners; they wanted geographic balance on the Law Review...I just didn't much want to do it. And all this time I was talking to this guy about the Law Review, I was looking at Hillary at the other end of the library. And the Yale Law School Library is a real long, narrow(room). She was down at the other end, and...I just was staring at her while this guy was looking at a book, and she closed this book, and she walked all the way down the library... and she came up to me and she said, "Look, if you're going to keep staring at me, and I'm going to keep staring back, I think we should at least know each other. I'm Hillary Rodham. What's your name?"*

Clinton had forgotten. A student of romance novels could not have done better in setting the stage for a relationship which would endure for years to come. "I was so embarrassed," Clinton told Allen, "but we've been together, more or less, ever since."

It's worth noting that Harvard economist Robert Reich, Clinton's Rhodes Scholar companion, maintains that he introduced Bill and Hillary to each other. Interestingly, Reich is missing from the account Clinton gave to Allen. I am, however, the first to admit that how the couple managed to get together is an issue that is somehow eclipsed by the fact that they remain that way.

Born in Chicago in October, 1947, Hillary and her two brothers grew up in Park Ridge, Illinois. In sharp contrast to Bill Clinton's background, Hillary's mother had remained at home to look after the three children. She graduated from Wellesley College in Massachusetts with high honors in 1969, having studied political science and psychology at the famed women's school near Boston. Then, having decided against attending Harvard, she headed to Yale, where she met Clinton. The year was 1971.

Clinton and Ms. Rodham spent two more years at Yale before their careers separated them. During the fall of 1972, both took time out from their studies to travel south to Texas and work in the George McGovern presidential campaign. Clinton, who says he was a "long-haired liberal" during his law school days, had opted for McGovern even before the Democrat had won his party's nomination for president. In the Lone Star State, Clinton served as state coordinator for the McGovern effort, staying in Texas from August until the election that November. Still, Clinton reportedly realized that the McGovern movement had lost touch with the Americans it was striving to win the right to serve.

During his sojourn in Texas, the future Governor met a state political activist named Betsy Wright. Although Wright has stated that at the time she was more taken with Hillary Rodham's potential for political success, she subsequently became Bill Clinton's campaign manager and top aide.

Following their graduation from Yale Law School, both Clinton and Ms. Rodham were offered prominent positions in the nation's capital. Both declined, although Hillary later accepted an offer to go to Washington and work for the House

Judiciary Committee, which was then investigating the potential impeachment of President Richard Nixon. She — and Clinton—had been recommended for the post by Yale instructor and Kennedy administration veteran Burke Marshall.

Ms. Rodham would stay at her post with the House Judiciary Committee until President Nixon resigned in early August, 1974. By that time, Clinton had returned to Arkansas and had been teaching at the University of Arkansas in Fayetteville for a year. Apparently, Clinton's teaching position was obtained via some sort of latter-day encouragement or afterthought. Recently, he claimed that all he ever wanted to be was "a country lawyer."

Indeed, he was headed home from New Haven to Hot Springs—Yale Law degree presumably close at hand—to become just that. Near Little Rock, just an hour from home, Clinton stopped by the side of Interstate 40 and called University of Arkansas Law School Dean Wylie Davis. Clinton told Davis that he had learned—via a Yale professor—that the law school had a pair of vacancies. Clinton maintained that he would teach anything, did not mind working, did not believe in tenure, and that Davis could get rid of him at any time. With an attitude like his, it's no wonder that Clinton got an interview, despite Davis' statement that Clinton, at 26, was too young to teach. As a rejoinder, the Yale graduate maintained that he had been too young for everything he'd ever done.

Quickly, Clinton found himself a member of the University of Arkansas Law School faculty. The position paid $25,000 per year—not a bad salary even in modern-day Arkansas, and especially good in 1973. Clinton's mother was unimpressed. "What's the deal?" Virginia recalls asking. "We've struggled for ten years to educate this man..." The fact that Clinton could have taken his pick of several high-paying positions on the east coast, but chose Fayetteville instead, demonstrated (at least to Virginia) that money meant little to him.

Fayetteville, Arkansas, is a relaxed college town which, as Patty Criner observed, is a great deal like New Haven, Connecticut Clinton thrived in both environments. During his two years' teaching at the University, Clinton sparked political ambitions in several of his students. Among them were David Matthews of Lowell, a small town just north of Fayetteville, who would become state representative for Benton County, and Lu Hardin of Russellville, who is currently state senator.

Hardin describes Clinton as "enthusiastic and dedicated," an instructor who displayed "a great deal of fairness" in the classroom environment. "He (Clinton) gave us the opportunity to tell him what we thought," Hardin told the authors. "It was a liberating and thought-stimulating classtime."

Other Clinton students have criticized their instructor for arriving for class seemingly unprepared for the discussion, and for paying attention to his political race against Congressman Hammerschmidt rather than to the class at hand. Hardin, on the other hand, thought Clinton well-prepared. He maintains today that Clinton went the extra mile to get to know his students.

Pine Bluff attorney Jesse Kearney told the Arkansas Democrat newspaper that he enjoyed going to Clinton's class, adding that the class offered him "engaging discussions of the issues of the day." Clinton, Kearney maintains, "was not the kind (of instructor) to read from a book."

Arkansas State Senator Morril Harriman told Allen that he first thought that Clinton, who was the instructor for Harriman's Agency and Partnerships class, was a fellow student because the teacher appeared so young. Harriman recalls that Clinton sometimes lectured off-subject, talking about the Watergate scandal then unfolding in Washington, D.C. Clinton and his students discussed the legal and philosophical issues behind the Watergate affair.

Other than the fact that Clinton was quite often rather late in posting his grades (Dr. Allen notes Lu Hardin's recollection of spring class marks finally being posted on Labor Day) Clinton's students seemed to have an appreciation for his teaching ability. Clinton no doubt cultivated their friendship by playing in pick-up games of half-court basketball with his students.

Fayetteville, Arkansas—in the northwest corner of the state—is an anchor in the heavily Republican third congressional district. The incumbent representative, John Paul Hammerschmidt, had been elected in 1966 on the Republican ticket, riding into office largely on the coattails of the anti-war backlash. Hammerschmidt's constituents ranged from the heavily-populated Rogers-Springdale-Fayetteville area down to the border city of Fort Smith. From there, the district slid eastward, passing through Johnson County, a Democratic stronghold, and Russellville in Pope County. Roughly, the district comprised a quarter of Arkansas' land area. Hammerschmidt himself hails from Harrison, a town near the northern border of the central part of the state. The congressman had not experienced a difficult reelection battle during his entire tenure in the nation's capital.

In the early months of 1974, Bill Clinton talked among his friends, trying to find someone who would challenge Hammerschmidt. In an interview, Clinton contended that he didn't intend to go up against Hammerschmidt himself and had asked a half-dozen qualified individuals to make the race before he decided that he would be the best candidate. Clinton turned down a job offer which would have allowed him to work on the congressional staff investigating the impeachment of Richard Nixon. In refusing the offer, Clinton told Allen that he said, "I'm going to stay down here and run for Congress because I can't find another living soul to do that." Clinton recommended Hillary Rodham for the job instead.

Clinton maintains that he was just making the adjustment to life in Fayetteville and had no intention of making an entry into politics at that time. In truth, he had only been teaching at the University of Arkansas for three months when he announced his candidacy against Hammerschmidt.

But the main problem with the argument that Clinton was reluctant to throw his hat into the political ring is that in the 1974 Democratic primary, he was one of four candidates. Apparently, the qualifications of the other three aside, someone else could have been found who was willing to run for Congress, and at least these three did manage to get their names on the ballot.

Had the other three announced their intentions after Clinton had entered the race, it would have been a relatively simple matter for him to withdraw his candidacy. This, of course, is not what happened. Clinton won the primary—albeit in a runoff election—and earned the right to challenge Hammerschmidt in November.

In the primary itself, Clinton won 44 percent of the vote, nearly outdistancing the other three contenders. He was forced into a runoff with State Senator "Gene" Rainwater, who had picked up just over 26 percent of the ballots cast, while David Stewart and James Scanlon finished third and fourth, respectively. Clinton soundly beat Rainwater in the runoff, amassing some 69 percent of the popular vote.

During the fall campaign, Clinton estimated that he met one hundred thousand voters. He also made dozens of solid contacts among influential third district Democrats who would help him in his race for attorney general two years hence. Many of those who worked for Clinton against Hammerschmidt—the elderly Jewel Phillips in Johnson County was an example—fairly gushed over the young man. "I think he's the greatest," Ms. Phillips said in 1976.

The Clinton for Congress campaign attracted dozens of young people—some too young to vote. At Lamar High School, Robin Robinson lobbied her teachers in Clinton's behalf. Robin's mother worked in a local government office, and the entire family gave Clinton its wholehearted support. The fact that Robin was not old enough to cast a ballot for her idol did not dampen her spirits. "Rockin' Robin," Clinton called her some years later, displaying his ability to recall the names and personalities of almost anyone who has helped him in a campaign effort.

During the campaign, Clinton criticized Congressman Hammerschmidt for putting the interests of Arkansas business ahead of those of his constituents, and noted that, as a Republican, Hammerschmidt bore the stigma cast upon the party by Richard Nixon's involvement in and resignation because of the Watergate affair.

Hammeschmidt, for his part, scored points against Clinton by pointing out that the young man had worked for the failed George McGovern effort two years before. Cryptically, Hammerschmidt alleged that the heavy hands of labor were at work in the Clinton campaign, mentioning that much of Clinton's campaign funds came from that source.

In Russellville, Clinton scored a coup of sorts during a political rally at the trailing end of the fall campaign. Every state and third-district candidate had been invited to the affair and given the opportunity to make a short three-minute speech. West Virginia's Senator Robert Byrd was there, speaking for Clinton's idol, Senator Fulbright, who would be defeated in his re-election bid by Arkansas' most popular governor, Dale Bumpers. Clinton was slated as the final speaker of the evening. He got his turn at the podium about ten o'clock.

I was standing near David Pryor, whom I had supported in the Democratic gubernatorial primary. I watched Bill Clinton—

in the space of 180 seconds — bring the tired, listless Pope County crowd to its feet. And I saw Clinton's political colleagues look upon his accomplishment with blank amazement. At 15, I was an experienced public speaker, having won several contests during the past year. I saw Bill Clinton's oratorical skill as a mark to strive for. I remember realizing, as my father drove me home that night, that Clinton was the only candidate I had not had the chance to meet. I would wait another year and a half for the opportunity.

On election night, Bill Clinton had badly scared John Paul Hammerschmidt. According to interviews, Clinton really didn't believe in 1974 that he could win the congressional seat, but he came quite close to proving himself wrong. He managed to attract 48 percent of the votes in the solidly Republican district, while Hammerschmidt won the election with 52 percent.

After the election, the Arkansas Gazette noted that Bill Clinton had made his mark as "a brilliant young law professor," and added that "it is regrettable that Arkansas did not quite add its own extra momentum to the national Democratic landslide..." The newspaper closed with the thought that "Bill Clinton very nearly made it to Congress, and surely he will be back in 1976." As it was, Clinton had run an impressive campaign, building a sound organization, and earning the endorsement of the powerful Arkansas Education Association in the process. Hindsight being better than foresight, it might now be argued that Clinton, following the lead of John F. Kennedy in 1956, won by losing, since his defeat by Hammerschmidt helped set the stage for a successful 1976 entry into Arkansas mainstream politics.

Clinton returned to his teaching post in Fayetteville, which he had retained without pay during his campaign absence, having begun to build his reputation as what Arkansas Gazette writer Ernest Dumas called "the boy wonder" of Arkansas politics. The man who had so nearly upset John Paul Hammerschmidt's well-funded applecart was only 28 years old. One might expect that Clinton's homecoming was a little less painful than it might otherwise have been for a defeated congressional candidate: Hillary Rodham had joined the University of Arkansas Law School faculty while the campaign was still in progress.

Hillary quickly adjusted to life in a small Arkansas town. Both aspects of her new environment were strange to her, but she freely admits that she quickly felt at home in Fayetteville and grew to love not only the law school and her colleagues, but the setting as well. She and Clinton taught through the balance of 1974 and into the spring semester of 1975. Somewhere along the way, the couple became engaged to be married.

The wedding transpired in October 1975 at Bill Clinton's Fayetteville home. At the private ceremony, the newlyweds exchanged rings — both of which were family heirlooms. Roger Clinton was there as his brother's best man, and the bride's brothers and parents also attended. During the reception, which members of the press attended, Clinton announced that he would seek office again in 1976, but that he remained unsure whether he would launch another campaign against Congressman Hammerschmidt or opt for seeking the state's attorney general post. Coincidentally, one of the wedding guests was the incumbent attorney general, Jim Guy Tucker.

Tucker, for his part, encouraged Clinton to select the attorney general's post as his next political goal. Tucker himself was intent upon vacating the office in an effort to win a congressional seat in another district. By early 1976, the Clinton organization was taking the field in an impressive show of force. Since the filing deadline passed without a Republican entering the race, each of the three contenders for the attorney general's office knew that whoever won the Democratic primary would, in effect, win the race.

Clinton faced opposition from a former secretary of state and an assistant attorney general. George T. Jernigan had been appointed to the secretary's post in the 1960s, while Clarence Cash had held his position for some years. Both men rightfully possessed an insider's knowledge of the Little Rock political environment, although this might have been a bigger handicap than an asset in the minds of Arkansas voters.

Clinton made an impressive showing in the primary, handling the challengers rather easily. Clinton drew more than 55 percent of the popular vote, winning the race without a runoff. Jernigan polled just over 24 percent, while Cash contented himself with a 20 percent showing. At the time he won the Democratic primary, Clinton was still three months shy of his thirtieth birthday. He was scheduled to take office as Attorney General in January 1977.

As like attracts like, Bill Clinton hired a young, idealistic staff to serve him as attorney general. He became extraordinarily accessible to the public—as I noted in the preface to this book, I once reached him in his office on the first phone call—and began to work on such important issues as prison overcrowding and consumer affairs. As the state's top lawyer, Clinton managed to weave an impressive thread into the tapestry of his political career. He had, indeed, begun to grow into the part of a master politician.

Arkansas Democrat editorialist John Robert Starr dipped his pen in acid some years ago to note that, while serving as the state's top lawyer, Clinton went out of his way to "cultivate" an anti-utility, pro-consumer image. In Arkansas, most residents feel nothing but disdain for the utility companies, since a large part of the workingman's paycheck goes to pay power and light and natural gas bills. The popular grassroots conception is that the utility officials are making away with vast sums of money while most Arkansans are barely scraping by because of inflated utility billings.

Part of Clinton's early success in Arkansas politics—winning the attorney general's race and defeating four opponents in the 1978 Democratic gubernatorial primary without a run-off—was due largely to public perception. Without a position of authority and without a mandate for change, Clinton could not initiate the sweeping reforms he would attempt during his first term as governor. It is a sad commentary on Arkansas' political mentality that, while Clinton could not by virtue of his position make any real attempt to change the way the state was run, voters across the state looked forward to bringing his youth, idealism and drive to power. Once in possession of the power necessary to bring change into effect, the populace as a whole rebelled against the changes Clinton tried to bring about—changes he had promised all Arkansans and changes they themselves had seemed to desire. Once portent had changed to power, dreams of real advancement were swept aside as most Arkansans reverted to the attitudes and behaviors which had served them so poorly for so very long.

3

THE END OF THE BEGINNING

★   ★   ★   ★   ★   ★

Arkansans, as a general rule, barely tolerate progressivism. Each of the state's seventy five counties is a political entity within itself, content to allow generations of carefully crafted tradition to create well-worn pathways for the future. Any Arkansas politician who contemplates a statewide race for elective office must come to grips with his homeland on a county-by-county basis. While the state can be divided into regions, they are at best ill-defined and irregular. The only way to win a popular election in Arkansas with any semblance of a mandate is to become an expert on each county...to come to know the structure, political power bases, problems, prejudices and opportunities that lie within each of the seventy-five separate dominions. This would be an easy task were it not for the fact that even adjacent counties are strikingly different. The only commonality is that all are equally frightened by the prospect of being dragged, kicking and screaming, into the twenty-first century.

In the Democratic gubernatorial primary of 1978, only one of the five candidates had recent experience in dealing with Arkansas on a county-by-county basis—and that candidate was destined to win without a runoff, something virtually unheard of in recent Arkansas Democratic decisions. The young man who prevailed over his four rivals was already known across the state, but that was not his only advantage: he was currently the attorney general, possessed charming good looks, an outstanding ability to communicate, and an intellect that rivaled any other ever seen in the service of the state. His name was William Jefferson Clinton.

Clinton and his four opponents were each gunning to replace Governor David Pryor, a former congressman who had served his obligatory two terms as governor and was now waging a campaign for a seat in the United States Senate. While nothing in the state's constitution limits sitting governors to two terms, Pryor had served his time and had done so with moderate distinction. His desire to move to higher ground was not without precedent; only two of the state's former governors—segregation-era mainstay Orval Faubus, defeated by Pryor in the 1974 Democratic primary, and the popular Jeff Davis—had served more than a pair of two-year terms. The odd result of this every-four-year phenomenon was that some capable Arkansas politician was, by virtue of a lost election, inevitably thrust out of work. Strange to say, the state's media never mentioned that fact. Nor did most Arkansans take notice of it.

The five Democrats who had thrown their hats into the primary campaign ring were a mixed lot. Three were lawyers, one was a former county judge, and one was a turkey farmer. This astonishing field represented nothing new or unusual in Arkansas politics, and would be succeeded by even stranger slates of candidates. But in the spring of 1978, these five candidates gave Arkansas Democrats a wide range of gubernatorial primary options.

The turkey farmer was a 75-year-old from Kingsland with the rather imposing name of Monroe Schwarzlose. He had run for state representative four years earlier—and lost. Nothing if not undaunted, Schwarzlose would appear with regularity in future contests for the governor's office. Of course, he would never advance beyond the primary.

Randall Mathis' claim to fame was that he had been former county judge of Clark County, the seat of which is Arkadelphia, where the Ouachita Baptist University is located. He was also a former president of the Arkansas Association of County Judges. In Arkansas, a county judge can't judge anything; he presides over the county's quorum court and directs county construction and improvement projects. The 47-year-old Mathis was well known as a cattle rancher and had a certain following in the south central part of Arkansas, but he lacked a statewide organization.

Frank Lady hailed from Jonesboro, the home of Arkansas State University. An attorney, the 48-year-old Lady had served as state representative and had been an unsuccessful candidate for governor back in 1976. Like Mathis, his strength was more regional than statewide; his popularity centered largely in the northeastern corner of Arkansas.

Joe Woodward was something else again. At 48, he had already been a prosecuting attorney, trial lawyer, and had served in 1973 as legislative assistant to the state's most popular governor, Dale Bumpers. Woodward, from Magnolia, came closer than any other candidate to fielding a large base for his campaign.

Except, ofcourse, for Attorney General Clinton. Already, the state press had singled him out as a force to be reckoned with in Arkansas politics. In Conway, the Log Cabin Democrat newspaper called the state's top lawyer "an attractive, articulate political leader," adding that Clinton's "record as attorney general has been studded with examples of hard work, consumer concerns, and a generally aggressive stance that has led him into a variety of situations with seeming zest."

All this was heady stuff, especially for a 31-year-old. Clinton himself had, before announcing his candidacy for the governor's office, published his own "Attorney General's Report" which, according to the Arkansas Gazette, lauded the achievements of Clinton's time in office in the same "glowing terms." Clinton used campaign monies to pay for the printing and distribution of the report.

Now the press was picking up the theme. Clinton, like any good politician, had been careful to cultivate the attention of the media during his two years as attorney general. Traveling around Arkansas, he succeeded in making a substantial number of speeches, and by the fall of 1977 was beginning to use some of those gatherings as impromptu campaign affairs. The people of the state responded in kind, rewarding Clinton's effort with warm handshakes, compliments, and pledges of support. At one early-morning rally in a small college ballroom, a young boy — the son of a friend — approached the attorney general and asked, "When you're governor, can I still call you 'Bill' or do I have to call you 'Mr. Bill'?" Clinton responded that the boy could continue to use the first name without modification.

All of Bill Clinton's hard work paid off in the Democratic gubernatorial primary of 1978. He faced his four opponents with one of the best political organizations ever seen in Arkansas. As a result, he swept the field clean, winning without a runoff—an incredible feat when one considers that five candidates were in the running. Clinton carried all but four of Arkansas' 75 counties and took sixty percent of the Democratic vote.

Despite the Rockefeller years, until 1980 winning the Democratic primary in Arkansas meant that the race was quite literally over. Only the recent organizational efforts of the state's

Republican faction have made the general election anything more than a formality. So it was in the fall of 1978, when Bill Clinton beat the Republican challenger, Lynn Lowe, by more than 140,000 votes. The margin might have been larger had not Clinton's effort appeared too well organized to many Arkansans.

Clinton put the time between the election and his inauguration to good use. First, he flew to the nation's capital to meet with President Jimmy Carter. The governor-elect wanted to open a state office in Washington, D.C.. He also discussed the state's executive budget with the President. Clinton was hopeful that the budget would meet Carter's anti-inflationary guidelines, but he was concerned by a proposal to raise teacher salaries, which might be considered counterproductive to that cause.

Clinton also seized the opportunity to moderate a discussion on the issue of national health care during the Democratic party's midterm convention in Memphis, Tennessee. Media representatives fairly flocked around Clinton, leading to rumors and speculation that Senator Edward M. Kennedy had chosen Clinton to be his running mate in an effort to unseat Jimmy Carter during the Democratic primaries of 1980. Others maintained that Carter himself was about to dump Vice President Walter Mondale to make room for Clinton on the 1980 reelection ticket.

The rumor apparently flattered Bill Clinton, but he told reporters that his first duty was to be a good governor and serve Arkansas to the best of his ability. The media, impressed with the young man's forthright attitude, had failed to observe the first rule of journalism. Someone had neglected to do his homework, which in this case would have meant quickly reviewing the U.S. Constitution. It states that if a president dies or becomes incapacitated, the vice president must, of course, be qualified to take his place. Clinton, according to the constitution, wasn't qualified. He wasn't old enough.

Clinton had turned 32 by the time he took office on January 10, 1979. National news programs and magazines called him "Arkansas' Boy Governor" and continually harped on the fact that he was the nation's youngest state executive. Foreshadowings of the future were there, just as in any political event, but few bothered to take the time to read them...including Bill Clinton himself. The result would be brutal—in two years' time, he would be the nation's youngest ex-governor as well.

At the moment, however, all was sweetness and light, especially in the Arkansas press. The now defunct Arkansas Gazette, then the state's largest newspaper, noted that the era of the "old-style political bosses" had apparently ended in Arkansas. "The old demon of race is nearly gone," the newspaper added with unsubstantiated optimism, implying that Arkansans were now free to pursue a more worthy agenda— "Better education, more roads, higher paying jobs."

During his inaugural speech, Arkansas' fortieth governor focused on education, which would become the cornerstone of his efforts to lead his state into "a new era of achievement and excellence" and "a life that will be the envy of the nation," rather than one of its saddest jokes. Clinton noted that Arkansas had spent too much time at or near the national bottom of teacher salaries in particular and education spending in general. "We must try to reverse that," the new state executive insisted, tapping his finger on the podium for emphasis. Clinton added that Arkansas needed "better accountability and assessment of students and teachers, a fairer distribution of aid, more efficient organization of school districts..." and noted that efforts continued to build programs for "kindergarten, special education, and gifted and talented children."

The inaugural address was broad-ranging. Clinton pledged his effort to address economic development, equal opportunity, abuse of power by government officials, emotionally disturbed children, tax relief for the elderly, and along that line, help for those Arkansans who were "old and weak or needy." Additionally, the new governor promised to establish a state department of energy and pledged to revamp the outmoded Arkansas Industrial Development Commission into an economic development group instead. (The outgoing director of the commission was a man named Frank White, who would clean Bill Clinton's proverbial clock two years hence.)

Clinton selected three young men to share power in his office. They were Rudy Moore, Steve Smith, and John Danner. Together, the modern triumvirate did little but create trouble and strife for Bill Clinton. Smith himself later admitted to political journalist David Osborne:

> We probably did too much head bashing in the first term. Part of it was that people like me on the staff were sort of smart (alecs), and angered a lot of people. We were after every dragon in the land. I used language like corporate criminals, which really did not endear the governor to the timber companies.

Arkansas Democrat newspaper editor John Robert Starr, a long-time Bill Clinton critic, noted that Moore, Smith, and Danner were "three young, bearded, impractical visionaries...they had not a shred of common sense among them." Across the state, business and political leaders came to the conclusion that the governor's staff was simply out to make them mad. In that regard, Moore, Smith, and Danner succeeded admirably.

At the outset of his term, Clinton began the effort to push through legislation aimed at raising motor vehicle registration and title transfer fees and gasoline and tire taxes. Most Arkansans paid roughly $15 for the auto licenses. Henceforth, because of the Clinton legislation, they paid about double. The fee increase was to generate revenue intended to pay for a major highway repair campaign.

In almost any other state, the residents would not have thought twice about such a small outlay for long-range rewards in road improvements. But in Arkansas, the citizenry reacted with rising alarm. This might have been forestalled if the system for collecting the tax had not been something reminiscent of the late middle ages. Residents made the rounds of their county offices each year, obtaining a vehicle inspection, paying the previous year's personal property tax, and submitting an assessment of their current personal property. The entire process was — and is — a purgatory of forms, surly, overworked county employees and long lines. To finally arrive at the end of the license tax line and be hit with a hundred-percent increase was, to many Arkansans, the straw that broke the camel's back. It made no difference what the money was to be used for. And rather than attack the system, which God himself apparently cannot change, Arkansans attacked the governor instead. They could change him — and they did.

Truth to tell, the tax increase hit hardest among those most likely to carry a grudge all the way to the ballot box — the rural poor. Here, residents usually drove older cars and trucks which, because they weighed so much, typically were the objects of larger tax increases. And the title transfer fee was an added burden to this class of Arkansans because, as Clinton biographer Charles Allen accurately noted, they were most likely to purchase an old auto, drive it until it wore out, and then purchase another old auto to take its place.

The problems with the Clinton administration didn't stop at the end of the license line. The governor became the target of local chambers of commerce, who contended that he was ignoring the task of recruiting industry to Arkansas. In fact, there was some truth to this charge because Clinton had abolished the old Arkansas Industrial Development Commission in favor of a Department of Economic Development. Rather than attempt to attract industry to the state, as had its predecessor, the new department spent time and resources on promoting agricultural exports, funding small farm projects, community development and small business consulting. Again, in any other state, these would all have been needed, helpful additions to state services. But usually, state economies must crawl before they walk, then walk before they run. Arkansas' own economic outlook has always been rather bleak at best, monopolized by large commercial interests which offer many jobs at less-than-average pay. Since most Arkansans are attracted to these industrial giants, the populace would rather have had the state's emphasis placed on finding more of them, rather than encouraging agricultural and business-related entrepreneurs.

Next, the governor came under fire from the state's physicians, who objected to the network of rural health clinics Clinton had established. Timber industry officials became upset by a series of public hearings on the subject of clear-cutting. And trucking and poultry industry magnates became increasingly concerned about higher taxes, despite the fact that the additional revenue was used to repair roadways traveled daily by their trucks and cargo carriers.

If there was a bright spot for Bill Clinton in his first term as governor, it was in the area of education. Here he fought another uphill battle, but emerged with only a few battle scars and some demonstrable results. The day after his inauguration, Clinton outlined to the Arkansas legislature his education plan, which contained a pair of controversial proposals: First, a bill requiring fair teacher dismissal procedures, coupled with legislation requiring all teachers to pass a competency examination before they could receive their certification to teach; second, a bill which called for mandatory achievement tests for all students in three grades each year. This testing system, Clinton maintained, would be a diagnostic tool of sorts, letting parents and educators alike use the information it yielded to make their decisions about the future of the state's educational system.

Bill Clinton's third proposal, school consolidation, was an ambitious undertaking initially assigned to a commission which would spend two years studying the issue. Arkansas, at the time, supported nearly four hundred school districts. The governor insisted that he had no desire to eliminate the smaller districts but wished to eliminate what he called "duplicative and inefficient administrative structures."

The new school consolidation package would be enacted into law, if the timetable held, sometime in 1981. After the plan was presented to the legislature, opposition grew, and the governor was forced to withdraw it from consideration.

During his Jan. 15, 1979, address, Clinton maintained that he wanted to modify the formula used to compute the Minimum Foundation Program Aid to Arkansas' school districts, vowing that the state had the funds to reform the program and at the same time provide each district with a funding increase. The aim of the reforms would be to narrow the gap between per-pupil spending in rich and poor districts.

The Arkansas legislature passed into law the governor's measure to require the state's public school teachers to take the National Teacher's Examination. While the Arkansas Education Association did not oppose the statute, individual teachers were, in some cases, quite vocal in expressing their displeasure. This was, in part, due to the fact that smaller Arkansas communities were utilizing local residents—some of whom did not even possess a high school diploma—to teach such classes as shop and driver's education. With the advent of the examination, those individuals could no longer be employed as teachers.

A year into his first term as governor, Clinton faced a crisis which threatened his plans to adequately fund Arkansas education. State revenues fell below projected levels, forcing a special legislative session in January 1980. Clinton and his staff devised a plan to change the way the state was collecting employee income tax withholdings from Arkansas employers. Rather than settling accounts on a quarterly basis, the system was changed to a monthly payment. The result was a "windfall" of about $40 million dollars, more than half of which went to the public school fund. Half of that amount was spent on teacher salary increases, resulting in an average pay raise of $1,200 per year for each Arkansas teacher. The Arkansas Education Association countered that the raise was not enough.

Failure and mismanagement continued to dog Bill Clinton through his first term as governor. The director of the state's new Economic Development Department, James Dyke, had ordered live plants as an office decoration—at a cost of $450 per month. At the Arkansas Democrat, Starr lost no time in pointing an accusatory finger at the Clinton administration. Dyke's order was subsequently withdrawn. Another article focused on the state's expenditure of $2,000 for an energy department employees' retreat at Lake DeGray. The governor defended the money spent, claiming that the conference was, in fact, due and needed.

Then, the Arkansas Democrat reported that Clinton's chief of staff, Rudy Moore, had been accused of abducting a woman from a Little Rock restaurant. It made no difference to editor Starr that the woman was Moore's girlfriend, or that she later dropped the charges. Another article appeared critical of the Special Alternative Wood Energy Resources (SAWER) Project, a vehicle used to provide employment to low-income Arkansans who cut wood and distributed it to the needy. According to the Democrat, the project had cost state taxpayers some $62,000 and had produced only three cords of cut wood. When the Arkansas Gazette launched a probe into the SAWER affair, Clinton fired director Ted Newman.

Meanwhile, political fever began to grip the state. Arkansas' two-year term limitation meant Bill Clinton would be open to challenge in the Democratic primary slated for the spring of 1980. Since the year also marked a presidential contest, it's surprising that he had only one primary opponent. He was retired turkey farmer Monroe Schwarzlose, who had succumbed to the Clinton onslaught only two years before. Many of us who were engaged in watching state political activity at the time thought Schwarzlose's bid somewhat ludicrous. We were surprised by how well he did — and should have been forewarned that a fall upset was in the making. Few of us — none, perhaps — picked up on it.

On the Republican side, Frank White, the former AIDC director turned Little Rock savings and loan executive, had filed in the gubernatorial primary, opposed by Franklin County's Marshall Chrisman. Although White rather handily defeated Chrisman in the primary on May 27, the fact that just over nine thousand votes were cast for the GOP candidates meant that his victory raised no eyebrows. Burdened by the characteristic track record left behind by other candidates from his party, White was given little chance of beating the Democratic incumbent in November.

The gubernatorial primary was set for Tuesday, May 27. The day before, Fort Chaffee, the military base near Fort Smith, Arkansas, became the setting for the drama which would drive the final nail into Bill Clinton's political coffin. Nearly 20,000 refugees from the Cuban "boatlift" had been confined at Chaffee by the federal government. On May 26, some 350 of these refugees decided they would no longer accept the camp's hospitality and began to roam through the surrounding countryside. Within three days, all had been recaptured by Arkansas State Police and local law enforcement officials. But Clinton was outraged. The federal officers at Chaffee had done little to either keep the Cubans on the base or to recapture them when they left. Clinton ordered 200 members of the Arkansas National Guard to the Fort, and demanded that the Federal Emergency Management Agency (FEMA) tighten security at the compound. He called President Carter and asked the embattled Democrat to issue orders that the army was to keep the Cubans on the base.

In all fairness to both the governor and President Carter, there were precious few other choices for locations in which to house the Cubans. The only other viable site was in Pennsylvania, and President Carter was quick to point out to Clinton that the climate there was unsuitable for individuals used to life in the tropics. Chaffee seemed the only logical alternative.

In Arkansas, much of the problem with the refugees seemed to be with how the survivors of the "boatlift" were perceived. Much media attention had been focused on Fidel Castro's use of the floating exodus to rid his island of criminals, drug pushers and the mentally and physically handicapped. Residents who lived near Chaffee, as well as those throughout the western half of Arkansas, were understandably frightened by the prospect of having nearly 20,000 such individuals close at hand. Not fully understanding the situation, they came to blame Bill Clinton for not "standing up" to the president and demanding that the Cubans be resettled somewhere else. In this case, however, little Clinton could have said to Carter would have made a great deal of difference.

The unusually warm spring rolled into an unbearably hot summer. Arkansas poultry farmers lost hundreds of thousands of chickens in the intense heat. The summer-long drought caused the deaths of thousands of head of livestock. Forest fires raged through the Ouachita and Ozark National Forests. A Titan missile blew up in its central Arkansas silo. "Every time you turned around," Clinton aide Patty Criner told Charles Allen, "there was a disaster."

Intrepid turkey farmer Monroe Schwarzlose was very nearly the political beneficiary of all this misfortune. In the Democratic primary on May 27, he racked up about 31 percent of the statewide vote — quite a showing for a 77-year-old who had campaigned on the issues of the SAWER fiasco and car tag fee increases. Indeed, Schwarzlose had circulated a campaign ad which featured the candidate himself standing beside his own woodpile, proof — according to Schwarzlose – that three cords of wood could be cut for a lot less than $62,000.

Four days after the primary, the Cuban issue exploded again. This time Arkansans saw their worst nightmares turn to reality as Fort Chaffee exploded into full-blown riot. While most of the conflict was confined to the base itself, some 200 Cubans headed down Arkansas Highway 22, bound for the small community of Barling, just outside of Fort Smith. They were turned back —by officers wielding nightsticks — about a hundred yards short of the town limits. Governor Clinton, appalled by the failure of officials to contain a federal problem, demanded once again that the army keep the Cubans on the base. Two months later, adding insult to injury, President Carter informed the governor that another 10,000 Cubans from other bases around the country would be transferred to Fort Chaffee.

For Frank White, the Cuban situation seemed manna from some sort of political heaven. That fall, the Republican nominee began running television ads which showed the Cubans rioting at Chaffee and criticized Governor Clinton for not standing up to President Carter. Carter's popularity in Arkansas — which he had carried in the 1976 election, due largely to Clinton's efforts – was at low ebb. The governor had done his best, but to reply that he had would be to invite White to rejoin that Clinton's best was apparently not good enough. The governor could do little but let Frank White score his points. As the campaign developed, that is precisely what happened.

For Bill Clinton, the political medicine ball was rolling downhill, and there was no way to stop it. The Department of Local Services had approved nearly a million dollars in grant monies to the Ozarks Institute of Eureka Springs. Locally, opposition to the program was spawned and began to grow, largely because Frank White inaccurately described it as an effort directed at teaching rural residents to grow gardens. Also, Steve Smith, the Clinton aide, had served on the Institute's board and was a close friend of its director, Edd Jeffords. Though the comments White made about the director proved untrue—and cost the new governor some $7,000 in a post-election libel suit—the issue was a political plus for Frank White.

Three weeks before the election, the Clinton and White campaign war chests were within a few thousand dollars of parity. The White campaign continued the refrain "Cubans and Car Tags" and carried it across the state; candidate White promised to repeal the car tag fee increases, which he called a source of "great pain" for Arkansans, especially those on fixed incomes. On a campaign swing through Russellville, the Republican candidate charged that Bill Clinton "should have sued them" when federal officials announced plans to settle Cuban refugees at Fort Chaffee. In almost any other state, the ambiguity of White's statement would have been its undoing. But that evening in Pope County, Arkansas, he received a healthy round of applause. By late in the campaign, anything anti-Clinton was fair game. The Republicans even turned Clinton's wife, Hillary Rodham, to their advantage, noting that she had declined to adopt her husband's name when they had married five years earlier. Somehow, many ultraconservative Arkansans reasoned, this omission on Ms. Rodham's part indicated either a lack of confidence in her husband's ability or a lack of Bill Clinton's ability to control his wife. Actually, Hillary kept her own last name for professional reasons and has since adopted her husband's last name as her own. But in the fall of 1980, it seemed that many Arkansans were just not interested in the facts—especially when they were about to exercise their franchise.

On election day, as Frank White took a commanding lead in the mid-evening returns, a reporter asked White if he thought the voters of Arkansas were trying to send a message to Bill Clinton. With his characteristic enthusiasm, White replied, "I think they're sending a message that they want me to be governor!," and rebel-yelled with delight. ABC Television, busy covering the already-decided presidential race between Ronald Reagan and Jimmy Carter, had early on projected that Clinton would retain his office. Late in the evening, they called the governor's campaign headquarters to assure Clinton, as if it mattered, that their projection still held firm—that he would win despite the latest vote tally. In the end, it made no difference. By the next morning, it was all over, including the shouting. Frank White had won the governor's office with a plurality of more than 32,000 votes. Nearly 840,000 Arkansans had cast their ballots. It was the first upset in an Arkansas gubernatorial contest in more than a quarter of a century.

In Little Rock, popular morning radio personality Ray Lincoln told KAAY listeners that he had run into "Bill and Hillary at the supermarket early this morning...they were hunting for boxes." That sort of joke prevailed across the state for the next few days, as anti-Clinton advocates and those who had supported Frank White—though the two were often not synonymous—celebrated their victory.

Frank White rode into the governor's office on the coattails of the Ronald Reagan/George Bush landslide. The mood of the times in late 1980 was a mandate for change. The old guard had tried, and it could not provide the answers. Perhaps the new guard could. As nearly always occurs in United States politics, the results certainly have been mixed.

Certainly, something other than the mood of the times defeated Bill Clinton. Reaction to the car tag fee increase—which probably would not have mattered in any state except Arkansas—and to the Cuban debacle certainly contributed to his downfall. But something bigger was responsible for Bill Clinton's loss to Frank White. Call it a public perception, a popular feeling, or a vague general impression. Most Arkansans felt that Clinton was too young, too arrogant, too ambitous, and too insensitive. The governor exhibited none of these traits during the campaign and immediately following his election. They all manifested themselves—in the public's mind, if not the governor's—after he had begun to serve.

Clinton himself told Charles Allen that he "simply didn't communicate to the people that I genuinely cared about them...I think maybe I gave the appearance of trying to do too many things and not involving the people as I should..." The governor said that he felt many Arkansans had swung their support to Frank White only in the last few, hurried days before the 1980 election.

Two years to the day after he had taken the oath of office, the Arkansas Gazette described Bill Clinton's emotional farewell to the state legislature. The article, titled "Clinton's leave-taking," noted that:

It was a poignant scene as Clinton appeared before a joint session of the legislature in a crowded House chamber, his wife, Hillary, holding their 10-month-old daughter, at his side. Just two years earlier he had taken the oath in the same chamber as the nation's youngest governor, one whose intellect and personality were soon to capture national admiration and credit for the state. Now he was beaten, leaving the state government after a narrow upset loss in November, asking the people to 'remember me as one who reached for all he could for Arkansas.

The article continued with a studied excerpt from Clinton's address:

It was an upstream speech, moving against the current of political fashion.But, as the governor remarked, Arkansas remains 51st—last—in the payment of state and local taxes: We pay less taxes than the people in any other state in the Union, not to mention the District of Columbia. Accordingly, we are at or near the bottom in the level of public services in nearly every category, from teacher salaries to higher education to unemployment compensation. There is but one answer—broadening the tax base—and the state will have to come to it, sooner or later, meantime settling for the barest minimums in the services expected in the American society...

The article might have mentioned that it had been Arkansans' refusal to decide that the time to broaden their tax base had indeed arrived and was largely the reason for this being Clinton's farewell article. The article closed with an appropriately sentimental note:

It is sad to see Clinton go, departing public life for an indeterminate period before the comeback campaign...that everyone

knows is certain. We have always thought of Bill Clinton as
something special. No one in Arkansas in modern times has
been elected governor so young with so much promise. If
circumstances joined with certain errors in political judg-
ment to deny him the customary second term, inevitably
Clinton has learned lessons that will serve him in the future...

Thirteen months later, Bill Clinton's first 1982 television campaign ad would hit the state's airwaves. Already less than thrilled with Frank White's performance as governor, Arkansans listened with new-found sensitivity and awareness as Clinton declared that he felt remorse for the errors that were his responsibility while in office, and that he wished again for the opportunity to serve. The former governor coined his own campaign phrase, "You can't lead without listening," which seemed to underscore this act of contrition. That May, Clinton beat back a challenge from State Senator Kim Hendren and Congressman Jim Guy Tucker in the Democratic primary, but managed only a runoff with former Lt. Governor Joe Purcell. Winning the runoff rather handily — although, to his credit, Purcell ran a clean, classy sort of campaign — Clinton thereby earned the opportunity to wrestle Frank White again. In November 1982, after a wildly seesawing campaign and the expenditure of nearly three million campaign dollars, the outcome was in Clinton's favor. He beat back the Republican effort, despite a fair bit of popular support and a George Bush endorsement for White's re-election bid.

But on that day in January 1981, when Bill Clinton walked away from the governor's office, his comeback triumph was almost too far in the future to be visualized. The defeated governor, his family, and staff had quite literally arrived at the end of the beginning.

4

THE YEARS AT THE HELM
1983–1988

★   ★   ★   ★   ★   ★

Bill Clinton returned to the governor's office in January 1983 without breaking stride. Judging from his behavior, chastisement by the voters and two years of solemn reflection had only served to strengthen his resolve to be a catalyst for change. Immediately, Clinton challenged the Arkansas legislature to join him in moving forward with a common purpose. Their goal would be to better the lives of Arkansans who had made the state's government the repository of their trust.

In mid-January, the governor delivered his State of the State address, which outlined a number of legislative reforms which would reach into the realms of business, education, and consumer affairs. Later in the year, Clinton would look upon the proposals with a mixture of pride and disappointment. Most politicians would argue that such a mixed result is inevitable. Bill Clinton, however, had never resigned himself to that attitude.

The governor told the state's lawmakers that he wanted to establish "enterprise zones" in disadvantaged areas of Arkansas, in an effort to help stimulate employment. Additionally, Clinton sought a one-time tax credit for employers who could demonstrate a net employment gain during the year.

Arkansas' industries have traditionally fallen short of the cutting edge in technology, and the governor sought legislative approval in his effort to attract high-tech companies to the state. Toward that end, Clinton sought to establish a special advisory group called the Arkansas Science and Technology Development Authority. Despite the rather ponderous name, the agency had a strikingly simple task—to coordinate the development of high-tech job skills and opportunities.

Of course, many industries in Arkansas relied on their own trucking fleets and the state's highways to transport their product. In an effort to help those firms, Clinton asked the legislature to increase truck weight limits on the state highways. This was a deceptively simple task, aimed primarily at garnering the state millions of dollars in highway funding. Clinton maintained that increasing the existing weight limits would help to increase the competition between trucking and shipping firms. While the lawmakers would reach a consensus on the truck weight issue, it would later become a source of great frustration for the governor. In fact, Clinton would later describe the initiative as one of the most disappointing episodes of the year.

The governor gave the legislative joint session detailed proposals for changes in school teacher contracts and teacher hiring and firing practices. Clinton told the lawmakers that education in Arkansas must become a top priority:

> *Over the long run, education is the key to our economic revival and our perennial quest for prosperity. We must dedicate more of our limited resources to paying teachers better; expanding educational opportunities in poor and small school districts; improving and diversifying vocational and high technology programs; and perhaps most important, strengthening basic education. Without competence in basic skills our people cannot move on to more advanced achievement.*

Eventually, Clinton would propose that the legislature allow Arkansas students to travel outside their home school
district to take advantage of classes offered elsewhere. Additionally, he asked the lawmakers to help expand regional educational service centers which would allow for the pooling of
resources from smaller rural schools.

The governor's efforts to improve education continued
through the regular legislative session and into a special called
session later that same year. This session in particular would
garner Clinton national attention because of his efforts to reform the state's education system and to legislate teacher testing. That issue in particular would provoke the ire of Arkansas
teachers and initiate a running battle between Clinton and the
Arkansas Education Association.

The tragic incidence of alcohol-related traffic fatalities and
the increasing number of driving-while-intoxicated arrests had
captured Clinton's attention as well. To the legislature, he
proposed tougher DWI laws, which he said would put Arkansas on the front lines in the war against drunk drivers. Today,
Clinton considers the stiffer DWI penalties enacted by the
legislature as one of his finest achievements.

Finally, Clinton pledged to attack the recurrent issue of
utility rate reform. The centerpiece of his package would be
legislation to revamp Arkansas' Public Service Commission.
The governor called for the PSC membership to be increased
from three to five, and that the panelists be elected, rather than
appointed. According to the Clinton plan, four of the five PSC
members would be elected from the state's congressional districts, and the fifth member would be elected at large by all
Arkansas voters and chair the group. In his address to the
legislature, Clinton pointed out that:

> *Nothing so clearly demonstrates what is wrong with the
> established order as the recent study by the Industrial Re-*

search and Extension Center which reviewed all utility rate-making systems and concluded that our present system of appointing the PSC... even the elected commissions have generally given proper, quicker decisions at lower cost, with lower rates in the end. The people do have enough sense to elect the PSC and a clear majority want the chance to do so. We should give it to them.

Finally, the governor issued a plea for legislative unity, saying that:

It will not be easy to balance the complex and often competing forces in our state to forge a forward march, but we can do it. Too often in the past, we have helped our old foe, "hard times," to defeat us by working against ourselves, by thinking too little of ourselves and what we can achieve... Admittedly, I have set an ambitious agenda for Arkansas in hard times. It has been criticized by those who say it is too full of promises. But politics is about the promises of today and tomorrow. It is far better to fall short of a lofty goal than to stand by in self-satisfaction while good people are pained by present conditions.

With his plan for legislative action set firmly in place, Clinton began the formidable task of convincing both the state's legislators and the legislative lobbyists that he had the best interests of the people at heart.

The legislature went straight to work, attempting to hammer out a badly-needed bill that would raise truck weight limits on the state's highways. Clinton held back his own proposal on the matter, waiting to see if rival factions within the legislature could bring themselves together and begin the process. For the governor, though, restraint was difficult at best. He had become convinced—and sought to convince the lawmakers—that unless the weight limit was raised from the existing 73,280 pounds to 80,000, the state would lose as much as $100 million in highway funds. In 47 other states, similar measures had already been adopted. Arkansas had to initiate the same sort of legislation just to keep pace.

The ensuing legislative debate brought two major lobbying groups into the hallways of the state capitol. One was the Forward Arkansas Committee, an industry coalition of shippers and truckers who wanted the advantage of being able to carry extra weight. The FAC was aided by poultry industry activists, who were used to winning these sorts of legislative battles and certainly anticipated another victory.

On the opposite side of the political fence was the Arkansas Highway Commission, headed by the formidable Henry Gray, who was a skilled practitioner of what might best be described as "button-hole democracy." Gray argued that the new federal weight laws—which necessitated this battle in the first place—were a double-edged sword, in that the statutes carried with them a tax structure which would cost the state even if the weight limit was increased. Additionally, Gray maintained that heavier trucks would cause greater damage to the state's highways, which would cost money to repair. Needless to say, the increased need for repairs would carry with it a rather hefty price tag.

Russellville's state representative, L. L. "Doc" Bryan, had long been an asset to the poultry industry's lobbying effort. Now, with the poultry industry aiding the Forward Arkansas Committee, the rotund, fast-talking Bryan stepped into the breach. His House Bill 192 would raise the truck weight limit to the requested 80,000 pounds, but failed to address any sort of revenue-generating measure which would be needed to pay for taxes and highway upkeep.

But Bryan had thought of that, too. His Mel Blanc-like voice echoing through the House chamber, the Pope County law-maker advocated a separate bill which would slightly increase licensing fees for trucks. The result—about $2.5 million in additional revenue.

For Clinton, Bryan's legislative initiative was a godsend. The governor embraced the twin measures with the passion of a hungry hound dog. The Bryan bill, Clinton maintained, best represented the state's goals. The fact that the Arkansas poul-try industry was the prime beneficiary—as much of Bryan's legislative efforts over the past several years—was somehow lost in all the political glad-handing which followed.

But the celebratory atmosphere was short-lived. A second revenue-generating bill was introduced which projected some-thing in the neighborhood of $32 million in road taxes. Those lawmakers who looked for benefit quickly saw that Senate Bill 220 would outweigh the benefits gained in Bryan's revenue initiative, even if one added in the $25 million Bryan's support-ers believed would come from the federal government.

Senate Bill 220 proposed a weight-distance tax to be charged to trucks entering Arkansas from other states. This 'ton-per-mile' tax received the immediate endorsement and backing of Highway Commissioner Gray. He literally set up shop in the halls of the capitol as he sought to convince legislators that they should take care of Arkansas first. No sort of retaliation, Gray maintained, would be forthcoming from other states.

Lawmakers did pass Bryan's House Bill 192, effectively putting an end to the weight-limit crisis. As the governor signed the measure into law in late January, he prodded legislators with the thought that the weight-distance tax—still backed by Chairman Gray and the Highway Department—would surely bring retaliation against Arkansas truckers as they ferried their freight across the country.

Clinton was quite correct in his assessment. Researchers had estimated that, since the weight-distance tax measure was aimed principally at out-of-state trucks, they would shoulder up to 80 percent of the financial responsibility. Continued controversy worked to stall the bill, as it had Bryan's initial revenue measure. Behind the scenes, Clinton began to work for a compromise.

By late February, the Forward Arkansas Committee proposed a revenue-generating measure which would effectively tax both in-state and out-of-state truckers alike by adding 3.5 cents to the cost of each gallon of diesel fuel. Additionally, a registration fee of about $1,200 would be applied to every truck authorized to carry 80,000 pounds in weight.

Henry Gray met the proposal with nothing short of flat negativity. On February 23, he told Arkansas Gazette reporter Carol Matlock that the new compromise was "just a smoke screen." Gray further maintained that the Forward Arkansas measure would never make it through the state legislature.

Additional comments from Gray were more to the point. He accused Doc Bryan of being a paid lobbyist for the Arkansas Poultry Federation. The fact that Bryan was employed by the APF certainly added validity to Gray's charge. Bryan, of course, had been hard at work with both the governor and the Forward Arkansas Committee as the compromise legislation was being designed.

Clinton's desire to better the lives of Arkansans began to manifest itself as the governor introduced his much-touted utility reform package. At its heart, the eight-bill effort carried the proposal to elect members of the Public Service Commission, rather than continuing to have them appointed. Additionally, the legislation would give the PSC authority to suspend utility rate increases in times of economic difficulty.

Starting with the 1984 elections, House Bill 467 would mandate that PSC members be elected by the voters. The legislation harkened back to a 1982 campaign promise in which Clinton maintained that he would work to make the PSC more accountable. The companion legislation, House Bill 453, would give the PSC authority to set aside rate increases during tough economic times.

As one might expect, reaction from the utilities themselves was something more than immediate. In fairness to the utilities, they had their point—commissioners should be appointed rather than elected so they could be free from political pressure and might better safeguard the interests of the utility customers.

Clinton's response showed his frustration with the entire process. On February 12, 1983, he remarked:

> I believe that an elected commission is preferable to our present system. In the last five years, increased utility rates have had a much larger impact on our pocketbooks than increased taxes have. But taxes can be raised by elected legislators, while utility rates are raised by Public Service Commissioners appointed by the governor. I find that many citizens don't even know the people who voted to raise their rates.

Clinton's comments harkened back to Frank White's single term as governor. Critics accused White of being a utility pawn, appointing PSC members who were, at the least, openly sympathetic to the utilities themselves. But the effort to have the commissioners elected meant more to the governor than just a vehicle to attack the policies of the previous administration. Rather, it grew to symbolize a covenant Clinton had made with Arkansans—that he would grant to them the right to decide their own economic destiny.

The day after the governor made his comment, Arkansas Gazette reporter John Brummett told his Sunday readers that, while Clinton might be frustrated and downhearted, he was not ready to abandon his efforts to reform the PSC. Indeed, the governor's office had sent a mass mailing to voters across the state, urging support for an elected PSC. Beginning with "Dear Friend," the letters were sent to individuals who had aided Clinton's campaign for reelection and to those Arkansans who had demonstrated a strong interest in utility reform.

Public support to the contrary, House Bill 467—now in the hands of the Insurance and Commerce Committee—faced tough opposition. At the next meeting of that group, the governor brought in an elected PSC official from North Dakota who told panel members that the citizen-election measure had brought his state great benefit. Attempting to calm some Arkansans, who apparently feared that an elected PSC would damage the state's business climate, the North Dakota official announced that the measure had not damaged the commercial interests of his state. As a final touch during the two-and-a-half hour meeting, Clinton added a thought of his own—he had investigated utility rates in North Dakota and found them to be lower than those in Arkansas.

At the very least, Clinton's appearance before the Insurance and Commerce Committee helped to belay a "do not pass" recommendation. It also managed to send a signal—to friend and foe alike—that the governor intended to continue to fight out the utility reform issues, opposition from the utilities themselves notwithstanding.

On February 19, Clinton addressed the august members of the Arkansas Press Association. He took the assembled reporters to task for failing to follow up on utility claims that electing PSC members would "politicize" the process. The governor asserted that politics was already a part of the PSC reform process, noting that Senator Clarence Bell—a member of the Senate Insurance and Commerce Committee—was the Industrial and Public Relations rep for Arkla Gas, the largest natural gas supplier in the state. In fact, State Representative Mack Thompson, who sat on the House version of the same committee, was the manager of the Arkla Gas outlet in Paragould. Arkansas Reporter Carol Griffee noted in the next day's Arkansas Gazette that the governor had issued a hefty challenge to the journalists when he said:

> You owe it to the people to ask, 'Isn't it true your employees sit on the committee? Let's not let people labor under the illusion that there's no politics involved now.

As hotly disputed as the commissioner election question was, the prospect of allowing the PSC to disallow rate increases during times of economic hardship became even more of a central issue. The Arkansas Chamber of Commerce joined with the utility interests in calling House Bill 453 a vehicle to harm economic development and dampen the state's business climate. Just how lower utility rates might bring about these conditions was never fully explained.

Cecil Alexander, a lobbyist for Arkansas Power and Light, became the most vocal opponent of the deferral measure. In late January, he called House Bill 453 "the most damaging" of all utility reform legislation, contending that AP&L and the other utilities had their own bills to pay and could not be expected to absorb "huge losses" during tough economic times.

Clinton was clearly frustrated. He had been sent back into office largely based on his promise to pursue utility reform, and now his course of legislative action was in grave danger. The best he could hope for, it seemed, was a partial fulfillment of his campaign promise. By early February, he was telling Arkansas Gazette reporter Carol Matlock:

> It's amazing to me the influence the utilities have on the Insurance and Commerce Committee. I mean, we had an

*election in which utilities were a major issue, and now it's
like we never had an election.*

By late February, it was becoming apparent that the election of PSC members would not become law in Arkansas. The legislation remained mired in committee and was pronounced dead in early March. The Benefit Insurance and Commerce committee had effectively killed the proposal by failing to give it a "do pass" recommendation. A similar fate would befall the governor's proposal to force utilities to "phase in" rate increases during tough economic times.

But Clinton had little time to mourn the fate of his two utility measures. His highway commissioner, Henry Gray, had just managed to re-energize the truck-weight issue, effectively resurrecting House Bill 220. The controversial weight-distance measure had nearly made it out of the Revenue and Taxation Committee, and frantic efforts were already underway to bring it to the House floor.

For the time being, the Highway Commission held the upper hand in the battle to raise highway revenues, since it had essentially beaten the proponents of House Bill 284 to the proverbial punch. However, legislators were being bombarded by claims that retaliatory taxes would soon be a fact of life for the state's truckers. Representative Bryan, who had been leading the fight for HB 284, handed lawmakers copies of a letter from Oklahoma which gave strong indications that retaliaton would be swift in coming. Bryan, arguing that lawmakers would have to deal with the retaliation issue now or later, maintained that legislators would have to return to Little Rock for a special session if House Bill 220 managed to pass. "We might as well get ready to come back down here (to Little Rock) in a very short period of time," Bryan intoned, "because that retaliation is what is going to happen." Bryan, who sat on the Revenue and Taxation Committee, told the Arkansas Gazette on March 16, 1983, that "this committee's greased."

Perhaps the lubrication was insufficient, because House Bill 220 survived the onslaught of the trucking and poultry industry lobby. With an amendment proposed by the governor, it was passed into law. After the session had ended, Clinton described the bill's passage as "a major accomplishment." His triumph was derided by those who believed that Clinton had remained on the fence, double-crossing legislators because he had supported both revenue measures at one time or another during the session. The governor responded with the belief that, by remaining a flexible mediator, he was able to facilitate compromise and work toward fulfillment of the pair of goals he had set for himself at the beginning of the truck weight battle. Clinton maintained that he had wanted to raise money from those truckers who benefited from the weight increase, thus bringing both sides together. While Clinton believed that he had, in fact, come close to achieving his ultimate goal, he had certainly not reached his objective in full.

In the area of utility reform, it must be said that Clinton achieved only limited success and had, in fact, lost a couple of battles. After the session, as the governor was relaxing, he told Arkansas Gazette reporter John Brummett that the utility reform measures were issues he felt quite strongly about. "I fought for them as hard as I could," Clinton stated. He added that he considered the just-concluded legislative gathering a "good session," maintaining that he looked upon it with "a great deal of satisfaction."

The 1983 regular legislative session had given Clinton the opportunity to address educational problems on a limited basis. Soon, however, he would have the chance to make his first substantial advance toward improving education in Arkansas. Since the controversy over the state's school funding formula had been raging unabated for some time, it finally resulted in a lawsuit filed by eleven of the state's school districts. The litigants contended that the current statutory formula was unconstitutional in that it did not guarantee equal protection under the law and did not meet the constitutional requirement that the state provide a general, suitable, and efficient system of education.

The lawsuit attacked Arkansas Act 1100 of 1979, known as the Minimum Foundation Program. Revenue distributed under the MFP constituted just more than 77 percent of all state aid. The program was made up of two major elements: base aid and equalization aid. The base formula, which accounted for the major portion of school funding, was calculated using the teacher-student population per district. When the base aid had been calculated, the second element—equalization aid—was distributed as a flat grant on a per-student basis. This second part of the equalization formula allowed state funds to be disbursed in such a way as to attempt to address disparity between Arkansas' rich and poor school districts. The equalization formula allocated something on the order of seven percent of the funds sent to the state's school systems.

The Arkansas Supreme Court issued an opinion which upheld a trial court's decision, which had previously condemned the formula as unconstitutional. The trial court decision maintained that the great disparity in property wealth among districts, and the relatively small amount of adjustment available via the state's equalization formula, had given rise to an unconscionable situation. In writing the majority opinion, Justice Steele Hays noted that "This great disparity among the districts' property wealth and the current state system, as it is now applied, does not equalize the educational revenues available to districts, but only widens the gap."

Justice Hays went on to expand his explanation of the court's concern, saying, "We find no legitimate state purpose to support the system. It bears no rational relationship to the educational needs of the individual districts; rather it is determined primarily by the tax base of each district. The trial court found the educational opportunity of the children of this state should not be controlled by the fortuitous circumstance of residence, and we concur in that view. Such a system only promotes greater opportunities for the advantaged while diminishing the opportunities for the disadvantaged."

Since Justice Hays had placed the responsibility for the funding system squarely in the lap of the state, the door was opened for a special legislative session. "We have discussed the two major problems faced in financing our state's educational system," the opinion noted, adding that "the first is the obvious disparity in property wealth among districts. That wealth is what primarily dictates the revenue each district receives and the quality of education in that district. The second problem is the manner in which the state determines how the state funds are distributed; and, as we have said, the current system is not a rational one. The end result is a violation of the mandates of our constitution. Ultimately, the responsibility for maintaining a general, suitable, and efficient school system falls upon the state."

Governor Clinton immediately announced plans to call a special legislative session to deal with the problems of Arkansas education. In late September, the governor addressed the people of the state via television. He stated that he intended to ask the legislature to congregate back in Little Rock on October 4 to begin the task of overhauling the state's education system. One of the major initiatives he intended to propose, Clinton said bluntly, was a tax increase. As he stated:

To put it bluntly, we've got to raise taxes to increase our investment in education. Arkansas is dead last in spending per child, and the Arkansas Supreme Court has just ordered us to spend more money in poorer districts to improve education there.

Clinton went on to outline a program with a price tag ranging from $158 million to $175 million. He told his constituents that the benefits to be gained far outweighed the cost:

I hope to be able to convince you that we have to raise this money for education if we ever hope to get out of the economic backwater of our country, that this expenditure can bring greater economic opportunities to us, and that my program will do just that.

Finally, the governor asked Arkansans to do two things: First, call their legislators and ask them to support the program; second, wear a blue ribbon displaying their support for a blue-ribbon educational system. Clinton maintained that the parents' actions would directly benefit the parents' own children:

We have been given an opportunity that we have never been given before and that, if we fail to seize we will probably never be given again. And I ask for your personal commitment because it will personally benefit you, your children, your grandchildren and the future of the state we all love so much.

Legislators spent the first week of the special session considering the governor's tax package and a revised school funding formula. At a Friday afternoon news conference which marked the end of the first week, Clinton said that he felt the tax increase for education was the most important task he had ever tried to accomplish. Reporter Bob Wells recorded the governor's observation in the October 8, 1983, issue of the Arkansas Gazette, noting that Clinton had said, "I cannot tell you how important it is to me personally. It is terribly important to me. It is more important to me than anything I have ever done in politics."

As one might expect, Arkansas legislators proved to be quite contentious when it came to approving a new school funding formula. Those lawmakers who represented districts with small schools wanted to make sure their constituents got their fair share of the proposed additional revenues. At the same time, those with larger systems in their districts wanted to make sure the smaller systems did not gain at the expense of their larger counterparts. As it developed, the search for a formula would take the legislature three long weeks.

Finally, House Bill 44—with the addition of a couple of late-breaking Senate amendments—passed the Arkansas House and landed upon the governor's desk, awaiting Clinton's signature. On October 27, 1983, the Arkansas Gazette noted Clinton's reaction that he "had felt the last couple of days the way I did just before my baby was born—that it would never happen. I feel like we can deal with the remaining issues in an expeditious manner."

The "remaining issues" Clinton spoke of were the tax increase needed to fund House Bill 44, and the question of teacher testing. Already, lawmakers had indicated that they would not agree to a tax increase without teacher testing.

Arkansas teachers did not enjoy questions regarding their competence. They began to besiege their legislators. On the same day Clinton regaled the Arkansas Gazette with the importance of the passage of House Bill 44, the newspaper carried remarks by Ermalee Boice, who was the assistant executive director of the Arkansas Education Association. Ms. Boice had told the House Education Committee—on behalf of many of her colleagues, the following:

House Bill 47 will single out Arkansas as the only state that believes that its teachers are so bad they have to pass a literacy test. I think Arkansas can do without that. I will guarantee to you that if this bill passes, you will lose more good teachers than you will weed out bad ones.

Alongside the articles concerning the governor and the remarks by Ms. Boice, the Gazette entered remarks by Hillary Clinton, the governor's wife and the chairperson of the state's Education Standards Committee. Mrs. Clinton maintained that teacher testing would clearly benefit the teachers themselves. As she had told the Arkansas Senate:

I think we have to hit head-on the widespread public belief that we have a lot of incompetent teachers because I don't think we can build a constituency for education unless we do confront that... I think it will clear the air of a lot of misconceptions and inaccuracies about our teachers.

With the breaking of the legislative logjam, Bill Clinton began to see a victory in the making that would eclipse anything he had imagined. Despite the overwhelming opposition presented by the state's teachers, the teacher testing bill was passed and sent on to the governor for his signature. And within a short time, the state lawmakers had approved a one-cent sales tax increase designed to fund the education package.

But even with the prospects of raises in salaries and improved classroom facilities, Arkansas teachers continued to voice strong opposition to the teacher testing law. Many lawmakers and Arkansans countered with the thought that the teachers were simply ungrateful for improvements in their condition. While the argument had merit, it made no impact. Even as the legislative session ended, the Arkansas Education Association announced its plans to legally challenge the new testing law. The statute, as enacted, called for teachers to take a basic skills test during the 1984-85 school year. If they failed, they would be required to submit to remedial programs aimed at helping them pass the test by 1987. If by that time teachers could not pass the exam, they would lose their certification.

Additionally, the testing law required a test in the teacher's certified area of specialty or a half-dozen hours of college study within the area itself.

Clinton immediately set about trying to mend fences, but the teachers would have none of it. The AEA declared that its membership was at "war" with the governor, and flatly stated that the organization would win the struggle. Across the nation, the teacher testing issue became a matter of continuing controversy.

In late January 1984, Clinton and AEA President Peggy Nabors were invited to appear on NBC's "Today" show. Their "debate" was the subject of a report in the January 25 issue of the Arkansas Gazette. During the discussion, the Gazette noted, the governor maintained that the teacher testing bill was not aimed at the majority of the state's teachers. "There are a small but not insignificant number of teachers who lack the adequacy of basic skills that every teacher should have and who should be required to improve those basic skills if they're going to remain in the classroom," Clinton said.

Nabors reacted by calling the bill a "quick fix" with "political overtones." She said that Clinton was simply looking for attention from the media. "The teacher testing makes good media headlines, but it's poor educational policy. Good media headlines do not make better education," Nabors concluded.

For his appearance on the "Today" show, the governor had remained in Little Rock, availing himself of the studios of KARK-TV, the city's NBC affiliate. On the air Clinton said that he did not enjoy the controversy that the teacher testing bill had generated, but he felt that testing was a course of action which would ultimately benefit the state's children. "No one has yet pointed out to me how a single child is going to be hurt by this program. We simply could not think of any other device by which we could quickly take an inventory of our teachers' basic skills."

AEA President Nabors told the national audience that a team from the National Education Association would be coming to Arkansas to examine the teacher testing law. Additionally, Nabors vowed that the AEA would not give up the fight against teacher testing. Asked about the arrival of the NEA team and their possible fairness in examining the testing issue, Clinton responded that since the NEA had already condemned him for the testing statute, he did not see how the organization could be objective.

In early 1984, Arkansas news accounts seemed dominated by those critical of Clinton. Arkansas Gazette columnist Ernie Dumas saw the governor's performance from a slightly different point of view. In the Feb, 5, 1984, edition, Dumas explained his analysis of the situation:

> *After a year of his second lease on political life, Clinton looks stronger than he has been since his first legislative session in 1979. He has three groups of unalterable foes—the truckers, utilities, and teachers—but in each instance the fights have proved [sic] to be a net advantage for him.*

Despite opposition from the trucking industry, Dumas accurately noted the weight limit had been raised on the state's highways along with a revenue package designed to pay for the damage caused by heavier vehicles. Clinton had kept his campaign promise to give truckers the advantage of carrying the extra weight and had found a way to forge a compromise with highway commission interests.

The utilities had created a fire storm of opposition to the reform measures Clinton had pressed for in the 1983 legislative session. Dumas noted that, when the dust had settled, the governor's appointees to the Public Service Commission had resulted in one of the toughest regulatory boards in the nation.

Finally, Dumas maintained that the education issue had resulted in a double advantage for Clinton. The double advantage was "a special session that enacted a tax program and a substantial education package (that) ended any prospect he would face any major Democratic foes." As it turned out, the 1984 primary season would prove Dumas' analysis correct.

By late February 1984, the state of Oklahoma had enacted a retaliatory tax on Arkansas trucks passing through the Sooner State. In discussing the $175 fee, Clinton said that he would begin exploring the possibility of negotiating a reciprocal agreement with Oklahoma and look at amending the weight-distance bill to allow Arkansas truckers traveling out of state to be reimbursed for out-of-state retaliation. Clinton indicated that he was strongly committed to the Arkansas trucking industry and was willing to work hard to find a solution to the retaliatory tax problem.

In March 1984, the National Education Association issued its long-awaited report on the teacher testing issue. The negative, stinging report pushed Clinton on the defensive. The governor maintained that he would continue to work with Arkansas teachers who wanted to improve education. Many of the state's teachers, he said, had given him a good deal of positive feedback about the education programs.

On the last day of March, the Arkansas Gazette carried an Associated Press report in which Clinton placed the blame for low teacher morale and discontent squarely on the shoulders of the Arkansas Education Association. He said that the AEA had mounted what he called:

...a deliberate, organized and systematic opposition to the testing provision, to blind people to the fact that if you flunk the test it just identifies a group of people who have to go through a development plan...

Clinton went on to say that Arkansans should be looking at what other states—and even other countries—were doing in the area of teacher testing:

We need to be able to say with confidence that we are going to have a nationally competitive system for certifying teachers, that we are going to have as modern, as adequate, as sensible an approach to our teacher education program as exists anywhere.

Some days later, the governor announced that a firm had been selected to implement the teacher testing program. Instructional Objectives Exchange—a Culver City, California, firm—would develop and administer a basic skills test for Arkansas teachers. The cost would be just less than $300,000. The test was scheduled to be given between March 15 and April 30 of 1985.

As Ernie Dumas had predicted, the 1984 primary failed to produce a significant Democratic challenger to Clinton. Franklin County's Lonnie Turner joined with turkey farmer Monroe Schwarzlose and Kermit C. Moss in bids to unseat the governor, but to no avail. As it turned out, Clinton won the primary without a run-off, taking seventy of the state's 75 counties and garnering some 64 percent of the popular vote. Clinton called the vote a "referendum on education."

But Arkansas Republicans were not idle. Their gubernatorial primary resulted in the nomination of Jonesboro contractor Woody Freeman to be Clinton's opponent in November. Freeman was a member of the state's board of higher education, and said that he would work to improve education in Arkansas, just as Clinton had. However, Freeman noted that he would not ignore other pressing problems, which he believed Clinton had left unattended due to his preoccupation with education reform.

During the summer of 1984, Bill Clinton received an invitation to speak at the Democratic National Convention in San Francisco. He was slated to deliver a speech during an evening session at the mid-August event. The address would be telecast across America to a prime-time audience.

With the convention under way, and party favorites Walter Mondale and Geraldine Ferraro poised to sweep the delegate balloting, the nation's youngest governor stood ready to display his political prowess to party loyalists from across the country. Clinton's speech was scheduled to follow on the heels of a convention film which praised the presidency of Harry Truman.

The Governor told the gathering that even though Truman had served the nation in the 1940s, his message then would still fare well in the 1980s. As Clinton put it:

He'd (Truman) remind us that 1948, like 1984, was a time of change, when new realities required new ideas and a willingness to stand up to interest groups both within and outside our party when the public interest demanded it. He'd tell us you can't please everybody in tough times and you shouldn't try.

After his oratorical debut, the governor told the Arkansas delegation that he was busy negotiating with a high-tech consortium—industries which specialized in genetic engineering—who were interested in moving to the state.

In the late summer of 1984, an issue that had nagged the Clinton administration for years demanded attention once again. Earlier that year, an administrative law judge working for the Federal Energy Regulatory Commission issued a finding that had the potential to force a large increase in Arkansas electric rates. The judge had ordered Arkansas Power & Light to pay some 36 percent of the cost of construction of the Grand Gulf nuclear power plant in Mississippi. At AP&L, spokesmen said the mandate would necessitate at least a 28 percent rate increase, and—when coupled with a rate increase already on the table—could result in a 40 percent rate jump for Arkansas customers.

The governor had said that he would seriously consider forming a public power authority to take over AP&L. Clinton said he would also begin action to overturn the judge's ruling. Additionally, he would travel to Washington for a visit with the Arkansas congressional delegation. Perhaps together they could find a solution to the problem via federal legislation.

Late in August, Clinton learned that AP&L and Mississippi Power and Light had been working on a compromise proposal which would allow the Arkansas utility to pay just 17.1 percent of the cost of the Grand Gulf plant. Clinton opposed the proposition, maintaining that AP&L should pay nothing at all.

The governor's resolve to protect the interest of Arkansas ratepayers echoed again during the Arkansas Broadcasters' Association convention in Hot Springs. His comments, reported in the August 10, 1984, Arkansas Gazette, demonstrated his belief that stockholders—and not ratepayers—should bear the cost of Grand Gulf:

> Management made the decision to build the plant and tried to stick us with it. You take chances in life. If you buy other stock, you don't know if you get a dividend or not. Most stock-holders can afford to live without dividends for awhile

a whole lot more than most Arkansans—whether business, industry, or elderly people on fixed incomes—can afford a 50 cent or a 10 percent increase.

While speculation abounded concerning skyrocketing electric rates, the governor's nemesis, the Arkansas Education Association, burst back onto the scene. President Peggy Nabors announced that the AEA intended to file a lawsuit—in November, of all months—to challenge the teacher testing law. To add to Clinton's image concerns, the AEA began to air "Teacher Alert" commercials on the state's radio stations, warning teachers about difficulties in the administration of the testing program.

On the heels of the AEA onslaught, Clinton found himself criticized for failing to work hard enough to bring about substantial industrial improvement in Arkansas. The attack came from Thomas McRae, who was president of the Winthrop Rockefeller Foundation. At a called press conference, McRae issued a foundation report which stated that Arkansas' industrial development was on the decline. Reporter Bob Stover, writing in the Sept. 27, 1984, edition of the Arkansas Gazette, noted McRae's conclusion that Clinton was crazy to quarrel with an obvious trend:

Anyone who doesn't know that industrial development is declining has had his head under a rock.

McRae added that the state's industrial development policy could be likened to a "blind hog rooting in the brush and occasionally finding an acorn."

The governor responded with the announcement that he had been working on a package designed to increase the state's industrial development. The program would be unveiled during the 1985 legislative session. Clinton noted that he had seen much success in the area of industrial development during his second term as governor, adding that the "blind hog" McRae had spoken of "has rooted out more jobs in the past year and a half than it has in a long time."

Clinton accused the Rockefeller Foundation of never having anything good or positive to say about Arkansas. McRae admitted that there was some truth in the governor's contention. On the other hand, McRae said:

...we have had little good to say about state leaders whose motivation is entirely political and who are ignoring the realities that are very clear to citizens in many parts of the state.

Clinton and McRae would have a number of opportunities to trade words during the next few years. The culmination of the battle would eventually be an unsuccessful bid on McRae's part for the Democratic nomination for governor.

At the moment, Clinton had reason to be concerned about the Republican challenge he would face in November. Nominee Woody Freeman espoused a no-tax increase philosophy and told voters, as Frank White had two and four years before, that he intended to run state government like a business. Freeman said he would correct Clinton's "mistakes" and repeal the tax on heavy trucks. The GOP candidate maintained that the election would be a referendum on Clinton's entire tenure in office.

Responding in kind, Clinton began to reveal more of his plan to foster industrial development in Arkansas. According to the governor, his 1985 legislative economic development package would cover job training programs, development financing and a plan to promote Arkansas nationwide.

Come November's general election, a small voter turnout helped Clinton defeat challenger Freeman with some 63 percent of the votes cast. The northwest Arkansas Republican stronghold was largely responsible for Freeman's 37 percent showing. For Clinton, the victory at the polls meant a third term in office, eclipsing the record of nearly all his predecessors before him.

Three days before Christmas 1984, Clinton was invited to participate in a broadcast interview on the ABC-TV affiliate in Little Rock, KATV. The next day, his comments were relayed in the Arkansas Gazette. The governor had taken the opportunity to express his confidence that the court challenge the AEA had begun—aimed at overturning the teacher-testing law—would eventually fail:

> I can't believe that a court of law would really rule that it is unconstitutional to determine the basic learning skills of a teacher and to require those who don't have those skills to improve in order to stay in the classroom.

The governor went on to say that he felt the AEA had overreacted to the entire teacher-testing issue:

> The leadership of the AEA sort of chose to make this their last stand and act as if it were the most important issue that had ever occurred in the whole history of time. It undermined their ability to fight for their own pay increases in special session, or for any substantive improvements.

Inauguration day 1985 dawned clear and cold as Bill Clinton prepared to begin his third term as governor of Arkansas—something that had happened only twice in the state's history. As tradition demanded, Clinton would meet briefly with a joint session of the legislature. The group would then adjourn to the steps of the capitol, where the governor would deliver his State of the State address while he and his audience shivered in the 30-degree weather.

In his opening remarks to state lawmakers, Clinton commented that he was especially proud to be sworn in by the new Chief Justice of the Arkansas Supreme Court, Jack Holt, Jr. Of course, Justice Holt's late uncle, Frank Holt, had given Clinton his first job in Arkansas politics. Working in Holt's gubernatorial campaign had been the catalyst for Clinton's successful political career.

Clinton told the legislators that he was ready to begin carrying out what he called "the people's business." That business, he continued, involved taking the next step in the process which had begun with the special education session of 1983. Clinton maintained:

I think we have an opportunity coming into this new legislative session to make the same sort of commitment to the economic development of our state, to increasing our capacity to bring jobs to our people, that we made to education in the previous two sessions. And if we view the two as two sides of the same coin, and if we muster that amount of dedication and concentration, I think we can have a very great legislative session and lay another great cornerstone in the future of our state.

The governor concluded his brief remarks by asking state lawmakers to look with him toward the future:

I believe as strongly as I ever have believed anything that, starting two years ago, we began a movement to put this state into the front ranks of the states of this country and that we will stick with it. If we will stick with the education program and develop an economic development program that is second to none in America, there is absolutely no reason we cannot do something that all generations of past Arkansans have not been able to do. That is, to bring our state out of the backwaters of American economic conditions.

The flurry of inaugural activities continued unabated through the afternoon as Clinton moved out onto the capitol's front steps to deliver his inaugural address. A crowd of about 850 well-wishers stood in the cold afternoon sunshine, listening to Clinton speak again of the future:

> We must believe in ourselves and our ability to shape our own destiny. Too many of us still expect too little of ourselves and demand too little of each other because we see the future as a question of fate, out of our hands. But the future need not be fate; it can be an achievement.

Only a few days passed before Clinton met again with the Arkansas legislature. The joint session heard the young governor lay out his plan for the future of Arkansas. Members of the state House and Senate were given a 312-page booklet that contained copies of the bills Clinton was proposing, along with a summary of each bill. The plan itself covered four major areas: economic development, education, crime and utility regulation.

The economic reform portion of the package contained initiatives that would allow creation of a state agency which could issue tax-exempt bonds to finance development projects. Clinton also wanted to encourage the state's three major retirement systems to invest no less than 5 percent of their assets in Arkansas. The success of these two programs could make available nearly 400 million dollars for economic development purposes. The governor asked for a public referendum aimed at securing voter approval for the sale of $150 million in general obligation bonds. These would be used to assure the state a better credit rating for other bond issues and to assure repayment in case riskier state investments failed.

In the area of education, Clinton proposed incentives to school systems which would voluntarily consolidate. He also sought to establish 15 educational service centers across Arkansas, helping school districts pool their resources.

Clinton's crime package included a speedy-trial law. This statute would ensure that a trial would be held within nine months of indictment. The package also included a bill which would enhance or protect the rights of crime victims.

In the utility regulation area, the governor proposed a bill which would require the use of data from "test year" cases—and not projections—in rate increase proposals. Another proposed reform would allow the state's Public Service Commission to consider management practices in rate cases. Another measure would allow the PSC to approve contracts between a utility and its holding company, in addition to contracts involving out-of-state construction.

Most Arkansas lawmakers looked upon Clinton's 80-bill package with favor, though a few legislators expressed concern over the seeming complexity of the set of initiatives. Committee members in both the house and senate were especially anxious about the governor's proposal to increase the size and scope of the state's bond issuing authority. Conservatives in both houses were worried about the possibility of the state becoming obligated to repay hundreds of millions of dollars in bond issues. As it developed, this concern would become a major source of debate in the days ahead.

As most Arkansans expected, the governor came face to face with his chief nemesis again, the Arkansas Education Association. In the opening days of the legislative session, State Representative William Mills introduced a bill which would allow teachers who had failed the teacher's basic skills test to keep their certification. Mills' colleague, Pat Flanagin, introduced a second bill that would allow teachers to take only the test in their area of specialization. Both bills were largely seen for what they were—efforts to gut the teacher-testing bill passed during the 1983 special legislative session.

Some experienced lawmakers, to be fair, saw these two bills in a different light. Some viewed the efforts made to eliminate teacher testing as a move to pacify the AEA. Additionally, some legislators had a political motive in mind—whatever bills they passed that would endanger the teacher testing statute would be quickly vetoed by the governor. Hence, these lawmakers would be free to propose and pass any legislation of this sort without fear of its becoming law. Finally, most would profess their support for the two bills simply as a tool to gain leverage with Clinton. By backing down from their advocacy of the two pieces of legislation, these legislators could gain his support for their own initiatives.

In late January 1985, Clinton was again called upon to be a spokesman for the Democratic Party. The governor had been chosen to moderate a half-hour response to President Ronald Reagan's State of the Union Address. The program would be produced and paid for by the Democratic Congressional Campaign Committee. The group had tapped Clinton as spokesman because, according to party insiders, he projected the "right image." In a word, they felt he best represented the young, articulate, progressive voter the Democrats needed to attract.

House Bill 178, the measure introduced by Representative Mills, appeared to be gaining momentum. Passed out of committee and onto the House floor, it passed there by a wide margin and was sent on to the Senate. In addition to allowing teachers to retain certification even after failing the basic skills test, the bill also exempted instructors from the 1983 Teacher Fair Dismissal Act. In essence, the legislation would allow local school boards to take whatever action they saw fit in the event a teacher did not pass the competency exam.

AEA President Peggy Nabors voiced the organization's unswerving support of the measure. In the February 6, 1985, edition of the Arkansas Gazette, Nabors told reporter John Obrecht that, if the bill did not become law, "teachers would be fired without any protection at all because of the score...on the examination." The AEA's position on the Fair Dismissal Act and teacher testing remained the same—more teachers would be hurt than helped.

While the Arkansas legislature pondered these issues, Clinton headed to Washington, D.C., to prepare for his national television appearance, orchestrated by the Democratic Party. The Democratic response to President Reagan's State of the Union Address was slated to air immediately following the conclusion of the president's speech to the joint session of Congress. Taping the program in advance, Clinton would be the moderator for a 30-minute program which would also feature Democratic standard-bearers from across the nation.

The governor was scheduled to open the program with a short statement and then move on to a discussion of individual issues. As Arkansas Gazette reporter Carol Matlock noted in the paper's Feb, 7, 1985, edition, Clinton stated that the Democratic Party "knows it has to change, and wants to reach out."

At the outset of his comments, the governor acknowledged the sweeping Reagan victory over the Mondale/Ferarro Democratic ticket. He noted, however, that Democrats still controlled a sizable majority in the House of Representatives and had made gains in the Senate as well. This, according to Bill Clinton, was a sure sign that a vigorous Democratic organization was still to be reckoned with in American politics:

> *Clearly, then, there is a Democratic Party in America which is alive and well, a party committed to prosperity and opportunity for all America, a party more concerned with the future than the past, a party convinced we are living in changing times which require us to go beyond the established dogmas.*

But Bill Clinton had little time to bask in the national lime-light. Back in Arkansas, the AEA was mounting yet another frontal assault on the teacher testing bill. State Representative Ode Maddox had introduced House Bill 616, which would serve to repeal the testing law completely. According to the Maddox bill, would-be teachers entering an Arkansas college of education would be required to take a basic skills test, and when they graduated, they would also be given a National Teacher Exam as well.

As one would expect, AEA President Peggy Nabors was quick to support this bill as well. In the February 8, 1985, edition of the Arkansas Gazette, Nabors maintained that the AEA did not write House Bill 616, but did support it. She called the bill:

> ...a reasonable and responsible approach to improving the (teaching) profession...it strengthens the education process. (Teacher testing) is not a political issue, it's an education issue. Testing, as it stands now, is a political issue, not an education issue.

Clinton was quick to counter with his own bill, introduced by State Representative Jody Mahoney. House Bill 511 would require all certified personnel to pass the basic skills test. Additionally, teachers who returned from a leave of absence, or moved into Arkansas, would have to take the test as well. The bill passed easily in the House, and was then sent to the Senate.

The governor lobbied actively for the passage of HB511. He told Arkansas Gazette reporters John Brummett and John Obrecht that the measure was designed to clear up questions about the original teacher testing proposal. On February 13, 1985, the two reporters filed their story, in which Clinton spoke to the issues raised by the countering legislation:

> The bill is important to me and I'm working hard to pass it, and contrary to some assertions that it is a slap in the face to

teachers, the bill is in fact designed to clarify some questions about the original law.

But the pressure to repeal the teacher testing law was unrelenting. In mid-February, some 3,500 Arkansas teachers left their classrooms and marched on the capitol in an effort to persuade the legislature to stop the "testing madness." Reporter Laura Newman reported the day's events in the Valentine's Day issue of the Arkansas Gazette. According to the article, Arkadelphia teacher Johnnie Sheeler was one of the featured speakers at the afternoon rally. She told the crowd that the testing law was an insult:

Pardon me, Governor, while I get personal. My teaching career is personal to me...I do not intend to take any test to keep something I already have, and yes, Governor, I take your insults personally. It's time all Arkansas [sic] took your insults personally.

Ms. Sheeler was one of ten plaintiffs in a lawsuit challenging the constitutionality of the teacher testing law. Two days later, Clinton pointed a finger at the AEA and their tactics: According to the governor, the AEA had:

...done a lot of harm to education by fomenting all the discord and trying to take advantage of it...and continuing to harp on it...and by most blatantly encouraging people to disregard the law.

The governor went on to liken the teacher uprising to the Air Traffic Controller's strike in 1981. In that case, of course, President Reagan fired all the workers who broke the law and went on strike. The governor, in a press conference, maintained:

I think most of our teachers are doing a good job and whether they agree with the law or not, most of them understand their obligation —all people have to obey the law.

Clinton stated his belief that teacher certification by the state was not "a right but a privilege."

Meanwhile, teachers across Arkansas were preparing for what could shortly become a reality in their lives. Nearly a thousand teachers attended workshops sponsored by the State Department of Education. Of course, that number was less than a third of those who had marched on the capitol.

The two-and-a-half hour workshops included test-taking tips and sample questions. Many teachers expressed the hope, once the sessions had concluded, that the test might not be as difficult as they had been led to believe. Most teachers carried printed material back to their schools with them, helping to educate other instructors about the testing process.

While the teacher testing battle raged on, Clinton was gaining ground in other areas. Amidst the fray, the Arkansas House passed and sent to the Senate a bill which would reimburse Arkansas truckers for retaliatory taxes levied against them by other states. This measure—House Bill 400—allowed funds collected under the Arkansas weight-distance tax to be used to pay back the truckers.

But the governor saw a setback in the making when the Senate Education Committee refused to give a "do pass" recommendation to HB5ll, the bill which would clarify the teacher-testing law. In the February 21, 1985, edition of the Arkansas Gazette, AEA President Peggy Nabors noted that:

Trying to correct errors in ACT 76 will only make matters worse. It is still a piece of bad legislation [sic] and trying to fix it will not help.

Clinton countered with the thought that he believed in the bill:

...and I believe that if you let the teachers in the state vote on every provision of the bill, the teachers would vote 3 to 1 in favor of it.

In the teacher testing battle, the governor's luck seemed to be going from bad to worse. By late February, the Arkansas House passed HB616, the bill designed to repeal the teacher testing law entirely. The measure passed by a two-thirds majority in the House, and went on to the Senate. Clinton quipped that if the bill passed the Senate as well, it would be one of the easiest veto decisions he had ever been required to make.

The 1985 legislative session could easily be described as a roller coaster ride. Clinton went from apparent defeat of his teacher testing package to a sweeping victory for his economic reform initiatives. Just a few days after HB616 was sent from the House to the Senate, both chambers brought the entire economic development package out of committee and onto the floor for an immediate vote. Without debate, the package was voted on and almost unanimously passed. It went on to the governor for his signature.

The entire economic development program was often criticized as being too difficult and complex to be adequately comprehended. The bill itself had languished in committee for more than a month. Across Arkansas, it seemed that no business interest had the courage to stand up, step forward, and work for the bill's passage—even though it would benefit the entire business community—except for the renowned investment firm of Stephens, Inc. With the addition of several amendments suggested by Stephens' personnel, the state was given a powerful tool in the quest for increased economic development.

Arkansas Gazette columnist Ernie Dumas noted on March 3, 1985, that except for the last-minute push from Stephens, Inc., the credit for passage of the economic development measure belonged to the governor alone. Dumas wrote:

Clinton and his staff carried the lobbying load almost alone. Although the bills greatly expand the public financing of business ventures, enlarge the powers of the banking institutions, authorize hybrid business financing entities, centralize control of public bond issues and give broad new tax incentives for business investment, little hard lobbying by anyone but the administration was evident. Clinton appeared at committee hearings and sat through testimony to answer questions and urge passage.

Dumas went on to write that there was not a great deal of disinterest in the measure, but some lawmakers had labored under a profound lack of understanding of the package and how it would work. Naysayers, Dumas noted, had expressed wariness at so innovative an approach, while contemplating the worst-case scenario of the state left with a huge economic albatross hanging around its neck.

Yet another strange turn of events saw the passage of the state's first bill banning abortion. The measure was sponsored by State Senator Lu Hardin of Russellville, along with Senator Bill Henly. The legislation—Senate Bill 35—was brought out of committee with almost no comment, voted on speedily by both houses and sent to the governor for his signature. Clinton signed the measure, saying that it was entirely appropriate given the recent Supreme Court decisions limiting late-term abortions. The measure became law on March 7, 1985.

A bit of explanation is in order here. Senate Bill 35 prohibited abortions after the 25th week of pregnancy. It also prohibited aborting any "viable" fetus. A viable fetus was described as one which could survive outside the womb via natural or artificial means after the 25th week of pregnancy.

The legislative roller coaster ride continued unabated when House Bill 616, the measure designed to repeal the teacher testing law, was suddenly killed on the floor of the Arkansas Senate. Three of the governor's top aides had been in the Senate chamber, working tirelessly until the bill came up for a vote. With considerable arm-twisting, the necessary votes were rounded up, and the bill was killed. AEA President Peggy Nabors was vocal in her disappointment, saying in the March 6 edition of the Arkansas Gazette that:

> *We are disappointed that we don't have a reasonable and responsible approach to determining competency. (But) we still have a court case. That's our avenue left open at this point. Otherwise teachers will have to be making some decisions about their professional lives in the next few weeks whether they want to particpate in an unjust law.*

Meanwhile, the Arkansas Department of Education was making preparations to administer the teacher basic skills tests on March 23, 1985. The Teacher Education, Certification, and Evaluation Committee had met and reported that they had arrived at a decision on minimum scores for each of the three sections of the test. The reading section would require a score of 50 percent, the math section 60 percent, and the writing section would be analyzed and given a simple pass-or-fail recommendation. Field testing had already been completed, and the results indicated that, out of 500 teachers tested, some 98 percent had passed the reading section and 93 percent had passed the math test.

The State Board of Education stepped in to change the minimum test scores when Clinton—and other testing supporters—claimed that the minimums were too low. Subsequently, the scores were raised, and the reading and math sections required a 70 percent score. From the field test results, education officials determined that, with the new minimum scores, some 26 percent of teachers who had taken the test would have failed. With more than 26,000 teachers certified to teach in Arkansas, this failure rate would have meant that there could be as many as 6500 teachers failing the basic skills test.

Then the see-sawing legislative battle took yet another turn in the governor's favor when the House and Senate passed House Bill 5ll, which strengthened the teacher testing law. This bill required all Arkansans who held a teaching certificate—and not just those teaching at the time—to pass the basic skills test by June l, 1987, or lose their certification. Teachers would also be required to pass a test in their area of specialty, or take an additional six college hours in that field.

Clinton's press secretary, Joan Roberts, told the Arkansas Gazette on March 12, 1985, that the governor was pleased with the bill and its passage, noting that the statute improved the testing program and was fair to all certified personnel. AEA President Peggy Nabors, however, did not react favorably. She noted that:

> *This country was founded by people who objected to unfairness, and I think the teachers will have to make their decisions about whether they want to participate...in an unjust law.*

The AEA obviously had a strategy to politically embarrass Clinton. Boycotting the teacher test was encouraged at every turn. In mid-March, the organization planned a double-barreled weekend event to encourage the state's teachers and voice dissatisfaction with the testing law. First, the teachers would gather for a Friday night candlelight vigil on the steps of the state capitol. On Saturday, they would march to the governor's mansion for an afternoon rally.

On March 16, 1985, Arkansas Gazette reporter Laura Newman described the candlelight vigil held on a chilly Friday evening. Several speakers denounced the governor's actions and called them humiliating. Others spoke again of boycotting the test altogether. They also talked about striking Mississippi teachers, who were trying to convince their state lawmakers to give them a raise. One of the speakers, Norma Justus of Walnut Ridge, Arkansas, praised her Mississippi colleagues:

> *Speaking of Mississippi, Governor, Arkansas teachers are very proud of them [sic]..we're going to be proud of ourselves on March 23rd. Do those words send a chill down your spine, Governor? Many of us are going to boycott your test.*

Several telegrams were read to the assembled gathering, including one from a New Hampshire teacher's group who promised to give Clinton an appropriate welcome when he arrived in their state that weekend to speak at a Democratic Party function.

Ironically, despite the effort on the part of the AEA, Clinton would not be in the governor's mansion when the teachers marched on the residence on Saturday afternoon. Clinton's New Hampshire commitment would take him away from Arkansas while the AEA continued to attempt to consolidate their boycott effort. On March 16, the Associated Press carried Clinton's personal reason for wanting to be out of state at the time of the demonstration: his daughter, Chelsea. He noted that:

> *I don't know that I could explain to her what's going to happen out there tomorrow without it having some impact on the way she feels and I don't want (that) to happen. It may be that I'll have to explain it anyway, but it's a personal decision that Hillary and I have made. We think it's better for her, and her attitude toward education generally, that she doesn't have to experience that.*

Some 4,000 teachers made the afternoon march to the governor's mansion, many wearing the official "test-buster" T-shirt. The 45-minute walk ended at the mansion's front gate. The afternoon's featured speaker was National Education Association Executive Committee member John Wilson of Raleigh, North Carolina. Wilson's remarks only proved that he was just as incapable of constructing a coherent sentence as his Arkansas counterparts:

> *Governor Clinton, where ever you are, I say you can't love Arkansas and you can't love Arkansas by assassinating the dignity of the public schools and the teachers of its children.*

Wilson ended his remarks by claiming that the teacher testing law was an insulting, simplistic, political hoax. He accused the governor of furthering his political ambitions at the expense of the state's teachers. The AEA again caught the eye of columnist Ernie Dumas, who wrote in the March 17, 1985, edition of the Arkansas Gazette that:

> *The rising militancy is not merely a bonanza for the AEA, although the AEA has harvested more loyalty among teachers—along with far more rancor from the public—by leading the attacks on the testing law. The AEA has gotten fresh critics from within the ranks for its strident handling of the controversy and from more militant teachers who have the impression that the AEA is mouthy and not much else.*

That weekend, Clinton was answering the call of his party in New Hampshire. His theme—carried through several fund-raising events—was echoed in comments at a brunch sponsored by the Democratic Business Council in Merrimack. There, the governor noted that:

We need to make some fundamental changes if we're going to be the majority party in this country. The reason we took a beating in the 1984 elections—apart from the perception (that) the economy was in pretty good shape and we weren't at war—has a little to do with the fact that the people don't perceive that the Democrats have a good economic policy, that we're pro growth, (and) that we understand what the country needs in terms of its long-term economic stability.

The New Hampshire spotlight quickly dimmed as Clinton headed back to Arkansas to continue his quest for change. In the days before his trip east, a situation had been developing which demanded his attention upon his return. A contingent of state legislators, with the assistance of Highway and Transportation Director Henry Gray, had proposed an increase in the tax on gasoline and diesel fuel to fund a rural roads program. The increase—four cents per gallon of gas and two cents per gallon of diesel fuel—would generate about $50 million in revenue, with some 70 percent slated for rural roads and 30 percent going to Arkansas cities and counties for street and road projects.

So far, the governor had been successful in resisting passage of the tax. Now, he found himself in a tough situation created by mere twist of fate. Although his economic development package had arrived on his desk and awaited his signature, Clinton had asked the House and Senate to recall the bill which established the Arkansas Development Finance Authority—the bond-issuing agency—in order that a minor change might be made. The bill, it seems, had been passed with an emergency clause making it effective when Clinton signed it. The governor, on the other hand, wanted to drop the emergency clause and to have an effective date of June 1, 1985, written into the bill.

When the bill arrived back at the legislature, it was immediately taken hostage, for lack of a better description. Gas tax proponents saw their golden opportunity to gain some leverage with Clinton, in an effort to force his support for their bill. The game of political chess that ensued, in addition to being one of Bill Clinton's best moves, was literally a spectacle. The Arkansas House and Senate passed versions of the gas tax bill and sent them to the governor's desk for his signature.

Not to be outdone, Clinton immediately vetoed both measures and sent them back to their respective sources. The legislature, not sensing Clinton's intent, quickly voted to override the governor's veto. This marked only the second time in nearly two decades that a major tax increase had been passed over the veto of the state executive.

It wasn't long before some of the more astute members of the General Assembly began to suspect that they had been outfoxed by Clinton. The governor, some members claimed, had not been opposed to the bill, but had vetoed it strictly for political reasons. The fact that the legislature had then overridden the veto—and enacted the tax—placed the political burden on their backs, rather than on that of the governor.

For his part, Clinton maintained that he was fundamentally opposed to the tax and felt that the public hadn't been properly informed of the need for such an increase. According to the governor, the fact that the legislature had, in such an historic move, overridden his veto only demonstrated the lawmakers' conviction on the issue. He praised the legislature for an excellent lobbying effort. The finance authority bill, incidentally, was held hostage until the last day of the session. It was then carried to the governor for his signature—without comment.

Arkansas Gazette columnist Ernie Dumas offered an analysis:

While the political risks of the gasoline tax seem acceptable,
standing alone, Clinton no doubt examined it in a broader
perspective. No matter what office he seeks next year, he is
apt to face a campaign that he has been responsible for more
new taxes than any previous governor. The veto of a tax that
was popular in the legislature will help blunt that kind of
attack and make Clinton appear to be anti-tax.

On March 23, 1985, teachers across Arkansas made their way to testing sites across the state. They were to take the nation's first basic skills test for classroom teachers. Two hundred seventy-seven designated testing sites were located in 147 Arkansas cities and towns. Some teachers wore black armbands to the testing room as a symbolic protest against the testing law. Though the AEA raised the specter of a boycott—up to 8,000 teachers were predicted as no-shows—the threat did not materialize.

The Arkansas Department of Education released figures that, of the state's 26,700 certified teachers, some 25,077 complied with the new law—a 94 percent turnout. There were some 3,000 absences—excused in advance due to family or personal reasons—and a make-up exam was scheduled in April. As it developed, only 1,600 Arkansas teachers missed or did not take the test.

Just before the test was scheduled to be given on March 23, a minor scandal erupted when an apparent copy of the exam was delivered to Little Rock television station KARK. The governor called upon the Arkansas State Police to investigate the matter and determine if the test had been stolen and what damage had been done to the integrity of the testing procedure as a result.

Clinton maintained that there was little time to widely distribute the test material and that it was unlikely that any widespread cheating would occur. He said he felt it was more likely an attempt to discredit the testing process and to cause him some personal embarrassment. Those who might be suspected of cheating, the governor said, would be asked to retake the exam.

In late May 1985, Arkansans learned of an article written by a reporter named Raad Cawthon which appeared in the Atlanta Constitution-Journal. The piece discussed the possibility of a presidential candidacy for Bill Clinton. Cawthon had spent a day in Little Rock following the governor about. The writer's intention was apparently to report on Clinton's political comeback and to shed light on the popular belief that he was a rising star in the Democratic Party's firmament.

"It would be fun to run," Clinton told interviewer Cawthon, "even if you lost. It would be a challenge to go out and meet the people and try to communicate your ideas and bring the different parts of the country together."

Asked by the Arkansas Gazette to comment on the Atlanta article, the governor replied rather candidly that:

> *You know how it is—a reporter comes here—and the one thing all reporters ask about is whether you want to run for President someday—and I told him, yeah, I'd thought about it. I think all politicians have thought about it—even if just in their wildest dreams.*

Clinton went on to tell the Gazette that he would probably run for governor again because he had fired people up about improving the state and that he felt he should stick with them.

The expected announcement came in late July 1985 during a gathering with friends at the governor's mansion. Arkansas Gazette reporter John Brummett covered the event in the July 24 edition of the paper. Borrowing a line from Ronald Reagan, Clinton told those present that he would "stay the course," adding that:

I have asked the people of this state to commit themselves to a decade of dedication. Over and over again I have asked you to work for that future. Over and over again you have responded, and today I can do no less. I cannot ask you to stay the course if I am willing to leave office before our programs are fully implemented..I want to stay home and finish the job.

What enticed Clinton to seek a fourth term as governor? One temptation may have been a constitutional amendment—approved by Arkansans in 1984—giving the state's constitutional officers four-year terms. If Clinton were to be re-elected, and if he served a full term, he would have spent a decade in the governors' office. This would eclipse the records of all other Arkansas governors with the exception of Orval Faubus.

In August 1985, Clinton journeyed to Boise, Idaho, to attend the National Governor's Conference. He and his colleagues expected that Clinton would be elected vice chairman of that organization. But during the course of the meeting, a partisan battle erupted over a fund-raising letter sent out by President Ronald Reagan. The letter pointedly criticized Democratic governors. The arranged election of Tennessee Governor Lamar Alexander as chairman was about to be blocked by the Democratic governors unless a compromise could be reached—and ruffled political feathers could be smoothed.

Clinton was asked to serve on a negotiating committee and to be its spokesman. After a heated three-hour session, an apology was offered by the Republican governors. The Democrats also secured a promise that the Republicans would not mail a second batch of letters to some 80,000 Republican supporters.

Clinton's comments after the Republican apology revealed some of the concerns shared by the Democratic governors. In the August 7, 1985, edition of the Arkansas Gazette, the governor is quoted as saying that:

We know anyone has the right to come into our states and send out fund-raising letters that we consider inaccurate— that's part of politics. But this (episode) went beyond that. If they (the Republican governors) had persisted in playing that way, all our efforts to build a bipartisan organization would have destroyed the organization as we know it.

By the close of the conference, Governor Alexander had been elected chairman of the National Governors' Conference, and Clinton had been installed as vice chairman. This honor paved the way for Clinton as chairman of the organization come 1986. Along with his election—a month earlier—to the chairmanship of the Southern Growth Policies Board, this new leadership position pointed to a growing national role for the young governor.

Clinton closed out 1985 with a trade mission to the Far East. He headed up a 13-member delegation from Arkansas. Their first stop was Japan, where presentations on the Arkansas business climate were given to groups in Tokyo and Osaka.

The governor maintained that the delegation's efforts in Japan were successful, largely due to the efforts of the Sanyo Corporation which had just completed an eastern Arkansas television assembly plant. Sanyo reps told their Japanese counterparts that they were very pleased with the Arkansas operation. In support of their claim, they cited the hard-working people of the area, along with the close working relationship the company had developed with the state government. After the first of the year, Clinton was again called upon to represent the Democratic viewpoint in a national forum. He was invited to appear on the MacNeil-Lehrer Newshour. The February 6, 1986, edition of the Arkansas Gazette carried the governor's criticism of Ronald Reagan's latest budget proposal. The nearly trillion-dollar budget called for another increase in military spending. Clinton disagreed with this sort of appropriation, saying:

> *This budget essentially says again that you get better defense if you spend more money; everything else is better if you spend less money.*

Particularly, Clinton mentioned some $40 billion in planned cuts in domestic spending—including cuts in farm programs, funds assistance for college students, law enforcement and aid to cities. The governor maintained that 40 states—including Arkansas—had been forced to raise taxes just to offset federal budget cuts and continue programs which had previously been federally funded.

Huge budget deficits were still occurring, Clinton noted, despite the Reagan administration's efforts to bring the budget under control. The Democrat noted that the budget should not:

> *...mortgage the educational future of our children or...undermine efforts to reach economic excellence. I think we have to keep moving forward in things that are critical for the economic future of our country and for human decency at home.*

As the 1986 gubernatorial primary approached, rumors of political confrontations swept across Arkansas. One of the more interesting rumors involved former governor Orval Faubus. According to the February 25 edition of the Arkansas Gazette, the rumors appeared to have solidified into substance. Little Rock-based political consultant Jerry Russell told the newspaper that "I think it can be said that his (Faubus') definite intention is to be a candidate for governor, but I can't say...when a formal announcement will be made."

How viable would a Faubus candidacy be? When asked the question, Russell replied that "it depends on how many people Bill Clinton has made mad."

Next, the Gazette contacted former governor Faubus. "I've talked to him (Russell) about helping in the campaign, if I get into the campaign," Faubus commented, adding "I'm definitely making plans." Clinton, told about the Faubus candidacy, had a one-word reply: "Wonderful."

The Little Rock district school board submitted a desegregation proposal to Judge Henry Woods, fast on the heels of a federal court decision forcing the city's school district to move toward desegregation. The measure required some $79 million in additional spending—for the first year—and about $51 million a year thereafter. Hearings to consider the school board's proposal were slated to begin within a few months.

Clinton said that the decision of the eighth Circuit Court of Appeals had placed a large financial responsibility on the state. As a part of a solution to the desegregation question, Clinton maintained, that burden was unconscionable. The governor noted that the expenditure would be unfair to other Arkansas school districts since they would have to give up funds to be used in dealing with Little Rock's problem. As it would turn out, the state's efforts to deal with the difficulty would result in another education first.

In late March 1986, former governor Orval Faubus threw his hat into the ring as a candidate for the office he had formerly held. The Arkansas Gazette sent reporter Marla Henson to cover Faubus' announcement, which took place in the state capitol rotunda. The 76-year-old Faubus presented a sharp contrast to the youthful Bill Clinton, but insisted to reporters and supporters that he was ready to face the challenge of governing the state:

Some say I have an uphill battle in this race I am entering. I was reared on a mountainside. Whenever I sought the top, I

had to climb. When I was away from home in the valleys, the
way home was always uphill. If this is an uphill battle, so be it.

Of course, reporters asked Faubus if his decision to bar blacks from entering Little Rock High School would come up in his campaign for governor. "That's nearly 30 years ago," Faubus said, referring to the 1957 incident, adding that "What we need to be concerned with now—all our citizens, rich or poor, country and city, black and white, or whomever—we need to be concerned with the here and now, the benefit of ourselves, and the progress of our state."

Within a few days, a Republican candidate had entered the gubernatorial contest as well. He was Frank White, who had ousted Clinton in the 1980 election, and had been himself defeated in 1982. His announcement that he intended to seek the Republican nomination came six years to the day after he announced his intention to challenge Bill Clinton in 1980.

White had been a life-long Democrat until he bolted the party in 1980. While the former governor did have a Republican primary ahead of him, he and his supporters were obviously intent on a rematch—the second of its kind—with Clinton. "When a governor gets too much power, it breeds arrogance," White claimed on April Fool's Day in 1986, "and arrogance breeds corruption."

Like the first Confederate shell exploding over Fort Sumter, White had just fired the first shot in what would be his third encouter with Clinton.

White's nemesis, meanwhile, was on his way to Salt Lake City to receive an award for his work in the field of education. The Democratic Policy Commission—an arm of the Democratic National Committee—had issued an eight-page report praising Clinton. The illustrated paper covered the governor's efforts to strengthen educational standards, raise teacher salaries, and to establish new programs aimed at helping teachers, students, and the disadvantaged. Paul Kirk Jr., chairman of the Democratic National Committee, joined with Policy Commission chairman Scott Matheson in praising Clinton and his leadership skills.

Of course, it came as no surprise to Clinton that the Arkansas Education Association endorsed Frank White as its candidate for governor; some Arkansas observers were shocked that the endorsement came before the primary elections and not after them. AEA President Ed Bullington told Arkansas Gazette reporter James Scudder that there would be no endorsement of any Democratic primary candidate. In Mr. Bullington's words:

We don't feel like the candidates in the Democratic primary for governor were committed to the issues that are of concern to teachers...

Asked for his reaction, Clinton candidly told the Gazette that "I assume that Mr. White's change of position from support to opposition of teacher testing was a major factor in the endorsement."

The largely uneventful primary races had predictable results. Clinton garnered 60.5 percent of the vote, defeating Orval Faubus and a third challenger, Dean Goldsby. Faubus managed 33.5 percent of the votes cast while Goldsby only received about 6 percent. In the Republican primary, White easily outdistanced three challengers to win the nomination without a runoff. Final tallies showed White with 61.9 percent of the Republican vote, Wayne Lanier receiving 20.5 percent, Maurice Britt with 13.9 percent, and Bobby Hayes only garnering 3.7 percent. Clinton reacted to the White victory by maintaining that he was glad the Republican primary had ended the way it had.

In August 1986, Clinton was elected chairman of the National Governors' Association. Arkansas Gazette reporter Scott

Van Laningham covered the event in the paper's August 27 edition. Clinton told his fellow governors that as far as he was concerned their agendas boiled down to a single item: The creation of jobs. The governor pointed out:

> Today I come as the first of the "over-the-hill" baby boomers to ask: Can we make America work again for her people? I believe we can, but only if we find ways for Americans to be able to work and have work. We must face squarely our responsibility to make Americans more competitive from the ground up and to reverse [the] tide of lost human potential in those who have fallen through the cracks of what I call America's "leaky bucket."

Earlier that same summer, Clinton had been asked to serve as co-chairman of the association's task force on welfare reform. In June 1986, he headed to Washington with a group of fellow governors, intent on listening to proposals by the Reagan administration. While the governors as a group fell short of endorsing the administration's program, they did agree that it had become necessary to restructure the welfare system.

Speaking for the group of governors, Clinton maintained that all were committed to working with the president on a bipartisan level. According to the governor, he and his counterparts had agreed on three major goals: First, put welfare recipients back to work; second, strengthen family bonds and responsibilities; and third, ensure adequate health care for young children.

The days leading to the November general election were filled with heated exchanges between Clinton and White. On election night, it became quickly obvious that White's comeback effort had failed. Clinton had gained a mandate with some 64 percent of the votes cast to only 36 percent for his challenger.

Gazette reporter Bob Wells was with the Clinton camp on election night. He noted that the governor appeared exultant in his victory speech. Clinton said:

In our 150th year, I believe with all my heart our best years are ahead of us. The tough campaign is over and now it's time for the hard work to begin on our problems and our opportunities. It's time for all of us to pull together as a family.

For Bill Clinton, his second defeat of Frank White was one of the most rewarding victories of his political career. For his part, White noted that he did not disagree with Clinton on many issues, but that he and his opponent approached solutions from a different point of view. Speaking to his supporters as he conceded the race to Clinton, White said:

As long as I'm a resident of Arkansas and continue to participate in the business community, I'll continue to work to better Arkansas and build a two-party system.

At this writing, Frank White has not made another political race in Arkansas. Gazette columnist John Brummett, writing the day after the election, told his readers that Clinton now shouldered an awesome responsibility:

This (the election) is a major story not only because of Clinton's margin; it is a major story because of what Clinton now has—this first four-year term in Arkansas in more than 100 years and a two-thirds mandate to boot. Pure, unadulterated power is what he now has. The state can only hope he uses it well, that some of the timidity, indecision and exercises in pure expediency will evaporate with what the voters have now given him.

Clinton's fourth term as governor of Arkansas began on January 13, 1987. For the fourth time, he addressed the traditional joint session of the state legislature before heading outdoors to the capitol steps to deliver his State of the State message to a crowd of waiting supporters. The governor told the group that he had been expecting to approach this inaugural day with virtually no excitement, then added:

But I confess I found myself this morning—I woke up at 4:30—more awestruck by the opportunity, more humbled by the responsibility, more grateful for the chance to serve than in any previous time.

Clinton shared with his listeners the immediate challenge that faced them all—raising enough state revenue to cover the expected shortfall. At risk, the governor maintained, were the new school standards which held the key to a brighter future for all Arkansans. The Education Reform package adopted in 1983 should not be delayed or abandoned, Clinton said, but should be given the opportunity to take root, grow and bear fruit.

Speaking to the state's lawmakers, he pointed out that the two-year-old economic reform measures they had passed were already beginning to take effect. Clinton said:

Two days ago, the press carried the report that last year, Arkansas ranked first of all the southern states in percentage growth of manufacturing jobs through August 1(1986). You can be proud of what you've done and what we've been able to do together. The question before us now is, are we going to keep our commitment are we going to recognize that we have got to finish this job in education? Are we going to spend a little amount of money to take on these initiatives and the major new investment it will take to get the school standards in? With a new, dynamic world economy the students of today must be given the opportunity to enter that economy ready to compete. The problem with doing what we've al-

ways done is there is no such thing as a status quo anymore. When times are changing like this, you either press ahead, swimming against the tide, or you get pushed back. There is no status quo. There is none and we can't hold it. It doesn't exist.

Clinton told the legislators that the real challenge was to face the reality of the future and to do what must be done now to meet it head-on. The need for additional revenue, which might mandate additional taxes, was a necessity he was prepared to meet side by side with the lawmakers. The governor said:

If you want me there, I'll be there. I'll stand up with you, I'll walk down the aisle with you. And I don't care if you are tall or short, black or white, male or female, or Democrat or Republican—if you support a way out of the problems we are facing, I'll be glad to tell the world you did it.

Arkansas lawmakers were presented with a 214-page report outlining the governor's proposals for the legislative session. Clinton's recommendations would not only ensure the on-time implementation of the new school standards, but it would carry the state through the next biennium without a shortfall. The governor had been touting a possible sales tax increase since earlier in January, but he told state legislators that he would not pursue that plan of action unless it became absolutely necessary. Apparently, Clinton felt that the lawmakers could reach their goals for the state by following the plan he had outlined for them. He noted that:

It won't be easy for you (lawmakers) to vote for this plan. I know that. Maybe you'll have a better one. But so help me, when we walk out of here, when this session is over, let's say "This will be the time when we were most alive, because we did our duty and we secured the future of this state."

Reaction to Clinton's challenge appeared mixed at best. In the January 20, 1987, edition of the Arkansas Gazette, State Representative W. F. "Bill" Porter said he was glad that the governor had laid aside—for the moment, at least—the notion of a tax increase. Porter maintained that:

I think (Clinton) had been talking to members of the General Assembly and found out that the people were against a major tax increase. Because of that, he came up with a very modest tax increase that will help the state of Arkansas. I think he realized that the economy is not good in the state of Arkansas at this time, and I think he wanted to be fair to the citizens of the state.

House Speaker Ernest Cunningham agreed that the school standards were important. Cunningham told the Gazette that:

I thought it (Clinton's plan) was very good...right on time. Arkansas has to continue the momentum we started. The salvation of our state is the educational system.

Five days later, Gazette columnist Ernie Dumas noted that despite some reservations expressed by state legislators concerning a tax increase, the concern did not appear to be politically motivated. Dumas noted that the chance of a voter backlash was virtually nonexistent:

The public apparently understands the custom and accepts it. Taxpayers rarely punish legislators—or governors—for doing their duty when they expect better services. In the last 30 years, during which taxes were raised significantly at seven sessions of the Arkansas legislature, voters at the next election never once defeated a larger percentage who voted for taxes than of those who voted against them.

With the session getting under way, the Clinton emergency revenue plan began to receive close scrutiny, especially as the governor began to introduce the individual bills. Bringing the Arkansas tax code with modern federal standards would be a major step which would provide the greatest amount of fiscal relief. Clinton also proposed deferring state contributions to the Public Employees' Retirement System for two years. He also wanted to exempt the 2 percent commission retailers were paid when they submitted their state sales tax reports every four months. Another measure would begin taxing interstate telephone calls and tax out-of-state firms that advertised in Arkansas or conducted catalog sales within the state. A fourth major revenue initiative would repeal the 4 percent sales tax exemption on cigarette sales.

Within a short time, all the measures—save for the tax code reform bill—had been approved. Setbacks, however, were on the horizon—setbacks which would slow the legislative session to a crawl. Senate Bill 203, suspending the discount to retailers for collecting state sales tax, was enacted without an emergency clause. Without the clause, the law would not take effect for 90 days, thus removing a major source of new revenue. Clinton's attempts to reinstate the emergency clause would spark considerable debate and succeed only in causing further delays in the bill's approval.

The measure to suspend state contributions to the Public Employees' Retirement System, although approved by the legislature and signed by the governor, failed to win the necessary concurrence of the board of trustees of the Arkansas Teacher Retirement System. Clinton rejoined that the panel's lack of support could backlash—resulting in a lack of support later in the session for a bill which would raise teacher retirement benefits. In the February 12, 1987, edition of the Arkansas Gazette, he noted:

> I'm disappointed that the board chose not to actively support making a contribution to public schools. The money is plainly needed to keep the schools open until the end of the year.

In mid-February, Clinton was asked to travel to the nation's capital, where he spoke to a group promoting cooperation between businesses and educational institutions. His growing reputation as a public official concerned with improving education had garnered him the honor. The governor seized the opportunity to offer some penetrating insights into the state of the nation's education system. American students, according to Clinton, were not on the same educational level as their foreign counterparts, especially in the critical areas of mathematics and science. Most disheartening, he noted, was the decline in the number of students able to demonstrate higher literacy skills:

> *...although almost all U.S. students easily meet the lower literacy standards of a generation ago, a majority do not meet today's higher standards.*

According to Clinton, part of the problem lay in the level of performance expected from students—a level he maintained was too low:

> *For decades, policy makers have focused their attention on minimum standards...but there are limits to what we can accomplish with minimums—oriented policies, and their effect upon teachers and administrators may sometimes be to prevent excellence as well as mandate minimum performance.*

Clinton concluded his speech with the thought that more attention should be given to a complete restructuring of the nation's educational system.

Back in Arkansas, the governor faced a slow-moving legislative session. Already, the press had dubbed the gathering of lawmakers as the "nowhere fast" session. An example of this "do nothing" attitude was the battle over Senate Bill 203, which would exempt the sales tax collection fee for four months. Since it meant they would not receive their usual percentage, retail merchants from across the state opposed the bill. Consequently, efforts to ramrod the measure through the legislature quickly became uphill battles. On four separate occasions, lawmakers made efforts to amend the bill by adding an emergency clause, so the measure could go into effect immediately upon being signed by the governor.

But newly-elected state representatives were another reason for the slow-moving legislative session. More than two dozen members of the House, who apparently felt it their duty to pore over state agency budgets with the proverbial fine-tooth combs, managed to keep the committees and the House floor relatively quiet. This group, then, was responsible for holding up appropriations bills while it conducted its own budget reviews. To those who complained, Clinton replied that the legislators in question were only doing a good, thorough job.

By late February, Clinton was again jetting to Washington, D.C., this time for the annual meeting of the National Governors' Association. He had worked on the NGA's welfare reform committee, and presented the group's findings to the White House. After the meeting, Clinton and NGA Vice Chairman John Sununu of New Hampshire—who would later become George Bush's embattled chief of staff—held a news conference. The two governors announced to the press that they had found broad-ranging support for welfare reform during their White House meeting. The consensus was that welfare recipients should enroll in work programs and that federal spending for education and job training should be increased. During the White House news conference, Clinton said:

*We want to create a (welfare) program that is fundamentally
a jobs program...to move the person toward independence.*

Arkansas Gazette reporter Carol Matlock noted that the
governor spoke confidently about the difficult task of convincing the White House and Congress of the need to fund rather
costly welfare reforms. Clinton maintained that while the tim-
ing for welfare reform had not been right in years past, the
right opportunity had indeed arrived; sound investment strategy would outweigh the high initial costs of funding the reform project. Additionally, Clinton said that he expected support from the nation's business community because, under the
current system, able-bodied welfare recipients constituted an
obvious productivity drain.

After a careful review, President Reagan endorsed several
key welfare reform proposals. Reagan said he agreed that the
educational and jobs programs should be expanded and that
those receiving welfare should be enrolled in some type of
work program. Finally, the President said he endorsed the
requirement for welfare recipients to sign a contract which
would spell out their rights and responsibilities.

Clinton expressed great pleasure with the endorsement,
and added that obtaining the President's approval was a major
objective of the NGA. Clinton was chosen to present the reform proposals to the House Ways and Means Committee at
its upcoming hearings.

Before Clinton left the capital, Washington reporters asked
him again—if he intended to run for President. The February
22, 1987, edition of the Arkansas Gazette quoted Clinton responding to a question about the recent announcement of New
York Governor Mario Cuomo. Cuomo, in a statement much
like the one he would issue nearly five years later, declared

that he would not be a candidate for the Democratic presidential nomination. In response to the Cuomo statement, Clinton said:

> It makes it easier to get in, if your objective is to see if you can finish second in Iowa or New Hampshire. It looks good for people who thought it (the candidates) would be Hart and Cuomo, and the best they could do was third.

Back in Arkansas, Clinton told a Gazette reporter that he didn't think he could responsibly run for President and serve as governor without a popular mandate:

> I don't think a sitting governor could enter into a campaign like that unless the people thought it was a good thing, unless they supported it...the people would have to feel it's something they were proud of, something they wanted. Not 100 percent, but a significant percentage would have to feel that.

The governor maintained that his primary mission was to preserve and protect the newly adopted school standards:

> I have to do that over and above everything else. That's what the people elected me to do. And I don't think I have any business doing anything else until that's done.

Truth to tell, Clinton was not the only Arkansan being touted as a possible 1988 presidential contender. Senator Dale Bumpers was testing the political waters, and many pundits felt that he would indeed decide to seek the Democratic nomination. Certainly, the Cuomo announcement cast a favorable light on Bumpers' possibilities as a candidate. Many top fundraisers had already voiced support for Bumpers, and Cuomo's departure left several top-notch campaign professionals available for service.

At the Arkansas Gazette, columnist John Brummett was fairly sure that Bumpers would enter the race. But, in all fairness to Brummett, he declared in the paper's February 25, 1987, edition that he would have to hedge on his prediction. Short of being definitive, the best paragraph Brummett could manage was this:

> Sources close to Bumpers say he apparently has decided to become a Democratic candidate for president. At this time, and barring any unexpected changes, he is likely to formally announce in two weeks either his outright candidacy or the formation of an exploratory committee so he can begin raising funds for such a race.

Brummett said he saw only one major factor that could affect Bumpers' decision to enter the race...something he called the "Clinton Factor." Unfortunately for Gazette readers, Brummett did not elaborate on what this factor was or what it portended for the senator's political future.

But that didn't really matter, because Bumpers soon ended all the speculation. In the March 21 edition of the Gazette, writer George Wells detailed the senator's decision, relayed by press aide Matt James. In his statement, Bumpers said that he would not seek the presidential nomination because, in the senator's words, a campaign "would mean a total disruption of the closeness my family has cherished, and if victorious, much of that closeness is necessarily lost forever." Bumpers admitted that he had reached his decision "after great deliberation," adding that he had "considered every aspect of what a decision to run would mean."

Despite the many discussions across the state and around the nation regarding a Bill Clinton presidential candidacy, the governor still had to cope with the daily business of running the state. The ongoing legislative session was rapidly becoming a battle of wills and nerves. Senate Bill 339, which would align the Arkansas tax code with the federal tax code, was brought out of committee and placed on the floor of the State Senate. From there, it was thought, the bill would move quickly to the House. Nonetheless, the bill was defeated by a single vote and it appeared to be a dead issue. Clinton and his staff began a massive lobbying effort which, within a few days, effectively returned the bill to the Senate floor. A lengthy debate ensued—not about the merits of the bill, but about the procedures to be used in bringing the bill onto the floor in the first place.

Hours of debate resulted in three procedural votes before the bill itself was ever addressed. Finally, the bill was voted on, passed, and sent on to the House. But the governor's work was not yet finished, since the bill had landed in the midst of the Revenue and Taxation Committee. Clinton and his staff began to lobby the panel members one-on-one. Their efforts resulted in a 12-6 vote, moving the bill out onto the House floor.

Just as the full House was finally ready to consider the bill, yet another stumbling block arose. Representatives, intent on forcing a Clinton compromise, introduced a similar bill in the House. While Senate Bill 339 would adopt a large portion of the federal code as the state's statute, this new legislation would retain much of the old Arkansas code and adopt only certain portions of the federal code.

The basic difference lay in how much revenue the state would realize from the change. Clinton's proposal—Senate Bill 339—would raise about $35 million, while the House effort would generate only about $20 million. By now, clearly frustrated with the process, Clinton tried to bring both sides together. He advocated consideration of the second version...if several items he considered vital were added to it. The hybrid bill would raise about $26 million in state revenue.

Thus the compromise bill made it to the floor of the Arkansas House. There, it was soundly defeated. For the first time in his political career, Clinton succumbed to the tension the overlong session had already created. Standing outside the House chambers as the vote was taken, he became visibly upset. He told reporters standing alongside that the state lawmakers had lied to the children of Arkansas when they said they cared about the new education standards and improving the state's schools.

Of course, a reaction was forthcoming from the legislators—in particular, State Representative Lloyd Reed George from Danville. The Yell County lawmaker had introduced the legislation recommending additional funding for schools, and felt that the governor had personally insulted him. In the Arkansas Gazette, George demanded that Clinton apologize for calling him a liar. Of course, the fact that the Clinton's remarks were directed toward the legislative body as a whole did not lessen George's conviction that he had been wronged.

But Clinton did apologize. In a letter to Representative George, he noted that:

In calmer times, I would not have used that word (lied). I'm sorry for any personal offense I have given. I do not regret any effort to get legislators who voted for the school budget to assume responsibility for making good the commitment to standards that budget embodies.

But George's blood continued to boil. He met the governor next day in a capitol hallway, and the two men adjourned to a nearby office to discuss their differences. Apparently, George did not feel vindicated by the ensuing discussion. When the House went into session that afternoon, he stepped into the well to vent his frustration. "Up where I come from," George noted, pointing west rather than north, "people don't call people liars." He went on to say that he had only voted his conscience, which told him that he had "voted enough taxes on my people."

The governor's desire to pass a tax reform measure continued unabated. Clinton and his aides began to look for votes which might reverse the House decision. After an afternoon of intense lobbying efforts in the capitol hallways and on the House floor, the bill was brought up again and passed. Clinton's effort had caused 22 legislators to change their vote.

Although the compromise tax code had eventually been passed, the bill still represented a considerable shortfall in Clinton's attempt to raise additional state revenue. That nagging question—whether a general sales tax increase would yet be necessary—began to haunt lawmakers and the press alike.

In the March 8 Gazette, John Brummett discussed the tax question, stating that many Arkansans had been asking about the need for a penny education tax during the time in which the legislature apparently raised the sales tax in the 1983 special education session. Brummett explained that first the legislature had passed a new school funding formula:

> The sales tax went up to 4 cents and the new money was plugged into a new distribution formula. Many districts got more money. Others were simply held harmless and shored up. Nearly a third of the new money went to higher education, which had a role of its own to play in the betterment of the state's educational system. That was then; this is now...Some sizeable districts are in trouble and need to pass their enormous mileage proposals this week to stand a chance.

Even at that they will need more money from the state, too. A complication is that state revenues have become static, meaning inflationary growth isn't providing schools with once expected routine funding increases.

Clinton began to sense that a sales tax proposal would probably be introduced in the legislative session, and he began telling lawmakers that any proposal would have to be more progressive in nature if it were to gain his approval. The governor wanted to exempt utilities and food and to provide some tax relief for those with low incomes.

Already, the 1987 legislative session was the fifth longest in state history. There were no signs that the conclave would end soon. Raising revenue to fund the state's new school standards was a serious bone of contention. An effort to delay the implementation of the standards for two years was introduced, sparking Clinton's denouncement of the measure as "disastrous." The governor maintained that any attempt to delay the standards would also result in delaying the state's ability to field a competitive education program.

Facing the inevitable, Clinton introduced a sales tax measure in late March. This bill called for a quarter-cent sales tax increase. As an initial step toward passage of the bill, Clinton began running radio ads urging Arkansans to call their legislators to plead for support of the measure.

The governor addressed the Arkansas House and invited members of the Senate to attend the gathering. According to Clinton:

I feel sort of like General Grant at Vicksburg. They said he was drunk, no good, he didn't have any sense. He won the battle because he came to fight. You may go home Friday, but I'm going to be like the man at Vicksburg. I care more about this than anything else. I think it's more important to the future of our state than anything else, and I'm prepared to go on, and on, and on, and on, until we get some resolution of it.

As he finished this sentence, observers heard lawmakers about the chamber groan with anticipation. Clinton continued:

I honestly don't think there's a single person in this chamber that will ever lose his or her seat for doing what had to be done in this difficult time.

In a word, he had placed the ball squarely in the legislators' court. Now, he began a full-court press. The intense lobbying effort included Clinton's legislative aides, his wife Hillary, and state agency officials and educators as well. However, the anti-tax legislative mood proved to be too strong to overcome. On the 82nd and final day of the session, the bill was voted down and state lawmakers prepared to go home.

But all was not lost. Working behind the scenes with Arkansas' Revenue Stabilization law, which sets priorities for state funding, Clinton managed to find the funds to continue implementation of the school standards.

The legislative session just concluded had managed to find some $55 million in additional revenue, but the state was still facing a shortfall. By law, Arkansas could not engage in deficit spending. This fact necessitated a continuing effort to resolve the revenue problem. Clinton looked toward a special legislative session to solve the difficulty.

This special session was set for the first week in June 1987. Clinton spoke to the state via a Little Rock television station, describing the session as an emergency effort to meet the state's needs. He said he would center his efforts on revenue-producing measures but would also introduce bills in two other important areas. First, he would initiate a comprehensive study of the state's tax system. His goal, Clinton maintained, would be to design an Arkansas tax structure which would see the state into the next century. Additionally, he would work to develop an equally comprehensive code of ethics for public officials, as well as a lobbyist disclosure law.

In the revenue-producing area, Clinton told his listeners that he would not propose a general tax increase. Clinton stated that he knew the public would not support such a move. He added:

> *I accept that, but if we cannot afford to move forward, we can less afford to fall backward either. Doing nothing will guarantee a reversal for us. Reaching for the future is still frustrating for us. It's a moving target. To catch it you have to keep moving with it. If you stop trying, you fall further behind.*

The speedy special session which followed Clinton's clarion call resulted in some $21 million in additional revenue. That figure included nearly $7 million in additional taxes. Raising the state corporate franchise tax and accelerating the collection of state sales taxes were the major revenue-producing measures approved by the legislature.

In late July, Clinton traveled north to Traverse City, Mich., to attend a summer session of the National Governors' Association. As chairman of the group, he had worked on a task force with fellow governors assembling a welfare reform program. At the opening of the session, Clinton urged the passage of the reform package by Congress before the end of 1987. He intended to follow up his remarks by returning to Washington to give testimony before a congressional committee looking into welfare reform.

Along with Governor Michael Castle of Delaware, Clinton had been chosen to assist with the welfare reform problem in

135

another way. The two men were asked to help negotiate the differences in federal welfare reform proposals between Congress and the White House.

As the outgoing chairman of the NGA, Clinton was honored for his efforts by his fellow governors. Minnesota Governor Rudy Perpich presented Clinton with a plaque commemorating his leadership and called him "the best governor in the United States."

Clinton's successor, Governor John Sununu of New Hampshire, praised the Arkansan's efforts and mentioned that one of Clinton's greatest assets was his "style and capacity to deal with his colleagues and get results." In the closing moments of the meeting, Clinton told the group that:

> *The American people want us to work together and to take responsibility for our future. They know we share a common commitment to solving these problems, and they know that government cannot solve these problems alone or leave them alone.*

In the fall of 1987, a decision by the U.S. Supreme Court prompted Clinton to call yet another special session of the state legislature. The decision before the high court involved a Pennsylvania case which cast some doubt on the constitutionality of Arkansas' weight distance tax on large trucks. The governor addressed the opening session and told lawmakers that they had no choice but to take immediate action. In Clinton's words:

> *I'm convinced that the longer we put it off, the worse it's going to be (speaking of the weight-distance tax issue). Go ahead, take a deep breath, and take appropriate action.*

The two major factions who had presided over the enactment of the original bill were prepared for this new session with proposals to be introduced at the fall of the opening gavel. Arkansas Highway and Transportation Director Henry Gray and his supporters were prepared to do battle yet again with the combined interests of the poultry, agriculture, timber and trucking industries.

The AHTD and Director Gray were touting a three-cent-per-mile tax with an exemption for empty trucks. The Arkansas Poultry Federation wanted a straight, across-the-board two-cent-per-mile tax. Clinton had endorsed Gray's bill as "the best possible proposal." The only major difference between the two camps seemed to be the amount of the tax involved.

The only solution seemed to be a compromise. Following a dramatic hallway conference, with reporters and spectators surrounding the principals, the two camps reached an agreement that the tax would be two and a half cents per mile. Back to their respective chambers went the legislators, aiming for an immediate passage of the compromise bill and an end to the session. Although the lawmakers achieved their purpose, this battle would not mark the last time the weight-distance tax would be debated in the Arkansas legislature.

In early November, with the 1988 elections still a year away, Clinton told Little Rock reporters that the National Democratic Party had been seeking his help in its fund-raising efforts. The party's "Victory Fund" had just been established, and Democratic leaders were seeking well-known public figures who could travel about the country speaking at party fund-raising functions. Clinton admitted that he was considering the offer but that he would have to reconcile any duty he performed for the national party with his constitutional duties in state government.

A few days later, Clinton was off to Florida to deliver the keynote address at the Florida Democratic Party's annual convention in Miami. With his usual rousing speaking style, he targeted the Reagan administration and its campaign against big government. Clinton said that the administration had shown, despite the anti-government stance, that government programs were important. The November 8, 1987, edition of the Arkansas Gazette reported that Clinton added:

People know the politics of the President are inadequate...the chickens he has spawned may be coming home to roost. The cheery talk and the happy rhetoric sooner or later give way to the hard facts of life. If we really want a future, we have to pay a price to attain it. If we do nothing, the future will be painful...Let's re-create a new world economic order...secure the American people's role in it. America can't grow if the world doesn't grow.

Clinton's promise to the people of Arkansas to pursue both a public official's ethics code and a lobbyist disclosure law, resulted in the call for a special legislative session in late January 1988. A bill, written from the recommendations of the governor's ethics commission, was introduced on the first day of the session. Within a week, the State Senate had attached some 30 amendments to Clinton's proposal, and senators were reportedly at work on their own version of the same legislation. While the Clinton bill called for the formation of a permanent ethics commission and for the disclosure of a lobbyist's expenditures on individual lawmakers and public officials, the Senate version mandated a single-person "Office of Ethics Counsel" and eliminated reporting requirements for lobbyists.

That Clinton's original ethics bill was in serious trouble would have been a kind understatement. The bill was no longer recognizable because of the substantial number of amendments attached to it in the Senate. While the House of Representatives was kinder to the governor's proposal, it still found it necessary to attach some 19 amendments. Somewhat tongue-in-cheek, Clinton praised the members of the House for their dedication to better government and for their willingness to give his proposal a chance to succeed. Clinton promised the assembled representatives that he would spread the word across Arkansas that House members had helped him in his effort to bring accountability to the process of government.

Later, Clinton told reporters that he was concerned about the future of any proposed ethics measure and that he was seriously considering a petition drive to allow Arkansans themselves to decide the question. The governor's aim was to make the ethics bill an initiated act to be decided upon by the state's voters.

Amazingly enough, the special session of the legislature ended without any sort of ethics bill being passed, a circumstance which played straight into Clinton's hands. A clash between the House and Senate regarding the lobbyist disclosure section made it apparent that no compromise would be forthcoming. The lawmakers then adjourned themselves without having accomplished anything worthy of note.

Clinton, meanwhile, expressed great enthusiasm for the legislature's work, since it would lend great impetus to his petition drive proposal. Clinton noted that he expected a great deal of money would be spent by lobbyists and opponents of the bill in their combined efforts to defeat the initiated act.

Arkansas Gazette reporter Bob Wells noted that the state lawmakers had played directly into the governor's hands. In the February 7, 1988, edition of the newspaper, Wells noted that:

> If the special legislative session had been a movie, Governor Bill Clinton couldn't have been a more brilliant director, jumping in at just the right moment Friday to shout "cut."

Wells noted that what appeared to be a Clinton defeat was, in reality, a victory of sorts:

The session ended, instead, with Mr. Clinton now able to take an ethics bill to the public that would require public officials and lobbyists to make disclosures essentially identical to those recommended by the gubernatorial Code of Ethics Commission.

Clinton did indeed begin a petition drive, kicking the event off in late February with a rally in the capitol rotunda. Nearly a thousand Arkansans crowded around tables to begin signing petitions to have the ethics question placed on the November ballot. The governor addressed the crowd, saying:

I've heard about every argument in the world against this proposal, but I don't think we will ever have to hear the argument again that this is an issue nobody is interested in. What we're trying to do is to put a bill on the ballot that will impose some accountability on this (government) process.

Clinton's confidence in the people's judgment was not misplaced. Although proponents of the ethics measure would have to work hard—they gathered more than 55,000 signatures by the July 8 deadline—the state's voters would eventually finish the job the legislature had abandoned.

The summer of 1988 would mark the moment of greatest political embarrassment to Clinton. Asked by his good friend Michael Dukakis, Clinton agreed to give the speech at the Democratic National Convention, which would place the name of the Massachusetts' governor in nomination for the presidency of the United States.

Clinton, as was his habit, stayed up until 5:30 a.m. writing a speech. As he read it, the governor timed his efforts, and was satisfied with the 15-minute result. It should be noted that Clinton had worked through nine drafts of the talk and recorded and timed the final effort several times.

At the same time, measures were supposed to be taken to bring the convention crowd to a fever pitch when Clinton introduced Governor Dukakis. Unfortunately for Clinton, the crowd began to cheer each time he mentioned Dukakis' name. Of course, this added substantially to the length of the speech.

Like a good trooper, Clinton continued through the speech as the crowd kept interrupting. These spontaneous demonstrations ate up minute after minute. Finally, Clinton had been on the rostrum for more than a half hour, and the crowd was vocally impatient for him to bring the speech to an end. To the governor's credit, he did attempt to bring the situation back under control. "Now I want you to calm down," he admonished the crowd at one point, "so I can tell the rest of the country why they should want Mike."

The speech was being carried nationwide by all major networks. When Clinton breached his preimposed time limit, the anchors and analysts got nervous. Finally, both NBC and ABC cut away from the proceedings and began to voice their criticism of Clinton. "I am afraid," John Chancellor noted, "that ...one of the most attractive governors just put a blot on his record."

For Clinton's part, the most rewarding moment of the evening came when he began to bring his speech to a close. The moment he uttered the phrase, "in closing," the convention floor erupted in applause. Both CBS and CNN had carried the entire speech live. When Clinton had concluded, both networks joined their competitors in criticism of the Arkansan.

After the speech, Clinton told an Associated Press reporter that, in good Roman tradition, he had fallen on his sword. "It was just a comedy of errors," he interjected, "one of those flukey things." The media's orgy of Clinton-bashing—better focused on the candidates—continued unabated the next day. In the Arkansas Gazette, reporter John Brummett noted that:

Clinton's developing national reputation as a gifted speaker, presumably the basis for Dukakis' selection of him as the lone nominating speaker, suffered a severe setback.

Brummett had the fortune—good or bad, according to your point of view—to sit across the aisle from Clinton during the plane flight back from Atlanta. At first, Clinton did not appear talkative and only nodded in response to Brummett's comments. Finally, apparently feeling the need to get some things off his chest, he began to describe to the reporter his thoughts and feelings as he stood at the podium. He faced, of course, millions of Americans and literally all of the nation's press.

Clinton had a growing concern, as he stood at the rostrum, that he would have to deal with a situation which had gotten out of hand. He told Brummett that his instincts told him to throw away the speech and get off the platform. But if he had done so, Clinton feared Dukakis' wrath for putting his ego ahead of the laudatory things Dukakis wanted him to say. His decision—like that of the ragtime band aboard the Titanic—was to be a good soldier and finish the task, no matter what the risk.

Even Johnny Carson castigated Clinton for his performance. "The surgeon general," Carson reported in his Tonight Show monologue, "has just approved Bill Clinton as an over-the-counter sleep aid. What a windbag!"

The Tonight Show's producers, perhaps fairer than their host, extended an invitation to Clinton to appear on the show the following evening. Clinton decided to accept. His appearance on the show—perhaps a watershed event—went a long way toward repairing his damaged national reputation. Carson had opened the program with a mimic of Clinton's convention speech, including the "in closing" comment which was met with applause.

After Clinton was introduced, he and Carson began to talk about what had transpired at the convention. Clinton asserted that he had delivered the doomed speech "on purpose—I always wanted to be on this show." He jokingly mentioned that Dukakis had called and wanted him to deliver the same sort of nominating speech for George Bush.

In a serious vein, Carson asked Clinton how the people of Arkansas had reacted to his convention speech. Clinton replied that his constituents had "reached out and embraced" him, admitting that instead, they might have maintained he had embarrassed them. Clinton described the preceding days as "one of the most wonderful weeks of my life."

Clinton highlighted his Tonight Show appearance by playing his saxaphone with Doc Severinson and the NBC orchestra. The evening, for Clinton at least, ended on a high note. He attended a post-show party in his honor hosted by Arkansas native Harry Thomason and Linda Bloodworth-Thomason, of "Designing Women" fame. The event was held at the Thomasons' Hollywood home. Fellow Arkansans Gil Gerard and Mary Steenburgen were also on hand. Today Clinton's brother, Roger, works on the "Designing Women" set.

Back in Arkansas, an occurrence full of dire portent was unfolding. By mid-September 1988, Clinton was aware of a situation involving a state employee and several allegedly unauthorized telephone calls. Larry Nichols, the marketing director for the Arkansas Development and Finance Authority, had made calls to known leaders of the Nicaraguan Contras. The 142 calls resulted in charges of $165 to a state telephone, prompting the observation that at least Nichols kept the calls short.

Nichols maintained that the calls had all been authorized by Wooten Epes, the director of the AFDA. According to Nichols, Epes had instructed him to use his contacts with the Contras to gain access to conservative congressmen and lobby for legislation on mortgage revenue bonds.

143

Nichols was also alleged to have made some 390 calls to political consultant Darrell Glascock, who had been Republican Frank White's campaign manager. According to Nichols, he and Glascock were discussing a contract to do work for the state of Arkansas. The calls to Glascock, who also had Contra connections, resulted in additional charges of more than $400, all billed to a state telephone.

Nichols resigned, apparently at the request of Epes. Nichols told Arkansas Gazette reporter Mark Oswald that he had quit his post "because of a complete lack of support from my superiors who could have set the record straight." He described himself as the victim of a "hatchet job." Nichols told Little Rock television station KARK that:

I guess my knowing the Contras poses a problem for Bill Clinton because of his position with Dukakis. I guess I was an embarrassment. I can say I've been destroyed, my family's been destroyed, for doing my job.

Obviously, Nichols' comments spoke of a growing resentment over the entire situation and of his desire to affix the blame on Clinton. Nichols would soon begin a course of action which would later catapult him into the eye of the Gennifer Flowers storm. A lawsuit filed in federal court named his former boss, Wooten Epes, and the governor as defendants. The suit contained allegations that Clinton had engaged in illicit relationships with several women. These allegations, although completely unsubstantiated, would later form the basis for the media circus which would revolve around Clinton on the 1992 presidential campaign trail. Although Nichols would later drop his suit, the controversy—largely a media creation—would continue to swirl around Clinton.

Election day 1988 brought Bill Clinton a victory in his battle for an Arkansas ethics law. Voters approved an initiated act containing both a code of ethics for public officials and a lobbyist disclosure law as well. More than 60 percent of Arkansas voters had voted for the law, despite the massive advertising campaign—which Clinton had predicted—mounted by opposing forces.

An example of the advertising campaign was a series of televison ads run by a group calling itself "The Committee Against Higher Taxes." The ads claimed that the ethics law was somehow a part of an effort on the part of the governor to raise taxes in the 1989 legislative session. Clinton countered with an ad campaign of his own, telling voters that these "big bucks" lobbyists were telling a "big tax lie" to draw voters' attention away from the real issue at hand.

On election day, Clinton got what he—and the people of Arkansas—had long wanted and needed. Clinton told Gazette reporter Mark Oswald that the ethics and disclosure measures had been "a passion of mine for ten years." The governor added that the voters' mandate "is just a big step forward in the quality of government in Arkansas."

5

THE YEARS AT THE HELM
1989–1991

★   ★   ★   ★   ★   ★

Clinton opened the 1989 legislative session with his most ambitious reform package to date. The broad-based effort was anchored with a controversial penny sales tax increase. Even before the session was officially opened, many state lawmakers were already throwing up their hands in frustration.

Aware that he would have to convince the legislature of the wisdom of his proposals—and help them find the courage to proceed—the governor began the first day of the session with a special news conference. Clinton had gathered about him a group of what he called "real people." The large gathering in the capitol rotunda had the opportunity to meet these "real" individuals and to hear their respective stories. In some way, each had been helped by the educational or economic reform measures enacted by the legislature during the last six years. Some had also expressed a desire to help solve some of the state's problems.

The range of stories offered was extensive. The governor introduced a barber who had served in World War II and had attended barber school on the G.I. Bill. One day, this barber confessed that he could barely read and expressed the desire to improve his skills. He enrolled in an adult reading program at an area vocational/technical school. In seven months, he progressed from a fourth-grade reading level to seventh-grade status.

On the platform with the governor stood a farmer who told the crowd that he was brokenhearted at the thought that people he employed to run a $150,000 piece of farm equipment could not read the operator's manual. As president of the local school board, this man was ready to lend a hand—and pay additional taxes—if he could offer his employees a brighter future.

Clinton also introduced a young woman who had been a welfare recipient and was now working full time. A state work-development program had found her a job, then arranged for her to enter another state program to earn her GED. This young woman was now starting college and looked forward eagerly to earning a degree.

The other four people introduced told similar stories. When they had finished, the governor began to make preparations to introduce these "real" individuals to the state legislature as a part of the ritual "state of the state" address. Clearly, Clinton wanted to communicate to the lawmakers the need to continue on the course they had followed for the past six years.

The governor began by telling legislators that his package—which contained some 90 bills—centered on education and human services reform. The sales tax increase, which would generate a projected $211 million, would help the state cover another revenue shortfall. This tax hike, Clinton maintained, would help bring the state into the 21st century. Additionally, it would help make up for the loss of federal funds.

The governor admitted the existence of formidable opposition to his program—and the tax increase—and readily suggested that his plan be implemented over a period of several years. But the problem, as Clinton admitted, was that by the time the legislature had enacted the multi-year program, it would be academic, irrelevant, and outmoded, because, as the governor noted, "everyone else is moving too."

At this point, Clinton introduced his seven guests, calling them "a piece of anecdotal evidence" with which to plead his case. The governor commented:

I brought them (the seven "real people") here...because they represent—to me—the human side of this legislative program and what is at stake for our state.

Clinton maintained that he wanted to give Arkansans the opportunity to develop their potential via education. This development, the governor said, would translate into economic progress. This strategy, he said, would prepare the people of the state for the competitive nature of a world economy:

The number one determinant of American economic life is how we fit with the rest of the world. How do we compete with the rich countries, the Germans, and the Japanese and the others who are as wealthy as we are, who have better educated workforces and are investing more money in people and econonic development? The new development strategy of every state has got to be to develop people and to diversify the economy so that you can get low unemployment and high income. The places that do will be rewarded; those that don't will be punished. It is as simple as that. And those of us who start behind have to work harder and do more.

But while Clinton was asking lawmakers to look at new ideas and keep pace with a changing world, his battle to institute reform was being bogged down by an extraordinarily conservative status quo. The formidable Arkansas Highway Commission had announced that it intended to ask for a major tax hike, which would pay for a system of three and four-lane

149

roads. The commission's proposal would raise the tax on gasoline and diesel fuel by some seven cents a gallon. Since both the governor and the AHC felt that their tax program must be introduced first in order to have the best chance of passage, considerable maneuvering ensued to see which proposal could be most immediately brought before the legislature.

Though the Highway Commission appeared—at first—to be deferring to the governor, it soon jumped into the fray by introducing it's bill on the second day of the session. Clinton remained confident that his package would be considered first. The next day, his prediction proved correct. Representative Jody Mahoney urged some 35 members of the Arkansas House to pledge that they would not vote on the gasoline tax increase until the governor's proposals had been given consideration. Mahoney's support held sway.

The most controversial element of the governor's human-services reform package was introduced early in the session. The bill called for the establishment of additional school-based health clinics. Already, fourteen such clinics had been placed in operation around the state. The bill gave local school boards the authority to decide what services would be offered in their respective clinics, and it contained a provision making it necessary for students to get their parents' permission before they took advantage of clinic services.

Right-to-life forces jumped at the opportunity to oppose the bill, maintaining that the school clinics would somehow be used to refer students to abortion clinics. Additionally, these groups opposed the dispensing of contraceptives at the clinics.

The health clinic proposal—Senate Bill 25—was passed out of the Senate without fanfare or amendment but found the House tougher going. The House Public Health, Welfare, and Labor Committee adopted an amendment banning distribution of contraceptives at the clinics. Dr. Joycelyn Elders, director of the Arkansas Department of Health, was quick to point out to committee members that "Our main issue must be to save our children when we have the highest teenage pregnancy rate in the world..."

Dr. Elders continued to battle for passage of the bill alongside Governor Clinton. Both admitted that they preferred the legislation in its unaltered form.

While criticism mounted from all sides, Bill Clinton seized the opportunity to discuss his legislative program with a group of bankers meeting in Little Rock. In response to critics' allegations that the governor knew only how to throw money at the state's problems, Clinton replied that the assertion was "the biggest load of hogwash I've ever heard." He added that he would continue to proceed as he had, maintaining that he was only doing what he thought best for the state.

One criticism—seeming to touch a nerve—involved the operating costs of the Governor's Mansion and the cost of providing security for the state's first family. Little Rock businessman Sheffield Nelson advocated having the governor live in a conventional home to cut costs associated with the mansion itself. Since Nelson was being widely touted as a potential Republican candidate for governor in 1990, Clinton directed his response directly at him when he said that he was "sick and tired of seeing school children and the future of this state being held hostage by a few cheap-shot artists." Nonetheless, Nelson's criticism would continue unabated throughout 1989 and into 1990. In the election year, he and Clinton would face off in a bitter gubernatorial contest, and Nelson would prove to be a rather sore loser.

Another of the governor's key reform proposals involved the removal of more than a quarter million low-income individuals from Arkansas tax rolls. The House Revenue and Taxation Committee finally gave House Bill 1130 a do-pass recommendation. The measure also included a tax increase for those Arkansans making more than $100,000 per year.

When HB 1130 arrived on the floor of the House, the governor—and a score of friends and political allies and lobbyists—stood ready. Their intensive effort ensured the passage of the bill. The governor rebel-yelled when the House vote was announced, and he told those nearby that the bill was one of the most important pieces of tax legislation to be considered in Arkansas in the past two decades.

But a harsher-than-anticipated welcome awaited Clinton in the State Senate. After it had been voted out of committee, the bill failed twice to win enough Senate votes for passage. The governor responded with the thought that if he couldn't win passage of the bill, circumstances would be considerably altered:

> Then the sales tax bill that I've proposed would not be appropriate, because even if you could pass the sales tax, you'd be giving relief to the middle-income people but not to the lower income people.

Already, talk of a special session to deal with Clinton's tax proposals was sweeping the capital. The failure of HB 1130 in the Senate merely added more fuel to the rumor fires.

Next, Clinton attempted to gain a bit of ground when he addressed the legislature's Joint Budget Committee. The governor maintained that neither the committee nor the general public really appreciated the gravity of the state's financial problem, adding that Arkansans faced "serious shortfalls" in their efforts to meet education and human services needs.

Budget analyst Bill Goodman—who worked for the committee—said that the administration's posture was basically correct, and that budget projections conformed with the figures the committee reviewed the previous fall. Goodman added that, gauging by the way in which revenues had been received, Clinton's gloomy economic tidings were "in the ballpark."

Senator Knox Nelson, a long-time committee member, voiced a growing concern on the part of many state lawmakers when he said, "I hope we would make some type of concentrated effort to cut spending before we talk about increasing the sales tax or the income tax."

Clinton, for his part, replied that cutting the fat from the state's government had been a preoccupying task for the past six years.

In the February 17, 1989 Arkansas Gazette, staffer Mark Oswalt observed that the state's lawmakers were literally scurrying in every direction, seeking alternatives to raising the sales tax. Some legislators suggested exempting food or utilities, while several others suggested raising taxes on soft drinks. With nearly half the session gone, many of the politicians were coming to realize that not even current levels of state services could be maintained.

Talk of a special legislative session was now rampant. Lawmakers maintained that any tax package reached via compromise must have the governor's input, and that he must bear part of the responsibility of selling the plan to the people of the state. To reporter Oswalt, Clinton confided his major concern, saying, "I'm not willing to sell out our people and our future by making some token effort to save face and leave very serious education problems unresolved."

In the legislature, it was a time for desperate measures. The Highway Commission abandoned its seven-cent-per-gallon tax on fuel and opted instead for a sales tax which would be applied to gas and diesel purchases. The new proposal carried with it its own ray of sunshine in the fact that it required only a simple majority to pass, not the three-fourths needed for a new tax measure.

With so many naysayers predicting that the governor's ambitious—and progressive—legislative package was bound to fail, *Gazette* columnist John Brummett jumped to Clinton's defense. In his March 7 column, Brummett tried his best to explain the situation to his readers:

> *What happened was that Clinton proposed something so bold and massive—so right, I submit—that it overwhelmed the timid and smaller-thinking legislature. The idea is that expanding the state's educational and economic opportunities would enhance the state overall and give it a better shot at emerging from perpetual backwardness.*

Brummett believed that the idea of raising taxes on the well-to-do and on businesses, in addition to an increased sales tax, was a bold move—especially in comparison to competing legislation to raise taxes on fuels. The governor's plan, the reporter was careful to point out, raised money to be invested in the people of the state, while the gas tax monies would only go to fund something tangible, like a highway. Brummett concluded:

> *Instead, he (Clinton) proposed to invest in teachers, college professors, and other forms of human life, be they underprivileged kids who need a head start to keep up in school or adults who cannot read or are otherwise ill-trained for the modern world. He was trying to do something not because a court order forced him, or in reaction to a natural disaster or federal government mandate, but apparently because it seemed to him to be the right thing to do.*

In mid-March, the governor found time to travel to Philadelphia to speak at a meeting of the Democratic Leadership Council. He sounded a familiar theme by telling the crowd that education was the key to competing in an expanding world economy. Speaking of a need for a more rigorous school curriculum and longer school years, Clinton said:

We must do more, better and differently, than we have in the past. We have to have a nation full of Einsteins to stay even with the rest of the world.

The governor also advocated better pay for teachers who demonstrated better performance in the classroom. Additionally, he maintained that members of his party had to generate strong leadership in the area of education:

Democrats have got to take the lead. Political leadership in both parties talks a good game, but there's a gaping hole between rhetoric and reality.

The governor received a standing ovation at the conclusion of his remarks.

At home in Arkansas, the state had been ordered to pay part of the cost of desegregating the Little Rock School District. The ruling came in response to a lawsuit filed several years earlier. Governor Clinton had been working with the state's Department of Education in an effort to reach a settlement which would end the lawsuit and take the state out of harm's way.

Arkansas Gazette reporter Scott Morris chronicled the events in the paper's March 14 edition. A settlement—costing $119 million but spreading payment over ten years—had already been introduced. The Joint Budget Committee heard from H. William Allen, an attorney for the Department of Education. He told lawmakers that some type of settlement would be acceptable and should be submitted quickly. Lists of violations of the court-ordered desegregation order were already being compiled, Allen told lawmakers, and the state would face staggering costs if a settlement were to be rejected. The committee's budget analyst told members that he had projected the cost of the settlement to run as high as $258 million over the next eleven years. As it developed, the state was already obligated for some $80 million over nine years. This money covered the cost of developing magnet schools in the Little Rock district.

Since, by law, lawmakers could only budget two years at a time, they balked at a ten-year settlement. Attorney Allen said the legislature would be forced to continue to budget for a ten-year period or be subject to massive liability for not honoring any settlement approved by lawmakers.

The settlement measure was given a do-pass recommendation and sent to the Arkansas Senate. It met quick approval there, and went on it's way to the House. Governor Clinton spoke to the state representatives during their consideration of the measure, pointing out that their best course of action would be to approve the settlement quickly and thus limit the state's ultimate cost "It would certainly cost more to refuse to fund this settlement," he said, "and to let the court send us a bill year in and year out..."

On the first vote taken, the settlement funding measure failed, with more than two-thirds of the legislators voting it down. Clinton said he was not surprised. He worked for two days, contacting lawmakers personally in an effort to gain enough ground to ensure the bill's passage. After three more rounds in the Arkansas House, the measure was finally approved by a slender margin. The governor, however, was jubilant, saying that "central Arkansas is open for business again." Little Rock school board president Robin Williams, tears welling in her eyes, told reporter Morris, "I feel like the weight of the world has been lifted off my shoulders."

Danville's state representative, Lloyd Reed George, had been a leading opponent of the settlement. He attacked Governor Clinton's "high-handed tactics" which resulted in getting the measure passed. "I'm very disappointed, obviously," a dejected George said after the vote, calling the settlement "a terrible mistake."

With the passage of the settlement funding measure, the legislature folded its tent. While the governor's attempts to raise additional education funding had failed, he still considered the session a success. Many items that had not required special funding had made it through the House and Senate, and several others were passed contingent upon funding being available in future months.

The legislature had approved the creation of an Office of Accountability, to operate within the State Department of Education. The office would serve to grade the quality of education in the various school districts, issuing annual "report cards" to the schools themselves. Students were also allowed to choose the school district they wished to attend. The governor said he hoped this piece of legislation would foster competition among districts, forcing some to make improvements to attract students. Additionally, the legislature had given the Department of Education the authority to take over or supervise those districts where students had continually low test scores.

In the field of higher education, Governor Clinton had gained approval for a measure which mandated annual performance evaluations of college faculty members. An additional measure allowed the state's Board of Higher Education to terminate inefficient degree programs and to expand scholarship opportunities.

The governor also claimed a victory in his efforts to improve the state's criminal justice system. The legislature had approved a measure tightening the enforcement of child support laws, and another Clinton bill created a new juvenile justice system to replace the old system struck down by the Arkansas Supreme Court. Additionally, lawmakers had established a military-style "boot camp" for first-time offenders.

On March 25, Clinton told the Arkansas Gazette that the session was, overall, very productive, although he admitted that he was disappointed that a sales tax increase to aid teachers and college faculty was not approved. He said:

This session probably produced the largest number of positive bills of any one I've been involved in with the exception of the special session of 1983. I've just got to roll up my sleeves and go back to work. Unless something happens, we're going to have a special session on education.

As it developed, a special session would be called—but not for the purpose of dealing with education. A question had been raised concerning the validity of the appropriation measures passed during the recent session. Among those measures was the bill funding the settlement of the Little Rock School District desegregation lawsuit. The question ended up before the Arkansas Supreme Court. Since one of the appropriation measures dealt with salaries for the members of the court, the justices all refused to rule on the question and stepped down.

The governor then appointed a Special Supreme Court to rule on the matter. The new panel took the matter under advisement and, within days, issued an opinion that the bills were indeed invalid. Apparently, the Arkansas constitution required a three-fourths majority vote on appropriations. As previously mentioned in this account, it had been thought that a majority vote would suffice.

All the appropriations bills were again presented for approval, and all easily cleared the House and Senate—except one. It was the desegregation settlement funding bill, destined to be the centerpiece of a controversial chapter in Arkansas legislative history. When the Senate began consideration of the funding measure, in an apparent effort to stave off a defeat in the House, the lawmakers attached an amendment. The amendment earmarked a portion of the 1983 one-cent sales tax increase for educational purposes. This change then made it possible to pass the bill with a simple majority vote. The Senate did so, and sent the measure to the House.

There the bill was brought to the floor—and defeated twice. Both votes were close, and proponents of the measure were hopeful that passage would take place on the third try. House Speaker B. G. Hendrix began "sounding" the votes as they were recorded by the electronic display system.

At this point, fate stepped in. As Representative N. B. "Nap" Murphy was asked to enter his vote, he discovered that he was without the key that allowed him to access the electronic voting mechanism from his desk on the floor of the House. "Mr. Speaker," Murphy immediately called out, "someone stole my key and I don't appreciate it." Speaker Hendrix refused to halt the voting until Murphy found his key, prompting Governor Clinton—who was standing at the door of the House when the event occurred—to explode in rage. "What a rip-off," the governor exclaimed, adding that "you can't tell a guy he can't vote who's standing there yelling at the top of his lungs." Later, the governor added:

> The man was down there in the well...he was there screaming at the top of his lungs, trying to vote. And I think the people of this state will find it very hard to believe that because someone took a key off his desk he couldn't put a key into an electronic machine...they wouldn't count his vote.

Nonetheless, the bill had passed, and the governor decided several days later to sign it. Attorneys for the Little Rock School District immediately asked Federal Judge Henry Woods to approve the settlement, effectively capping the state's liability. Representative Lloyd Reed George, still the leading opponent to the passage of the settlement, announced that a lawsuit would probably be forthcoming.

As the session ended, attention began to shift to the upcoming 1990 election. In late June, Little Rock businessman
Sheffield Nelson—speaking to a convention of the state's Municipal League—confirmed the speculation that he would be a
candidate for governor the next year. He told members of the
league that he "sure would like your support."

Nelson, a lifelong Democrat, stopped short of saying that
he would bolt his party to seek the Republican nomination. He
maintained that the details of his entry into the race would be
announced at a later date.

Arkansas Attorney General Steve Clark, standing next to
Gazette reporter Patricia May, listened to Nelson's announcement. Then Clark made the rather cryptic comment, "Well,
that makes two of us, doesn't it?"

After the conclusion of his talk to the Municipal League,
Nelson met with reporters and admitted that he had decided
not to run in 1986 because the only way to unseat Bill Clinton
would have been with what Nelson called a "dirty campaign."
"I don't believe in dirty campaigns," Nelson allowed, adding
that "the way Clinton's running the state (now) will take care
of that."

Nelson has been president of Arkansas Louisiana Gas for a
dozen years and had served on the state's Industrial Development Commission for three years as well. He told reporters
that he had resigned his position as chairman of the AIDC in
1988 so that he could travel the state and assess his position as
a potential gubernatorial candidate.

Bill Clinton turned his attention to the settlement of the
Little Rock School District lawsuit. Specifically, the governor
wanted to ensure that all the work expended to approve the
settlement was not undone by a lawsuit. In late June of 1989, he
called the state's lawmakers back to the capital to consider a
measure designed to achieve this particular goal.

The bill Clinton had devised would change the way the settlement would be funded. It would authorize the Arkansas Board of Education to transfer money from the state's Budget Stabilization Fund—and some general revenue as well—to the Public School Fund. Under the Arkansas Revenue Stabilization Act, this would give the settlement top priority for funding.

Since the close of the first special session, the governor had been working feverishly to garner the votes needed to assure his measure's success. To further shield the settlement from legal action, he needed a three-fourths majority in both the House and Senate.

As it turned out, the governor's bill went smoothly through the legislature, gaining the necessary number of votes on each side. Clinton signed the bill, ending the dispute. Final figures, reflected in the bill itself, indicated that the state of Arkansas would end its liability at $131 million over ten years. In comparison to neighboring states, lawmakers were quick to observe that Missouri had already spent a staggering $700 million trying to settle desegregation lawsuits in Kansas City and St. Louis.

Opposition to the settlement, despite the governor's signature on the bill, continued unabated. State Representative L. L. "Doc" Bryan of Russellville allowed that Arkansas students were no longer responsible for something which had happened in Little Rock in 1957. Some, however—like *Gazette* columnist John Brummett—maintained that they approved of the governor's efforts to end the infamous episode. Brummett wrote:

> *Clinton deserves accolades for taking the responsible position in the first place, staying with the fight even when it seemed lost, devising a new plan, persuading a few balking House members and taking the political risk of calling yet*

another special session. Being a good governor, in other words.

By August 1989, Sheffield Nelson had put an end to speculation about which party's nomination he would seek in his quest to become governor of Arkansas. Nelson called the media to his family home in Brinkley and told them that he would seek the nomination of the Republican Party instead of the Democratic faction. He maintained that his decision to bolt his party was motivated by philosophical, not political, considerations. "I've done what I had to do," Nelson told the reporters, adding that his dissatisfaction with the Democratic party was due largely to a movement he perceived as being "more and more to the left."

According to Nelson, cutting the fat from state government would become a priority. He claimed that his experience as a private businessman would be a great asset for him as governor. He noted that, to his eye, that type of experience was sorely lacking in the Democratic camp:

I don't see anybody in the Democratic Party who's ever tried to run a business. All of them have been at the public trough for years.

In September 1989, another Arkansan tossed his hat into the political ring. He was Tom McRae, the former president of the Winthrop Rockefeller Foundation. McRae told *Gazette* columnist Brummett that he intended to run in the Democratic primary and seek the party's nomination for governor. By mid-September, McRae was telling Brummett that the reporter's fictitious candidate who could beat Bill Clinton was a characterization which fit McRae perfectly. McRae contended that he was indeed a new face, representing a new vision for the state. Additionally, McRae said he believed that he could bring new leadership ability to the state's efforts to move toward prosperity.

McRae said he had been meeting with what he called "focus groups" to find out about issues and about what they thought of him as a possible candidate. He said he would continue to emphasize education, as well as tax fairness. Many people, he maintained, wanted assurance that they were getting their money's worth from state government. Thus, McRae said, he would make state accountability a priority if he were elected governor.

Running against Democratic incumbent Bill Clinton would be a formidable challenge for McRae, and Brummett asked the challenger how he felt he would fare. McRae replied, "I relish it (a tough campaign). I think I can be a pretty good street fighter. But more importantly, I think I can address issues in a way that will force other candidates to address them."

McRae would find his abilities to address issues put to the test when the primary season arrived.

Governor Clinton attended President Bush's national education summit in Charlottesville, Virginia. The September 1989 event was held on the campus of the University of Virginia. This summit, touted as a major beginning in a national effort to improve education, was reported by media across the nation.

President Bush and the attending governors worked for several days in the hope of issuing a joint statement giving an indication of their desire to work together toward improving America's educational system. That joint statement reflected the realities of trying to make major education improvements through the process of government. The statement read:

We understand the limits imposed on new spending by the federal deficit and the budget process. However, we urge that priority for any further funding increase be given to preparing young children to succeed in school.

163

Along with their joint statement, the summit participants had developed an agenda for beginning the process of change. Among the items mentioned was the establishment of a process for setting national goals, along with the search for greater flexibility and accountability in the use of federal funds. Finally, the President and the governors addressed state-by-state efforts to restructure schools.

Governor Clinton, who was credited with significant effort in developing the summit agenda, said he believed that the final statement was of extreme importance in developing a national education policy. Clinton said President Bush, "...embraced the concept of national goals and acknowledged that he should be held personally accountable for his work in helping meet those goals."

Bush, for his part, said that "I agree with Governor Clinton that this (statement) is a major step forward in education."

By the fall of 1989, it was becoming obvious that the 1990 gubernatorial primaries would be rather crowded. In mid-October, Arkansas Congressman Tommy Robinson announced that he would not run for re-election. Well-known for making unusual political moves, Robinson told supporters that he would seek the Republican nomination for governor. Just a few months earlier, President Bush had praised Robinson for bolting his party and joining the Republican cause. Robinson had been a long-time Democrat.

Reporter Cary Bradshaw told Arkansas Gazette readers on November 15 that Robinson was running true to his controversial form. Looking past any Republican opponents, the congressman was already attacking Governor Clinton. He described Clinton's tenure as "a decade of many unmet promises," characterized by "a gap between rhetoric and reality." Robinson maintained that the governor had failed to meet his goal to improve education. "After much talk," Robinson said, "massive legislative support and millions of dollars (spent), our educational system and adult literacy rates are not good enough."

Continuing to understate the problems Clinton had faced, and sounding decidedly Republican, Congressman Robinson said that the state's next governor must be someone who could solve problems, rather than merely "throw money at them." He continued:

We need a leader who is willing and knowledgeable enough to improve existing government services. Our current leaders have simply forgotten the management responsibilities of government and think that every government solution must center on the need for more taxes.

Taking little note of the growing number of gubernatorial candidates, Bill Clinton called legislators back to the capitol again. Their mission this time was to consider new measures to provide additional funding for education and finance Arkansas' war on drugs. As it turned out, the governor would find little popular support for his proposals.

On the opening day of the special session, Clinton addressed both houses of the legislature to explain what he felt was needed. He began by telling lawmakers that much-needed money for education could be found without implementing a controversial sales tax increase he had touted during the regular legislative session. By simply restructuring the state budget, lawmakers could give education a $50 million shot in the proverbial arm.

A small tax increase on cigarettes and tobacco products would fund the war on drugs and provide additional monies for the state's prison system. The tax hike would also affect whiskey and cigarette rolling papers. The result, the governor maintained, would be $21.6 million in much-needed revenue.

165

Legislators were already aware that the drug problem and the prison funding difficulty would require action. Members of the House and Senate had expressed the sentiment that restructuring the budget and utilizing natural budget growth would be more to their liking. Clinton countered the legislative opinions by saying that he objected to draining resources from the state's schools, which he believed to be a first line of defense against the drug problem.

After several days, it became readily apparent that legislators did not consider natural revenue growth a suitable vehicle with which to fund education and the war on drugs. In an attempt to find some nominal funding for the drug and prison problems, the governor proposed a temporary surcharge on personal and corporate income taxes. The surcharge would remain in effect for two years and would generate some $17 million annually.

The legislature was uncooperative. Once again, the Arkansas House proved to be a tough and unyielding opponent. Three times in three days, the tax surcharge measure was voted down in the House. Even though it was coming up for a fourth vote, most observers held little hope for a favorable outcome.

Governor Clinton asked for the opportunity to address the House before the fourth vote was taken. He told the lawmakers that:

> *Fifty-eight members of the House have voted to fund the program, and yet the newspapers are full of how we're in disarray, how this is a failure, a waste of time; we're squabbling. Let me tell you something. I care about this state... I try to get things done the best way I know, person to person. All I want is results. I don't care who gets the credit for it, I just want results.*

Moments later, the House voted the measure down for the fourth time. The measure's final defeat ended the special session.

1990 was already appearing to be one of the most active political years in the state's history. Gazette columnist John Brummett told readers on January 14 that there were already strong signals that Bill Clinton would seek an unprecedented fifth term in office. There had been some unfounded speculation that, largely due to his difficulties with the state legislature, Clinton might run for a congressional seat.

Brummett, in search of the truth, visited with some of the governor's closest friends. State Representative David Matthews said he had advised Clinton not to run, adding that he urged the governor to look for a high-profile job with the national Democratic Party. Even if Clinton did not seek re-election, Matthews said he knew where the governor's future would be:

> I think Bill Clinton has a chance to be president of the United States in the late 1990's, because I think by that time the nation will have come around to his thinking on what we must do for education in this country.

Brummett spoke with other Clinton friends, including first-term staffer Rudy Moore, who was a lawyer and a former member of the state legislature. Moore told Brummett that problems with the legislature should be a major factor in Clinton's decision:

> It's not whether he should run, because I think he is. It's not whether he can win, because I think he will be re-elected. The question is whether—if he is elected—can he be effective with the legislature. In my mind that is a very serious question. He seems to have run a string with the legislature that may have resulted in a dead end.

167

The governor was giving no clues about his own political future. In another Gazette article, he commented, I will say this—the last three months have been very good. I've enjoyed them. I'm at peace, whatever happens."

A few days after the governor made his no-comment comment, Arkansas Attorney General Steve Clark made his gubernatorial bid official. At a series of kick-off rallies across the state, Clark told supporters that he was the candidate who could make a difference for Arkansans in the decade of the 1990s. Clark noted:

The decade of the '90s holds for Arkansas great opportunity; that opportunity can and will be realized if we have a governor who is a leader.

The attorney general outlined a program that included building new roads, utilizing a five-cent-per-gallon tax on gasoline. Clark advocated an education initiative which would obligate the state to pay college or vo-tech tuition and fees for those students who kept up their grades and stayed out of trouble. He also promised $1000 across-the-board raises for the state's teachers. Speaking to Arkansas' large elderly population, the candidate said he would create the first state agency on aging. Additionally, Clark said he would be tough on crime, stating his belief that he could be "a leader who can win the war on drugs. We're not going to win (it)," Clark continued, "just by building prisons, prisons, prisons."

But Steve Clark's moment in the political spotlight would be short-lived. A few days after his announcement, Clark attempted to close the door on a controversy involving his expense account by writing the state a check for $4,000. His own sloppy bookkeeping, the attorney general admitted, had been the basis for mistakes in the account.

In Arkansas, constitutional officers are not required to file explicit documentation for expenses. Clark said he spent a half hour every two or three months reconstructing his expenditures from receipts, notes, his memory, and his personal calendar. He did compile more detailed reports in an effort to assist the state's Legislative Joint Auditing Committee in its review of government spending.

But the effort wasn't enough. In early February, Clark called a press conference to announce the withdrawal of his candidacy for governor. Standing just outside his office in the capitol, the attorney general read from a prepared statement:

After much reflection and discussion with my family and friends, I have reached the conclusion that the mistakes in my expense records and subsequent news coverage about those mistakes have virtually destroyed my ability to run an efficient and effective campaign for governor.

Visibly shaken by the ordeal, Clark returned to his office, refusing to answer questions from reporters. He remained in his office only a short time, then slipped out an exit on the roof of the capitol building, thus avoiding other members of the media.

Bill Clinton had yet to announce his political intentions. His only remaining Democratic opponent, Tom McRae, announced the formation of a 76-member statewide campaign committee. Holding a new broom in his hand, McRae told a gathering of supporters that he intended to make a clean sweep of state government, brushing away the rhetoric and the career-oriented politicians. Members of the press noted that his candidacy was not without precedent; McRae's grandfather had been governor of Arkansas during the early 1920s.

The state political picture continued to develop as U.S. Representative Jim Guy Tucker announced his intention to seek the Democratic gubernatorial nomination. The candidacy would mark Tucker's first step into the state's political arena since 1982. The tone of Tucker's candidacy was clear from the outset: Arkansans needed a change. The new candidate pointed out that Bill Clinton had been governor for a decade. "I think he's had a good ten years as governor now," Tucker told supporters, "and I really think that's long enough."

Tucker outlined a program of improvements in education, highways, and health-care costs. When asked about funding the changes he'd seek, Tucker said that, while not ruling out a tax increase, he would not endorse one, either:

> *I don't see the need for any tax increase at this time and certainly wouldn't want to suggest any tax increases in government where I know there are substantial savings to be made.*

Tucker began an aggressive campaign for the nomination, preparing to run television ads touting his candidacy and urging Bill Clinton not to seek another term. Strangely enough, a little over a month later Tucker would change his mind about the gubernatorial race and express a firm resolve to seek another elective office.

Bill Clinton had maintained silence. He repeatedly said he would let the people of the state know of his political plans at the right time. Of course, speculation had been mounting that the governor might enter any one of several races. Some claimed Clinton would run for Congress from Arkansas' second district, while others believed he would opt for a Senate race. The conventional wisdom held that Clinton was interested only in a national office.

All the speculation ended abruptly on March 1, when Bill Clinton announced that he would seek an unprecedented fifth term as governor. With Hillary at his side, Clinton told a press conference that he had made up his mind to run again "even though the fire of an election no longer burns in me."

The governor said he was aware of the concern expressed by many that he had been in office too long. He told the press:

We're going to be real careful to reach out in every county in this state to find new people to be part of our family so that none feels excluded from appointments and nobody feels excluded from other decisions of the Governor's office. And we know there is always the problem of arrogance of power, and we are bending over backwards to be as humble as we can in this campaign.

Clinton had spent a great deal of time deciding to seek another term. He said he liked being governor and felt that, among the candidates, he could still do the best job in the office. "In spite of all my reservations about the personal considerations, Clinton said candidly,"I believe that more than any other person who could serve as governor, I could do the best job."

Political opponents had mixed reactions to Clinton's announcement. Jim Guy Tucker refused to comment, saying the day belonged to Clinton. Tom McRae said he'd prefer not to run against an incumbent, but added that if he had to, he was glad to run against someone who had been in office for ten years and had the "negatives" Bill Clinton supposedly possessed. On a personal note, McRae said he liked the governor and considered him a gentleman.

Potential Republican opponent Tommy Robinson said a great deal more: "We're fired up in our campaign. We all applauded over here when he finally announced his intentions..."

And GOP front-runner Sheffield Nelson sounded a bit more analytical:

I personally felt it would be in some ways better, because an incumbent has a record to run against. It just so happens that in this case, the incumbent is the strongest candidate. I consider Bill Clinton a friend...

In late March, Clinton headed south to New Orleans to accept the chairmanship of the Democratic Leadership Conference. Back home in Arkansas, his gubernatorial opponents charged that the governor was taking time away from state duties to dabble in national politics.

On the last day of the DLC session, Clinton officially accepted the chairmanship and spoke briefly, outlining some of the group's current positions. His topics included welfare reform, educational improvements, and government in general. Three times his talk was interrupted by applause, but Clinton managed to bring his speech to a speedy end and adjourned the meeting.

By the end of the month, Jim Guy Tucker had changed his mind about running for governor. Instead, Tucker announced his candidacy for the office of lieutenant governor. Tucker said that to stay in the race against Clinton, "...would result in a highly divisive campaign, one that would be counter productive to the best interests of our state and my party, at a time when Arkansas needs unity, not turmoil."

Tucker added that a divisive Democratic primary would only help the Republican cause.

Financial World magazine ranked Arkansas 41st out of the 50 states in financial management practices. Quickly, Bill Clinton responded with a five-page news release refuting the article. The magazine, according to the governor, did not understand the state's budgeting process, and Clinton pointed out that Arkansas had "one of the most tightly controlled budgets in the nation." Clinton said the article incorrectly implied that Arkansas did not have a balanced budget. This, of

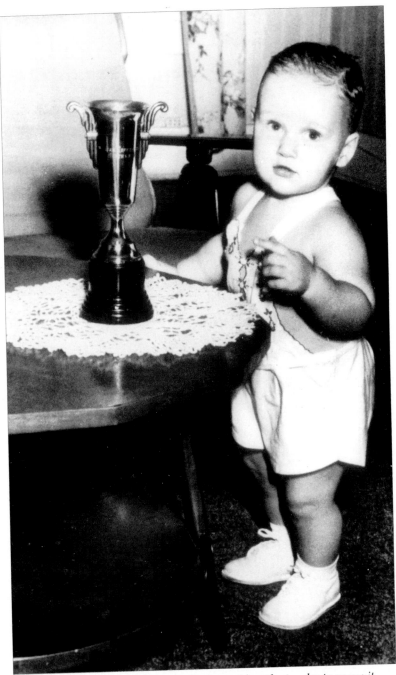

In 1947, Bill Clinton is a beautiful baby and has the trophy to prove it.

Already, in 1950, Bill Clinton was a young man in a hurry.

Bill Clinton has it all for high school graduation—cap, gown and a big smile.

Bill Clinton and a friend pose during a break from the 1963 American Legion Boys' Nation in Washington, D.C.

While attending the American Legion Boys' Nation in 1963, Bill Clinton shakes President John F. Kennedy's hand during a White House visit.

At 27, Bill Clinton begins his trek on the campaign trail, while seeking a term as a member of Congress.

Governor and Hillary Clinton attend the opening of a corporate day care center in North Little Rock, Arkansas.

A kindergarten student discusses his plans for an education with Governor Clinton.

Governor Clinton unveils his Youth 2000 Program to a class of kindergarten students.

Talking to reporters, Governor Clinton explains the environmental condition of Arkansas.

With his wife looking on, Governor Clinton receives an award from an Arkansas-based veterans' group.

During a quality management meeting, the governor discusses methods for government employees to be more efficient in their duties.

The governor receives approval from his wife after announcing his intentions of seeking re-election.

Former governor's mansion head cook, Liza Ashley, shares an umbrella with Governor Clinton during a Labor Day picnic.

Governor Clinton answers questions during a press conference at the Capitol building in Little Rock, Arkansas.

Governor Clinton and President George Bush join Terry E. Branstead, governor of Iowa, during the Education Summit Meeting in Charlottesville, Virginia.

Governor Clinton pays tribute to Martin Luther King on the anniversary of the black leader's birthday in 1991.

Wife Hillary and daughter Chelsea share the excitement as the governor announces his candidacy for the office of President of the United States.

Governor Clinton smiles as he receives a question from a reporter during a press conference.

A cup of coffee and a bit of conversation do not erase the weariness of campaigning from the governor's face.

During a visit to a Mississippi school, the governor discusses the importance of a good education with the students.

Young Man in a Hurry

course, was impossible, since the state was prohibited by law from engaging in deficit spending.

Magazine editor Richard Greene explained that Arkansas' low ranking was due to the lack of a "rainy-day fund" for use in emergencies. If the lack of such a fund was not considered, Greene maintained, Arkansas would probably fall into the middle range among other states. Clinton responded by saying that the fund idea had been considered a poor management tool by state officials.

Instead, the state chose to use its Revenue Stabilization Act, passed every two years by the Arkansas legislature. This act, according to Clinton, "mandates a true balanced budget by tying spending to revenue received." The governor added that the act sets priorities for spending, and money is allocated as it becomes available.

The Financial World article did give Arkansas high marks in the areas of job creation, investment in—and maintenance of—its infrastructure, dealing with deficits and surpluses, projecting revenue estimates several years in advance, and competitive bidding.

By mid-April, the governor was responding to another challenge. His appearance before the Arkansas AFL-CIO convention was marked by increased tension, since 1990 marked the first time the organization had failed to endorse Clinton's candidacy for governor.

A group of convention members had drawn up a resolution condemning the governor. In part, it said that Clinton:

> ...decieved us with broken promises of support for Worker's Compensation, right-to-know and other benificial legislation. (He has) tricked us on taxes and has further rigged the tax system against workers with more special interest exemptions and loopholes.

In his speech to the labor gathering, Clinton sought to address the concerns brought forth in the resolution. Said the governor:

The most appalling suggestion of all is that I somehow tricked you on taxes and tax reform. I raised this issue and we lost. And what was the response? Bill Clinton jumped off the tank on tax reform.

The resolution raised another issue concerning the governor's role in securing a $300,000 loan guarantee for a plastics firm. According to the resolution, the firm "used it (the money) to build an inventory as strike protection." Clinton responded by explaining that the minority-owned business employed 410 Arkansans, who were threatened with the loss of their jobs. He noted that the company sold almost exclusively to Ford Motor Company. As it developed, Ford had sought to terminate a contract with the firm if the company did not have a two-month inventory on hand as protection against a possible strike. Clinton concluded by saying, "My job is to save jobs. I don't ask you to agree with me. Just put yourself in my position."

The condemnation resolution was withdrawn after the governor spoke, largely because it might have provoked a divisive debate from the floor.

Next at the AFL-CIO podium was President J. Bill Becker. Becker told the assembled group of union leaders that Clinton "will pat you on the back and p—down your leg. He just twisted the facts to suit himself."

Becker said the loan guarantee was the "straw that broke the camel's back." But even those harsh words did not preclude Arkansas union locals from endorsing Clinton. Two weeks later, 18 locals broke away from the AFL-CIO position to give the governor their blessing.

As the 1990 gubernatorial primaries headed toward election day, one of the most talked-about events in state politics was about to take place. While governor Clinton had traveled to Washington, D.C. to release a report of the Delta Commission to Congress, Democratic opponent Tom McRae seized the chance to hold a news conference in the capitol. McRae chided Clinton for being absent from the state, and he intimated that Clinton had thereby refused to debate him. McRae insisted that it was only proper for him to pose questions to the governor, and, in Clinton's absence, provide the answers himself.

At that moment, Hillary Clinton stepped from the back of the crowd and said:

Do you really want an answer, Tom? Do you really want a response from Bill when you know he's in Washington doing work for the state? That sounds a bit like a stunt to me.

The intrepid Mrs. Clinton then produced a prepared statement which quoted from Rockefeller Foundation reports for the past fourteen years. Most of the quotes praised Bill Clinton for his work as governor. "I went through all your reports," she concluded, "because I've really been disappointed in you as a candidate and I've really been disappointed in you as a person, Tom."

McRae responded with the unique contention that the issue was not whether Clinton had "done good things." Rather, the challenger insisted the issue was whether someone else—namely, McRae himself—should be given a chance to try. He continued by criticizing the progress in state education over the past decade, noting that Arkansas teachers were still the nation's poorest paid. Hillary Clinton conceded that there was still work to do, adding:

For goodness sake, let Arkansas stand up and be proud. We've made more progress than any other state except South Carolina, and we're right up there with them.

Later, reporters asked McRae if he considered Mrs. Clinton's interruption rude. "On one level, yes," the candidate replied, adding that:

I think that her coming out, in a political strategy sense, it makes some sense. You send her out there, she knows the issues and she doesn't have an accountability—and she takes me on. That's fine. And she's probably more popular than her husband.

Learning of the exchange at the McRae press conference, the governor conceded that he and his wife had discussed the situation via telephone the night before. When Hillary broached the possibility of attending the press conference, the governor told her he had no objections.

A forceful, emotional Bill Clinton went on the offensive against Tom McRae. At a Democratic rally in Washington County, the governor said McRae

...went around telling people that I gave tax breaks to out-of-state industry, and I am still waiting for him to say what tax break that is. He won't be able to tell us. You know why? Because there is no such animal.

McRae had been criticizing Clinton for spending ten years in the governor's office. Clinton responded by asking the crowd:

You know how long Tom McRae was director of the Rockefeller Foundation? Fourteen years, and after ten years he said, "give me another term so I can finish what I set out to do." I'm just asking for the same thing Tom McRae asked for.

On election day, Clinton easily defeated McRae. The governor waited until just after midnight to claim his victory; he had spoken to McRae by telephone. In his victory speech, Clinton told his supporters that the real gubernatorial race "begins tomorrow." He also spoke of McRae in glowing terms, saying:

> *He ran a very clever campaign. He got people to focus on the ten-year issue and to look at him as an alternative. I took him very seriously. He had a clear strategy and it was plainly the right strategy.*

In his concession speech, McRae told supporters that he had "absolutely no regrets." He praised those who had worked for him, adding that "what you've done is make this campaign something special." McRae admitted that he didn't intend to make a campaign out of negative comments and issues, but added that his advisors told him he had to "be mean and tough." The challenger decried the problem of running a more positive campaign.

In the Republican primary, businessman Sheffield Nelson had handed Congressman Tommy Robinson his first political defeat. Robinson blamed his defeat on Governor Clinton, alleging that the incumbent had somehow "meddled" in Republican politics. He claimed that the governor had urged some of his supporters—as if Clinton had thousands to spare—to "cross over" and vote against Robinson in the Republican primary. Clinton wanted Nelson to win the nomination, Robinson believed, because the Democrats saw Nelson as the weaker candidate.

Sheffield Nelson, in his victory speech, thanked the media for even-handed coverage of the campaign. Now, he said, he would concentrate on defeating Bill Clinton in November. Nelson maintained that he would run on the issues, and against Clinton's "tax and spend" record.

By mid-September, former state employee Larry Nichols was proceeding with his lawsuit against the state and Governor Clinton. The legal effort sought some three million dollars as damages. Nichols, you may recall, had resigned under pressure when it was learned that he had made calls to contra leaders on a state telephone. While Nichols claimed the calls were authorized, his former boss at the Arkansas Development Finance Authority claimed they were not.

In his suit, Nichols alleged that Clinton and Wooten Epes had lied about the facts and had slandered Nichols as well. He claimed proof that Clinton had used agency funds to make out-of-state trips for improper purposes.

Just two weeks before the November election, the lawsuit file was sealed by Circuit Judge John Plegge. The magistrate said that the allegations contained in the lawsuit could cause irreparable damage before election day. The attorney for Nichols' former boss, David Hargis, had requested that the file be sealed, calling the allegations it contained "obnoxious."

Bill Clinton and Sheffield Nelson faced off in a pair of televised debates, the first airing in late September. The event took place on the Arkansas State University campus at Jonesboro before an audience of about three hundred students. The exchanges were typical election-time fare, with both candidates trying to score points at each turn. Nelson began by hitting Clinton for raising taxes, mentioning that tax rates had doubled under the Clinton administration. The incumbent replied that the tax revenues had doubled, not the tax rates. Nelson said that, despite Clinton's best efforts, teacher pay was still low and SAT scores were falling. Clinton maintained that national observers had been quite complimentary of the education effort in Arkansas, and he added that graduation ratios were up and students going on to college had increased by twenty percent.

Clinton jabbed Nelson for flip-flopping on a tax increase for education. Clinton noted that the Republican had supported the increase until he began running for governor, then changed his mind.

Nelson warned viewers that giving Bill Clinton four more years in office meant four more years of taxes as well. Additionally, Nelson said that another term would give Clinton "absolute power" in Arkansas.

Two weeks later, the second debate took place at the University of Arkansas at Fayetteville. Nelson sounded a familiar theme, warning the audience that Bill Clinton was interested only in furthering his political ambitions:

> *He wants to go to Washington, D.C., he wants to go to New York, he wants to go to Hollywood. I just want to stay in Arkansas and be governor.*

Clinton, taking the cue, slammed Nelson about his chairmanship of the Arkansas Industrial Development Commission, complaining that Nelson had promised to travel and use his business contacts to bring jobs to Arkansas:

> *He didn't make a single trip. Even when I begged him to go places, he wouldn't do it. He was too busy traveling around the state promoting himself for governor.*

Election day 1990 saw Bill Clinton win a fifth term as governor of Arkansas, garnering some fifty seven percent of the statewide vote in his re-election bid. Sheffield Nelson offered a short concession speech and then met with reporters, saying that the people of Arkansas had spoken:

> *The people said they wanted Bill Clinton for four more years, and I don't think it would have made any difference who was against him. He was just that strong.*

Across town, Clinton's supporters heard the governor wax philosophical in his victory speech. The governor told the excited crowd that, "I have looked into the eyes of the people of this state, and I have seen a yearning to do what is right and best for the children, to move forward."

6

'NO EXCUSES' HILLARY

★   ★   ★   ★   ★   ★

Depending upon your perspective, Hillary Clinton can seem a woman filled to the very brim with contradiction. Witness the fact that, entering Yale University to study law, she was a confirmed conservative, thanks largely to her upbringing, her years growing up in Chicago, and her education at Wellesley. By the time she graduated from Yale—the same year in which Bill Clinton graduated—she was a liberal's liberal, yearning to champion idealistic causes and to make the world a better place.

That desire to help others has not left her, although she now tends to be a political moderate. Having experienced both ends of the political spectrum, Mrs. Clinton may well be the essential expert on the fine art of political purpose and achievement.

When she married Clinton in October 1975, Hillary retained her maiden name of Rodham. Those closest to her suspect that, in choosing not to adopt her new husband's last name, Hillary was exerting her independence, letting it be known rather loudly that she was her own woman. She still is her own woman, of course, although, since Clinton's comeback effort in 1982, she now uses her husband's last name.

Today, with Clinton in hot pursuit of the right to run for the highest office in the land, Hillary is quick to come to her husband's defense. Many Clinton observers have voiced the opinion, seconded by the candidate himself, that Mrs. Clinton would probably make a better candidate than her husband. Arkansas political insiders say that this sentiment has its place, since the governor apparently consults his wife in advance of most major decisions, and her opinion is a source of considerable interest to him.

While she may never possess Barbara Bush's folksy charm, she can and does relate rather well to almost anyone. Years ago, when she was just coming into her own as the wife of a rather successful Arkansas politician, Hillary grasped the fine art of talking at length with almost anybody about almost anything. On the campaign trail, this is an invaluable asset, and time has only allowed her to master the technique.

While it is true that Arkansas' Byzantine political structure can exert pressures on the players out of keeping with the state's laid-back image, one finds it doubtful that Hillary Clinton ever seriously entertained the notion that, with the Democratic nomination seemingly within her husband's reach, she and her marriage would be subjected to the kinds of tough, biting, and personal questions that inevitably haunt presidential candidates. In Little Rock, she has borne up under the intense public scrutiny as best she could. On a national level, however, she is what she is and makes no apologies for it. With Hillary Clinton, more so than any other potential or actual first lady in recent history, there are no excuses. What you see is what you get.

And with Hillary, you get a lot. She is a keen competitor—even at games like Pictionary and pinochle—playing with such ferocity that her friends often feel compelled to remind her she's only playing a game. She dotes on her eleven-year-old daughter, Chelsea. She oversees the Governor's Mansion in

Little Rock, playing hostess to some 20,000 visitors every year. And, she is a partner in a well-known capital city law firm.

Hillary grew up in the Chicago suburb of Park Ridge, Ill. Her father owned a textile firm. Every summer she held a job at a local park and pulled along a wagonful of sports equipment each day. She earned every Girl Scout badge available. Elected president of her high school class, she garnered so many honors that she apparently felt uncomfortable at graduation. At home, she rounded up the neighborhood kids and staged sports tournaments and the like in an effort to raise funds for migrant farm workers.

After her undergraduate work at Wellesley, Hillary moved on to Yale, where, according to a Time Magazine account, she first noticed Clinton as he held forth in the student center, convincing his fellow students that Arkansas wasn't such a bad place to visit. The article continues with Hillary mentioning:

I remember him boasting that Arkansas has the biggest watermelons in the world...

Later, Hillary repeated this same story to Sam Donaldson on ABC television's "Prime Time Live" program. Like Time Magazine, Donaldson never bothered to mention that Clinton, having spent his earliest years in Hope, would know watermelons better than most, since his hometown is widely regarded as the "watermelon capital of the world." (In this case, at least, Clinton was not boasting. Having attended the watermelon festival held in Hope each year, I can attest that watermelons larger than the home-grown variety are literally unimaginable.)

The Time article goes on to detail with marvelous economy of words how Bill and Hillary first met. Time did not bother to mention that Hillary Rodham first met Clinton during her freshman year at Yale. Apparently, they spent a few weeks eyeing each other before she introduced herself. But here an inconsistency of sorts emerges. According to the magazine, after Hillary noticed Clinton in the student center, she didn't see him again for some time. One day, he literally ran into her as she was registering for classes. Hillary says:

> *He joined me in this long line, and we talked for an hour. When we got to the front of the line, the registrar said, 'Bill, what are you doing here? You already registered.'*

While this scenario appears slightly more romantic than Clinton's own version, one fact remains readily apparent. Either they met in the Yale Law Library, as Clinton maintains today, and Hillary left the story of the original meeting out of her account as given to Time magazine, or the library meeting itself was and is a figment of the governor's imagination. Of course, if the incident were, in fact, made out of whole cloth, one would assume that Clinton would not admit to having forgotten his name when Hillary asked it.

Harvard economist Robert Reich has also claimed the honor of introducing Bill and Hillary. I asked Clinton which version was correct: Reich's sparse account, the scenario involving the meeting in the library, or several other more improbable versions. He hastened to assure me that he and Hillary did, indeed, meet in the law library at Yale, and, since Reich was a friend to both him and Hillary—his Rhodes Scholar companion set up their first date. "Bob knew Hillary pretty well," Clinton told me, "and he arranged for us to go out. We've been together ever since."

By the governor's own admission, the union has had its rough spots. This could be due to the fact that, as they were dating, both he and Hillary quickly realized that they were headed in vastly different directions. Hillary desired a law practice in some thriving metropolitan area while Clinton wanted to return home to Arkansas to become a "country lawyer." Nonetheless, they managed to spend an inordinate amount of time together at Yale, arguing together as lead attorneys in a mock trial, which they lost and heading to Texas to manage George McGovern's ill-fated presidential campaign in 1972. They were aided in their efforts by writer Taylor Branch and by Texans like Betsy Wright.

Wright, who later became Clinton's chief aide during his initial tenures as governor of Arkansas, freely confesses that she had never met anyone quite like Bill and Hillary before. "I'd never been exposed to people like that," she told the Arkansas Democrat-Gazette, adding that young Mr. Clinton and Ms. Rodham "spent the whole semester in Texas, never attended a class, then went back to Yale and aced their finals." Betsy gushes, "they were breathtaking."

The McGovern effort was hopeless. And, it seemed for a while as if the Bill Clinton-Hillary Rodham relationship was hopeless as well. Point blank, Hillary was, at that time at least, a fierce feminist, and her friends recall that she had enormous difficulty in choosing between her own career in politics and Bill Clinton.

She told Time magazine that she's glad she "followed her heart" to Arkansas, although she made the decision to head to the Land of Opportunity only after going to work first for the Children's Defense Fund, and then serving on the House Judiciary Committee's staff during the Nixon impeachment hearings. When that job came to a screeching halt on August 9, 1974, Hillary decided to see if she could adjust to life in a small Arkansas college town. What she found in Fayetteville was a setting quite similar to New Haven, Conn., where she and Bill had attended Yale University.

Like Clinton, Hillary taught at the University of Arkansas law school until the couple moved to Little Rock for her husband's single term as attorney general. Getting settled in Fayetteville, according to Hillary, was quite an experience, especially since Clinton was running against John Paul Hammerschmidt for Congress at the time she moved to Arkansas. "We had a very interesting first couple of months there (in Fayetteville), " Hillary told Charles Allen, "and I loved Fayetteville...I loved the University. I loved the law school. I loved my colleagues. I made some of the best friends I ever had in my life. It was an adjustment in the sense that I'd never really lived in the South and I'd never lived in a small town, but I felt so immediately at home..." Part of the down-home, small-town feeling, Hillary told Time's Margaret Carlson, was having Fayetteville locals stop her in the grocery store to ask if she was "that lady professor at the law school."

A year after she made the move to the University of Arkansas, Hillary Rodham and Bill Clinton were married. The small, private ceremony took place at Clinton's home in Fayetteville. Roger Clinton was Bill's best man, and Hugh and Tony Rodham, Hillary's brothers, also attended the ceremony. Both young men were students at U. of A. Hillary's parents were on hand, as was Bill Clinton's mother, Virginia.

Within a year, the couple were making final preparations to move to Little Rock. With her husband as attorney general, and widely touted as the best candidate to succeed Governor David Pryor, Hillary got her first taste of living life in a proverbial fishbowl. It was during Clinton's two-year stint as the state's top lawyer, so the unsubstantiated stories go, that he began his dozen-year affair with an ex-cabaret singer named Gennifer Flowers. Those who argue that the Flowers allegations are true conveniently overlook the fact that Bill and Hillary had only been married a short time, and that Clinton, in particular, was so consumed with his career and political prospects that an illicit relationship would probably have been the last thing on his mind.

Additionally, Hillary had been in Indiana during much of early 1976, helping orchestrate Jimmy Carter's primary fight there. Back in Arkansas, her husband was taking charge of the state's Carter campaign. It's doubtful that Clinton would seek the companionship of another when his wife had been away for an extended period of time and had only recently returned.

Of course, Clinton did win the race for the governor's mansion in 1978, and he and Hillary moved there in January of the following year. During the second year of her husband's first term in the office, Hillary gave birth to their only child, a baby girl named Chelsea. The baby apparently received this name largely because of her father's fond memories of his years in England.

By the time the baby was 10 months old, the state's new first family was on its way out of the mansion. Ousted by Republican Frank White, Clinton spent the next year in relative seclusion from public life as he got acquainted with his daughter, forged a solid relationship with his wife, and pondered what had derailed the Bill Clinton political express.

The answers to that question were many and varied. Two points on the home front were Hillary's insistence on retaining her maiden name and the fact that the family did not seem particularly religious. Within a year and a half, when Clinton kicked off his comeback campaign, both problems had been solved: Hillary Rodham was now Hillary Rodham Clinton, and the couple and daughter were regular worshipers at Little Rock's Immanuel Baptist Church. Clinton won his second chance as governor with some 55 percent of the state vote.

I recall asking Clinton about Hillary's refusal to adopt his last name. My question came during the first year of the Frank

White administration. The former governor told me that he felt Arkansas voters were making much of nothing, and I agreed. He maintained that whether Hillary kept her maiden name or not, the matter would not be a significant issue during the next campaign. I thought at the time that Clinton's reply meant he didn't intend to ask his wife to adopt his name. "That's all right, boy," I remember saying, "don't be governor next time."

Apparently, Clinton and his wife subsequently subscribed to the notion that Hillary's continuing use of "Rodham" was a political liability. It wouldn't have been a liability in any other state, but in Arkansas it surely was. "I gave it up," Hillary told *Time* magazine, referring to "Rodham," adding that her use of her maiden name "meant more to them (the voters) than it did to me."

Now, with the presidential primaries under way, Bill and Hillary Clinton have a decade in the Governor's Mansion behind them. Hillary has yet to slow down. On the campaign trail, she is taking time away from the Rose Law Firm, where she is a senior partner and earns something on the order of three times her husband's salary as governor. Twice, she has been named one of the top 100 attorneys in the United States by the National Law Journal. She serves on nearly a score of civic and corporate boards, and is chairwoman of the Children's Defense Fund. Her hair is still blonde, and she rides a stationary bicycle for exercise. She hardly ever misses one of Chelsea's school functions.

When Clinton announced his intention to seek the Democratic nomination for the presidency, the Arkansas Democrat-Gazette treated the candidate's wife better than it treated the candidate himself. The paper noted:

First lady Hillary Rodham Clinton is one of Arkansas' most
influential women, admirers and critics agree, and could be

governor if her husband didn't already have the job. Often credited with being the more decisive of the two, she is none- theless Governor Bill Clinton's most ardent and loyal sup- porter. By all accounts, she is the governor's most influential adviser. He makes few, if any, major decisions without con- sulting her.

But not everyone has been so admiring. John Brummett, a columnist for the paper, noted that the producers of "Prime Time Live" had contacted him for information about Hillary. He mentioned his belief that Ms. Clinton "had undergone physical make-overs to augment the governor's career ad- vancement, (and) how she appeared to have spent two years at cheerleader camp to learn the adoring gaze between Clinton's defeat in 1980 and his comeback in 1982..." After finding out that the Prime Time segment would focus on Hillary, and that his comments would probably be used, Brummett added his belief that it was "a good time to be out of the country." As it developed, he was on his way to Moscow, covering a trip being made there by another Little Rock lawyer. The cartoon accom- panying Brummett's column features a desk clerk, holding a telephone receiver to his ear, and telling Brummett that he has a long-distance call from Hillary Clinton, who, according to the clerk, "doesn't sound real happy."

But if Hillary isn't quite used to this sort of thing by now, she is well on her way to achieving that status. As Time magazine's article noted:

With her marriage being held up to the light for cracks, Hillary Clinton wonders how much of her private life a political spouse has to offer up. "My marriage is solid, full of love and friendship," she says, "but it's too profound to talk about glibly."

When the Gennifer Flowers story broke, Hillary jumped to the defense of her husband. To her, at least, there was little doubt about the forces behind the emerging scandal. She told the Democrat-Gazette's Jane Fullerton that:

It's really unfortunate that political opponents of Bill's... make charges against him. The people of Arkansas didn't believe them. All of these people (the women named as having had illicit relationships with Clinton), including that woman (Flowers), have denied this many, many times. I'm not going to speculate on her motive. We know she was paid.

Asked if the charges would affect her husband's campaign for the Democratic nomination, Hillary told Ms. Fullerton:

No, because I think my husband has a very strong public record. We have a very strong marriage, and we're committed to each other. We're just very much involved in each other's lives. We're just going to let the American people make their own decisions about these accusations. They're going to judge us and make their judgments over the course of this campaign, and that's what we're going to rely on.

But Mr. and Mrs. Clinton apparently felt compelled to help the American people along a bit, appearing on the popular "60 Minutes" television program less than three days after Hillary spoke so eloquently about "letting the American people judge." During their taped appearance, watched by some 40 million viewers, Hillary noted:

I'm not sitting here because I'm some little woman standing by my man, like Tammy Wynette. I'm sitting here because I love him and I respect him, and I honor what he's been through and what we've been through together. And you know, if that's not enough for people, then heck...don't vote for him.

Apparently, Hillary's remark deeply offended Tammy Wynette, who promptly demanded an apology. Ms. Clinton replied that she "didn't mean to hurt Tammy as a person," adding that she happened to enjoy country music herself.

Hillary seemed mystified over the continuing media pursuit of the Flowers story, such as it was. She told Newsweek magazine that she and her husband were the victims of a strange sort of double standard:

> If Bill Clinton and I had been divorced three or four years and he were running for president, no one would ask him anything. So from my perspective, a lot of it doesn't make sense.

Thanks to the "60 Minutes" interview and to the efforts of Time magazine and such television programs as "Prime Time Live," Americans have come to see two sides of Hillary Clinton—both as an achiever and as a wife. Most people have yet to have the opportunity to reconcile these two with a picture of Hillary Clinton as a mother.

Twelve-year-old Chelsea is, according to Hillary, a priority within the Clinton family. With her tied-back brown hair and oversized glasses, the youngster is a familiar fixture at Clinton political events. Two years ago, her father took a week away from his duties as governor, fulfilling a promise to his daughter to spend five days with her at Walt Disney World in Florida. Hillary told Charles Allen that:

> Rather than quality time, I feel strongly that kids need routine time. Bill and I try very hard for one of us to be here if the other is gone. We've worked very hard on that because we'll always feel our primary job is being parents, and I take that very seriously. We have really worked hard to try to give her (Chelsea) a sense of herself and be respectful of her interests and not try to mold her into some sort of little public image.

As much as Hillary is a doting yuppie-type mother—once, as I was driving her to a fund raiser, she spent 20 minutes telling me about Chelsea's baby clothes—she freely admits that her husband is a doting father as well. At a Democratic dinner "roast" honoring National Committee Chairman Ron Brown, Hillary was asked by host Larry King, "It's ten o'clock...where's Bill Clinton?" She replied that her husband was with the "other woman in his life." This comment, coming on the heels of the Flowers' revelations, caused a brief stir in the crowd. Hillary continued, "He's with his daughter, Chelsea."

The governor, however, is quick to give credit where credit is due. He told Charles Allen that:

I think she's (Chelsea) a remarkable child. I mean, I have to give more credit to her mother than to me. She has her mother's character and intelligence, and she looks like she's going to have my energy level; and if she gets that, she'll have the best of both worlds. She'll have, you know, a massive constitution to endure long years of effort and have Hillary's character and intelligence. She'll be in good shape.

Chelsea is attending a public magnet junior high school. Both her parents believe she is bright and well-adjusted to living life in the Arkansas spotlight.

Whether she becomes first lady of the land or remains first lady of Arkansas, Hillary Rodham Clinton has a great deal going for her. She is, according to Arkansas Democrat-Gazette columnist Jack Kilpatrick, "a knockout," although Kilpatrick decries her apparent inability to compare with Nancy Reagan as a "rapter," a wife who stares raptly at her husband. For what it's worth, Kilpatrick notes that, "as a potential White House daughter, Chelsea in braces and pigtail is far better material than the Little Clogger of Plains." No doubt, his comparison between Chelsea and Amy Carter will be repeated again and again in months to come. For his part, Clinton claims Hillary's adoration for him might be misplaced. In early February 1992, he noted:

I'm not sure people aren't right when they say she is the one who ought to be running. You know, we like each other. You can watch me watch her speak sometimes, and I've got the Nancy Reagan adoring look.

Clinton candidly admits that his wife represents a good reason for voting for him. When Mr. and Mrs. Clinton were in Florida, campaigning among the delegates there, Dottie McKinnon, a delegate from Palm Beach County, gushed over the Clintons, saying:

He's a good guy. He's got a lot of experience. Don't you like him? Heck, you (Arkansans) elect him all the time. In fact, though, if his wife was running against him, I'd vote for her. She's pretty great, too.

It's no wonder, then, that Bill Clinton regards his wife as his own right hand. On the campaign trail, he once introduced Hillary as the woman on his right. In fact, Hillary was sitting to her husband's left. To his right was an empty chair. Some of us were reminded of the inaugural ceremony when Clinton held up his left hand and placed his right on the Bible. It should have been the other way around.

But small matter. Intelligent, attractive, witty, and secure in herself and her marriage, Hillary Clinton is quickly emerging as something of a media darling. Some enterprising businessmen have even seen her as an image with which to sell products of all sorts. Recently, Hillary found herself the involuntary subject of a new ad for designer blue jeans. Appropriately enough, the jeans bear the label, "No Excuses."

7

THE EDUCATION GOVERNOR

★　　　★　　　★　　　★　　　★　　　★

In the fall of 1987, Governor Bill Clinton traveled back to New
Haven, Connecticut, where he had spent three years as a student at the Yale Law School. Clinton had left New Haven, law
degree in hand, in the spring of 1973. Now, he was returning to
address an alumni dinner as governor of Arkansas.

During the last few moments of his speech, Clinton talked
about his childhood, from which stems his desire for education
reform in his home state. He said:

> When I was a little bitty kid, I lived for four years with my
> grandparents. My mother was a widow and she was off going
> to school trying to get to where she could earn a living to
> support me. I think my grandparents, who had very little
> formal education, set in motion the process that brought me
> to this wonderful law school.
>
> When I was two and three years old, they would sit me up in
> the high chair at breakfast and tack playing cards on the
> baseboards of the windows and make me count, and teach me
> to read, to add and subtract. I can still remember my grand-
> father saying, "You have got to do this. You have to learn
> these things so you can do better than I've done..."

The other day my wife and I went to my daughter's school, a public school in Little Rock. It's mostly a black school, a lot of poor kids in it, and it's a good school. I was looking at her, thinking, you know, I want her to do better than I did. Believe me, if you're governor of Arkansas, it's not hard for your kid to do better than you have done, economically. But, anyway, it's not as simple as that anymore. I not only want her to do well, I want all of those other kids to do well too. Not just for them but for me. Because the idea that my grandfather passed on to me was based on the assumption that the American economy would grow forever and that our country will always be strong and the question was who would win and who wouldn't...

Five years later, as a presidential candidate, Clinton is urging national education goals which will help ensure that all students win. They include apprentice programs for students who elect not to go to college, preschool for all children and parental choice of the schools their children attend. (The last goal is a voucher program which would pay money to parents to send their children to the school of their choice, and it is supported by the Bush administration. Clinton, however, argues that the program should be limited to public schools, while Bush advocates that it be applied to both public and private schools.)

Clinton also wants to implement a national examination system for all elementary and secondary schools, designed to "push" students to "meet world-class standards in math, science, and other core subjects." Additionally, he frequently calls for a sort of "domestic G.I. Bill," whereby money for college would be loaned to anyone who is willing to pay the money back either on a percentage-of-income basis or through some sort of national service. The service work Clinton mentions revolves around nursing, teaching, child care, and law enforcement.

Critics respond that the "domestic G.I. Bill" means that, as president, Clinton would first have to "reach out and tax someone." The governor, on the other hand, maintains that the measure would be funded by a congressionally mandated national trust, which would take money from the defense budget's so-called "peace dividend" and pool it with funds from the student loan program currently in place.

As governor of Arkansas, Bill Clinton has thrown his weight behind measures designed to enhance the early-childhood experience, including, of course, early childhood education. As a study of his tenure in the governor's office indicates, he increased teacher salaries, while at the same time insisting on a controversial competency test. Parents who fail to attend meetings with their child's teacher can be fined $50. He has expanded the Head Start program and instituted health clinics in Arkansas' public schools. And starting in 1993, failing students will not be allowed to obtain a driver's license.

In Arkansas, Clinton has championed the cause of adult literacy, demonstrating that his passion for educational excellence surpasses the usual child-oriented considerations. Across Arkansas, the program has made an impact. In another 1987 speech to the Little Rock Board of Directors for the NAACP, Clinton recalled:

The other night, at my first PTA meeting at the Booker Arts Magnet School, another parent came up to me and said, "Governor, I've been hearing you give those speeches on adult literacy, and I work for a company here in town, and I can't read. Do you think you could get me into one of those programs?" I took his name down and we got him into a program. The last thing I told him was, "Man, that is noth-

ing to be ashamed of. You ought to think about this and see if you can't go back to work and find everybody else that's in the same boat you are and get them involved in the literacy program. You can do that."

As president, Bill Clinton would spread the success of the Arkansas Adult Literacy program throughout the country. In a campaign position paper, he notes that:

In an era in which what you earn depends on what you can learn, education and training have to continue throughout everyone's lifetime. We owe every American the chance to get ahead.

For adults shortchanged by the educational system in the past, we will ensure that every state has a clear, achievable plan to provide adult literacy services to everyone who needs them, give everyone with a job a chance to earn a GED, and wherever possible, to do it where they work.

The governor's interest in continuing education is evidenced by his commitment to help those in the workplace continue to train and sharpen their skills:

For every American worker, we will ensure opportunities to learn new skills every year. Today, American business spends billions of dollars on formal training programs— the equivalent of nearly 1.5 percent of their payrolls— but 70 percent of it goes to the ten percent at the top of the ladder. We'll require employers to offer every worker his or her share of those training dollars, or contribute the same amount to a national training fund.

These provisions for lifelong learning and lifelong training make good business sense, because better-trained workers are more productive, and higher productivity means both higher wages and higher profits. Workers will get the training they

*need, and companies will discover that the more they train
their workers, the more their profits increase.*

The "educational shortchanging" spoken of by Clinton
evidences itself rather clearly in his home state of Arkansas.
The students there have always ranked at or near the bottom in
testing and surveys. As a child, Clinton became dismayed by
the education statistics, and his mother recalls his asking her,
"Aren't the kids in Arkansas born with the same brain as
people in other states?"

They are, indeed, but the educational system in Arkansas
has, since its inception, failed to provide the same sort of
excellence, commitment, and intellectual stimulation provided
for students in other states. This is largely due to the fact that
the state's many school systems have refused to burden themselves with the additional efforts, expenses, and challenges
dictated by progress. As a former student in an Arkansas
school system, I can attest that lackluster teacher performance
has largely been accepted instead of high professional standards, and that the day-to-day operations of many districts
remained unchanged from the early days of this century. Those
few progressive professionals who do attempt to institute
change are usually held in check by an autocratic school system, to which progress and forward-thinking individuals are
an anathema. The school districts in Arkansas seemed to oc-
cupy their time and allocate their scanty resources in the re-
lentless pursuit of mediocrity. The fact that Bill Clinton, an
intellectual and scholar by anyone's standard, hails from Arkansas only indicates that, with his educational accomplishments, he is very much a rarity in his own homeland.

Clinton himself recognizes this and blames the educational
failures of his fellow Arkansans largely on attitude. In a speech
during his second term as governor, he spelled it out:

Do you believe the way so many people in Arkansas seemed to have believed for as long as I've been alive, that in some sort of strange, cosmic way, God meant for us to drag up the rear in the nation's economy forever?

The interdependence of economic success and sound education can readily be seen in Arkansas. In 1989, the state fell to 48th in median household income, 48th in the percentage of residents qualifying under poverty guidelines, 49th (in 1990) in average weekly factory worker wages, and next to last in youth unemployment. The 1990 statistics show that the teenage jobless rate stood at just over 23 percent.

By 1989, Arkansas had fallen to 25th (out of 28 states surveyed) in ACT scores. The state continues to rank at or near the bottom in the area of teacher compensation. Confronted with the reality posed by these statistics, residents of the "Land of Opportunity" are hard-pressed to find the opportunity that purportedly lies therein.

All of this is scarcely Bill Clinton's fault. His detractors may note that, under his tenure as governor, Clinton has not exactly distinguished himself by leading the state upward in a successful quest to improve those statistics. However, the nay sayers generally refuse to reckon with or admit to Arkansas' peculiarity as both a state and a culture. That Clinton has been able in an environment like the "Wonder State" to accomplish anything at all should rank him with the saints as a modern-day miracle worker.

In his first inaugural address, on January 9, 1979, Governor Clinton set the tone for what would become a sweeping package of educational reform by noting that, as Arkansans:

...we have lingered too long on or near the bottom of the heap in spending per student and in teacher salaries. We must try to reverse that. However, we must be mindful that higher

quality education will not come from money alone. The money must be but part of a plan which includes better accountability and assessment for students and teachers, a fairer distribution of aid, more efficient organization of school districts, and recognition of work still to be done in programs for kindergarten, special education, and gifted and talented children...

Because his term in office was constitutionally limited to just two years (since changed to four), Bill Clinton had scarcely begun his educational reform program when he was defeated by Republican Frank White. But by the time Clinton regained the governor's office in early 1983, the mood of the entire nation seemed to be sweeping toward just the sort of educational changes the governor was poised to recommend. In just the two years from 1982 until 1984, some forty states strengthened their graduation requirements, another three dozen increased the testing of students, more than twenty had implemented some sort of performance incentives and nearly all 50 states had substantially increased their teachers' salaries.

In Arkansas, the basic problem had been money. The state had been spending relatively little on public education, and the results bespoke the substandard contribution of the average Arkansas taxpayer. When Clinton first took office, in early 1979, the average amount of money spent on each student in the state's public school systems was about half the national average.

But the problem was not a modern one. Indeed, substandard teacher salaries and low amounts spent per student were economic legend in Arkansas. As far back as the pre-Civil War era, Arkansans had been complaining about the state's inability to provide adequate school systems. A 1921 legislative study concluded that "for thousands upon thousands of children, Arkansas is providing absolutely no chance." In the two decades leading up to Clinton's first term in office, progressive governors like Winthrop Rockefeller and Dale Bumpers had tried to address the education problem, but to no avail. Even Clinton's predecessor, David Pryor, had been forced to literally squeeze dollars from the state budget in order to increase teacher salaries. Arkansas, Pryor later noted dryly, is "poor but friendly."

Part of the problem lay in the fact that small school districts, which constituted more than a hundred of Arkansas' 370 school systems—boasted a student enrollment of fewer than four hundred students. As a result, the state at the outset of Clinton's second term as governor ranked 17th in administrative costs per student.

That same summer, however, marked a golden opportunity for education reform in Arkansas. The severe recession which had plagued the state— with its attendant high unemployment percentage— began to lift. Other states were passing new tax increases designed to improve their own school systems. During 1983, just over half the 50 states increased sales taxes, usually with the intention of spending the money on teacher salaries and better schools. In fact, Arkansas had become dead last in teacher salaries and per-student spending, since Mississippi had raised its gas, sales, and income taxes to boost its own spending figures in those two areas.

Additionally, the National Commission on Excellence in Education had issued its ominous and threatening report citing the poor condition of the nation's schools as a whole. The national press gave the commission's report quite a bit of coverage. Also, the Arkansas Supreme Court had struck down the state formula for distributing education funding. The high court believed that the state's plan was unconstitutional because it failed to provide equal educational opportunities for students in every district across the state.

All of these events took place during the period in which the Education Standards Committee, chaired by the governor's wife, Hillary, was conducting public hearings in each of the state's 75 counties. An average of a hundred witnesses in each county had testified before the committee, which had been formed pursuant to a legislative mandate in early 1983. In essence, the Arkansas Supreme Court decision gave the governor the opportunity to enact several important educational reforms.

Having learned his lesson in his last bid for re-election, and knowing that any education reform meant breaking a no-taxes pledge, Governor Clinton moved into what observers called a "listening mode" during the summer of 1983. It lasted nearly four months. He conferred with all but two of the state's 135 legislators, spoke to interested groups and individuals across the state, and—in an effort to attract public attention—dropped broad hints as to his intentions and coined themes he would later use during the legislative session.

In late July, the governor noted that he "was preparing to lead the state in a dramatic and once-in-a-lifetime effort" to break the bonds of self-imposed ignorance and isolation. That same month he told an audience that the state's school systems would require more tax money but that Arkansans shouldn't have to foot the bill until they could see what benefits they would receive in return. By mid-September, the governor had the benefits package ready for Arkansans to evaluate. Clinton announced that he intended to speak to the state on television on September. 19, when he would reveal the contents of his education reform plan.

Across the state, residents tuned their televisions to the dozen-odd Arkansas stations and, at the appointed hour, beheld their young governor ready to address them. Clinton began his speech:

My fellow Arkansans, I want to talk to you tonight about the real problems we have in education. They are costing us jobs today and damaging our future. To put it bluntly, we've got to raise taxes to increase your investment in education. Arkansas is dead last in spending per child. And the Arkansas Supreme Court has just ordered us to spend more money in poorer school districts to improve education there...

Depending upon how one viewed the situation, the last sentence might not have been exact truth. The high court did overturn the state's school funding system, but an alternative might have been to re-distribute money to the state's school systems without an increase in funds. For Clinton, this move would have been political quicksand, because it would have meant reducing funds to some poorer districts, or shutting down rural districts altogether. Apparently, it was easier— and safer, politically— to opt for the Supreme Court ruling as a mandate to spend more money than to interpret it as a proposal for what Dan Durning later called "downward equalization."

This "downward equalization" virtually ensured that the governor's plea for a tax increase would be successful. Legislators from rural areas, faced with the possibility of their school districts losing badly needed state funds, would be more likely to risk the wrath of their constituents and vote for an increase in taxation on the pretext that it would provide a more equitable distribution of state funds to every school system.

Citing the fact that Arkansas had for too long, been the land of "lost opportunity," the governor began advocating that Arkansans change their way of thinking. A tax increase to benefit education was not, he said, "just a tax increase." Rather, Clinton maintained that the higher taxes would be "an investment in the future of our children and in the economic development of the state."

The day before the governor made his speech on television, the Arkansas Gazette indicated that Clinton had his work cut out for him:

> *One should not underestimate the magnitude of the legislative task Governor Bill Clinton has assigned himself: trying not only to raise taxes a few months before primary (the 1984 election) season, but also to devise a new formula for distributing money to public schools that will satisfy enough diverse education interests to pass.*

In his televised address, the governor set forth the basic points of his effort to reform education in Arkansas. In addition to ensuring a more equitable distribution of state funds to Arkansas school districts, Clinton advocated adopting some of the standards suggested by Hillary Clinton's education commission as law rather than allowing the Department of Education to take its time in implementing them. These mandatory standards allowed for the increase of the school year 5 days to 180 days total, increasing the school day a half hour to five and one-half; mandatory kindergarten requiring students to pass proficiency examinations in the eighth grade before they could be promoted, and raising the age of mandatory school attendance to cover 6 to 17-year-olds. This increased the mandatory time in school by a year in either direction.

In 1975, President Gerald Ford asked Americans to join him in wearing large, red "WIN" buttons. The buttons were designed to promote the concept that by working together we could somehow "Whip Inflation Now." While the net result of the campaign was less than impressive, the political effect was a positive one. Clinton, having learned that images and popular themes speak louder than a governor on the stump, asked Arkansans to join him in wearing blue ribbons to promote his educational reform package.

The blue ribbons were the popular symbols of a larger theme: "Let's put our kids in first place; support blue-ribbon education in Arkansas." The so-called "Blue Ribbon" Committee, along with its counterpart, Arkansas Partners in Education, blitzed the state with television, radio and newspaper ads. The "Blue Ribbon" Committee, in particular, mailed brochures to 100,000 Arkansans asking for support of the governor's program, and promoting the blue ribbon theme. Both individual and corporate donations were solicited to fund this campaign; both the "Blue Ribbon" group and APE spent a total of $100,000 in the process.

The governor, of course, could not remain idle if his plan for reform was to have a chance of success. Across the state, Clinton did go on the stump, attending meetings and whipping up support for the education package. Having learned his lesson in the fall of 1980, the governor realized that he would have to sell the education package to his constituents if he hoped to pass a sales tax increase and still retain his office.

But the campaign had an additional benefit for Bill Clinton. The Arkansas legislature, like many other coequal bodies across the United States, can hardly be called a professional organization. Nearly every one if not all of the members of the Arkansas House and Senate were, of necessity, part-time politicians. In all fairness to the lawmakers, it is extraordinarily difficult to live on the salaries the state pays them. The state representatives and senators can be an independent lot; courting them takes not only a considerable amount of time but often considerable mental energy as well. The "Blue Ribbon" campaign succeeded in convincing many legislators that Arkansans supported Clinton's education reform initiatives. Because the state's lawmakers got the message via popular perception, Clinton and his staff were spared an agonizing and time-consuming ordeal convincing them to vote for the governor's package.

Not one for taking chances, the governor commissioned a firm called Precision Research to poll Arkansans and ask their opinion of the proposed sales tax increase. More than 63 percent of those responding said that they wanted their state legislator to vote for the tax hike. As Dan Durning accurately noted, many Arkansas lawmakers got the message — that it might be more dangerous politically to vote against the sales tax increase than to vote for it.

On October 4, 1983, Arkansas lawmakers gathered in the state capital at Little Rock for a special session. At the dinner hour, Governor Clinton opened the session with a speech which once again set forth his program for education reform and presented the popular arguments in its favor. "Our people are sick of excuses," he told the members of the House and Senate, adding that Arkansans "want action." The blue ribbon the governor wore was conspicuous particularly because only about a dozen lawmakers in the crowded chamber had bothered to wear theirs.

This special legislative session had been divided into three parts. As it turned out, the first of the three subsessions took up much of the time allocated for the entire special session itself. But, as most Arkansans had guessed, the battle for the new school aid distribution formula was intense and protracted. Much of the time lawmakers were listening to representatives from specific school districts arguing for as much state money as they could get.

The second subsession dealt with the issue of teacher testing. In any other state, probably any other group of state-paid professional civil servants would have had little problem with displaying that they were, indeed, qualified to earn their paychecks. In Arkansas, however, the teacher testing issue constituted the most hotly contested battle of the entire special session.

The governor's own polls showed overwhelming popular support for the teacher testing measure. The measure was certainly innovative enough; at the time, no other state in the nation required its teachers to prove that they could communicate on an eighth-grade level and pass a standardized test in their area of expertise. Since the Arkansas educational reforms, though, many states require new teachers to take the National Teacher's Examination, and others implemented their own teacher evaluation programs.

In late 1983, however, such a progressive attitude was strongly lacking in the Arkansas educational community. The Arkansas Education Association—the state's branch of the National Education Association—opposed the teacher testing part of Clinton's reform immediately. Take a moment to consider that the majority of the teachers in Arkansas— three quarters belonged to the AEA—were going to benefit from another plank in the platform in that the tax increase would help fund salary increases. Nonetheless, most Arkansas teachers remained opposed to any legislation which would force them to demonstrate that they were qualified to receive those additional tax dollars.

Spending the number of years I did in an Arkansas school system would go a long way toward convincing even the most skeptical that the educators in Arkansas certainly needed to demonstrate their accountability. I recall one instructor who told me when I was in the ninth grade that he became a teacher because he felt it was the only profession in which he could "play around" and still earn a paycheck. That gentleman, incidentally, is now—by accident of local history—the superintendent of my former school system.

Even those educators who desired to demonstrate their accountability behaved questionably. The Arkansas Association of Professional Teachers— a rival group with about four hundred members— requested that its members actively promote their own willingness to take the competency and subject tests. A letter to the members read:

> *The too much publicized campaign of the AEA against teacher testing is doing irrepairable [sic] harm to our profession...*

The fact that the letter supporting Clinton's teacher testing program— presumably written by an educator, or several of them— contained a misspelled word and a grammatical error did nothing but strengthen the governor's case.

According to the Arkansas Education Association, the state's school teachers were "at war" with Governor Clinton. Group President Peggy Nabors wrote that the organization's members were "being laid on the alter [sic] of sacrifice for political expedience." Other than widespread public support, however, there was nothing politically expedient about the entire teacher testing issue. The governor himself responded that he felt that taking an examination was "a small price to pay for the biggest tax increase for education in the history of the state and to restore the teaching profession to the position of public esteem that I think it deserves." Clinton expressed the same sense of wonderment and consternation felt by many Arkansans when he added, "It's a mystery to me that the AEA could put in peril the largest teacher salary in history merely to keep teachers from having to take a test."

Hillary Clinton herself commented, "the problem of teacher accountability begins in higher education, and we (the Standards Committee, which she chaired) think teacher education is inadequate in many respects." Mrs. Clinton added that "The governor is quite properly looking at teacher accountability in the context of his overall recommendations."

Clinton stood his ground. He maintained that without teacher testing there would be no sales tax, no teacher salary increase, and in essence, no real reform outside of redistributing state funds at their current levels. AEA Executive Director Kai Erickson complained that Clinton was "hot and overreacting," adding that she considered his actions "irresponsible."

Truth to tell, Governor Clinton was threatening to kill his own education reform initiatives if Arkansas teachers remained unwilling to yield on the teacher testing issue. For a politician to order killing his own legislative effort seems, to most of us, absurd. Let no one say that Bill Clinton lacked conviction in the matter. For him and for many Arkansans the battle lines seemed clearly drawn.

In a rejoinder, Clinton maintained that the AEA leadership was willing to sacrifice teacher raises, more money for standards, and additional funds for higher education. Quite bluntly, he accused Director Erickson of being hired "solely to protect a few teachers who might be incompetent." The AEA, on the other hand, held fast to its conception that the teacher testing issue represented some sort of governmental "witch hunt."

Halloween, 1983, was a day of great celebration for Clinton. The teacher testing bill passed both houses of the state legislature. At the end of that same week, after a short delay caused by a disagreement over taxing food items, the sales tax increase sailed through both the Arkansas House and Senate, enacted with an emergency clause which allowed the tax increase to take effect immediately. Merchants began collecting the extra penny per dollar spent on Monday, November 7. Arkansans would pay four cents per dollar rather than their usual three percent sales tax.

The special session of the legislature then dissolved itself while lawmakers' ears were still fairly ringing with Governor Clinton's praise and thanks. The governor was fortunate to have been able to move the education reforms package through during a special session rather than during a regularly scheduled conclave. The reason for his good fortune was simple: Arkansas lawmakers are unusually inconvenienced by special sessions, which take them away from their usual income-producing activities; they are usually motivated to finish their legislative business as quickly as possible in order to return to the prosaic practice of making money.

But the battle over teacher testing continued to be fought even after the legislators who had enacted the concept into law had left Little Rock for home. An Arkansas Gazette writer noted that the relationship between the governor and the AEA had narrowed to one of "harsh public bitterness and nasty private name-calling, totally the result of Mr. Clinton's insistence on requiring teachers to take a basic skills test in exchange for the nice raises most of them will likely get from his tax program, the AEA's fervent opposition on the basis that teachers were being insulted and the entire teaching program degraded, and Mr. Clinton's public denouncement of the AEA for opposing him."

AEA President Peggy Nabors alleged that the governor had used the state's teachers as a "scapegoat." Ms. Nabors maintained that many good teachers would quit their jobs rather than take the competency tests. How the teachers in question might benefit from such a course of action was not immediately clear.

Despite the withdrawal of the test the governor intended to use—the Educational Testing Service announced that it would not allow its test to be used to evaluate teachers who were currently teaching—and the announcement by the National Education Association that it would consider challenging the teacher testing statute in court, the testing actually began in March 1985. The AEA's threatened test boycott and mass teacher walk-outs did not occur. When the testing had been completed, something on the order of 3.5 percent of Arkansas' teachers had failed to pass. More than 1,300 teachers had been forced out of the state's school systems because they could not make the grade. Admittedly, the failure rate among black instructors was higher than for their white counterparts.

The first teacher testing session had taken place in the spring of 1985. By the next year, Bill Clinton was chairman of the National Governors' Association, aiding in the development of a report he labeled the "second wave" of school reform. The brief documented the steps the nation's governors could take to improve their state's school systems.

Arkansas now boasts the lowest high school dropout rate in the South, but as the governor noted, "...the bad news is it's still nearly one in four." In adult education, the state has significantly increased its financial commitment. The wave of education reform begun in Arkansas during Clinton's second term has now spread throughout the South and across the nation. Today, on the campaign trail, the governor continues to point out that American youngsters are going to face a declining standard of living during the next decade unless the nation's educational systems do more to promote high-technology concepts and learning in the classroom.

During the first week of December 1991, Clinton addressed the leaders of the National Education Association. Rather than being the target of criticism and abuse, the governor was warmly welcomed by the NEA executives. Eight years before, of course, the NEA would have given him the boot— but good.

During his speech to the NEA leaders, Clinton generated clear-cut support as he described his achievements in the arena of Arkansas education. To some who were attending the conference, his reception might indicate that he stood a chance of picking up the endorsement of the association.

To do so, the governor would be forced to upstage Iowa Senator and rival presidential candidate Tom Harkin. Harkin heads up the Senate appropriations subcommittee dealing with Health and Human Services, Labor, and Education. For the NEA to pull the rug out from beneath Harkin, it would be forced to practically endorse the fact that Clinton opposes collective bargaining for teachers, while Harkin supports such a measure. Additionally, the senator's placement on the appropriations committee gives him hands-on control of the money pipeline. Governor Clinton, of course, is an outsider to Washington politics and therefore possesses no similar advantage.

Although a number of labor organizations seem surprisingly warm to Clinton, the NEA endorsement could be a big advantage in a fall campaign. The last candidate the NEA aggressively backed was Jimmy Carter in 1976. With someone possessing Clinton's concern for education heading a ticket in 1992, the organization might be equally responsive once again

In retrospect, Governor Clinton's actions during his second and third terms demonstrate his masterful ability to handle a particularly difficult political situation. Perhaps the AEA played into his hands by hotly contesting the teacher testing statute; at any rate, that debacle became the crux of the education reform movement for Arkansas taxpayers who would support it. Indeed, the teacher testing crisis helped refocus public attention on the debate over instructor accountability, allowing a tax increase far larger than the doubling of car license fees to pass the legislature unobstructed.

The teachers, of course, bore the burden of Arkansans' emotional catharsis. They became unique symbols for everything that was wrong with Arkansas' school systems. Of course, many career instructors found this sort of symbolism both degrading and demoralizing. Unfortunately, the success of the

Arkansas education reform movement which made scapegoats of the teachers in the first place, depended upon their subsequent performance in the classroom.

Those who view the Arkansas education reform movement from a distance are usually struck by the question of how much might have been done had Clinton not been governor. While the good political scientist knows that he cannot predict a negative exclusion with any degree of certainty, the situation nonetheless invites closer study. Had someone without Clinton's ability to work with the state legislature and to candidly take his case to the people been in a position of authority, the reforms might never even have been advanced to the legislature. But there is another consideration to be weighed.

Bill Clinton is a man of commitments. He had no idea in mid-1983 that the emerging battle over teacher testing would help draw critical attention away from an impending sales tax increase. Nonetheless, he felt strongly enough about teacher testing in particular— and Arkansas education reform in general— to move ahead toward the adoption of the Standards Committee's recommendations. While the legislature did not, in truth, give Clinton everything he wanted in terms of generating revenues for Arkansas schools, they did put most of the badly needed school standards into motion.

Many of the reforms Clinton initiated within Arkansas' school districts are already law in other states across the country. Nevertheless, he scores a valid point today when he maintains that the educational system at large is failing to prepare today's students for the challenges of tomorrow. Based on his track record during four terms as governor of Arkansas, even his critics are forced to acknowledge that Clinton, in a position of national authority, would probably continue to advance the cause of education with as much fervor as he has demonstrated in his own home state.

Governor Clinton's critics doubtless will attack the depth and scope of his achievements in his efforts to reform education in Arkansas. Outsiders looking in will often opt for the thought that much more could be done, and truthfully, much more needs to be done. Nonetheless, as someone who spent his grade-school and high-school days attending classes in an Arkansas school district and later attended Arkansas universities, I feel more than qualified to express my opinion that Bill Clinton's grandfather would be proud of the effort his grandson has made to ensure that each Arkansan has the opportunity to learn and advance.

8

BILL CLINTON AND THE PRESIDENCY

★　　　★　　　★　　　★　　　★　　　★

What would Bill Clinton do if elected President? Already, his track record on education issues strongly suggests that he would be an education-oriented chief executive. On the economic front, Clinton is proposing sweeping changes in the way in which we deal with and compete with other nations to ensure funding for an ambitious domestic agenda. And on most other issues, Clinton sets himself apart from the other Democratic presidential candidates by reiterating positions which place him to the right, more towards Republicanism, on the Democratic Party's political spectrum.

In his campaign's outline, a booklet titled "A Plan for America's Future," Clinton boldly declares that the future of the nation is in serious jeopardy and that he has suggestions, answers, and solutions to the problems which face us. Unlike the rhetoric and high ideals spouted rather freely by past and current Democratic and Republican presidential hopefuls, his plans are usually specific and to the point. In the booklet, Clinton declares:

I am running for President with a specific plan for economic change, a plan to jump-start our economy in the short term and a new long-term strategy to turn our country's economy around and restore the American Dream for all.

Later in the introduction, he maintains that:

It's time you had a President who cares, takes responsibility, and knows what he wants to do for America for a change. You deserve more than slogans and 30-second TV commercials. You deserve more than political rhetoric and outdated proposals...

What makes the Clinton presidential agenda patently unique is that it is at once relatively specific, stretchingly realistic and workable, while being, for the most part, free of the cliches and high ideology which have clouded the concepts and strategies of the hopefuls of the past.

Like any good Democrat, Clinton is careful to point out that under the George Bush administration the United States has suffered economically. Statistically, the nation has suffered enough to make one harken back to pre-Depression memories of Republican Herbert Hoover. As Clinton sees it, middle-class Americans are working more and earning less and shortchanging their families in the process. At the same time, costs of housing, education, taxes and health care have all seen dramatic increases. The result is a middle class that has been squeezed out of the economic equation.

This adds up to a powerful altar call for those Americans who see themselves as having fared worse during the past decade, watching with arms akimbo while the upper class, large corporations, and federal bureaucrats alike seemed to have reaped considerable benefits. Additionally, for those who see the American family in a continuing state of decline and blame that decline for a large number of the country's social ills, the Clinton platform has a great deal to offer. These individuals are of necessity largely members of the so-called middle class: they work for a living, depend upon the federal government for protection and for economic help in troubled times, and, apparently, see their common American dream slipping away. For many of these voters, the decline in their lifestyle has done nothing but accelerate during the presidencies of Ronald Reagan and George Bush.

Consequently, most of the Clinton economic agenda is aimed at this disenfranchised middle class. Like most of the other Democratic Party standard bearers, he is advocating a tax break for typical wage earners, the shortfall from which would be compensated for by an increasing tax bite on those earning more than $200,000 per year.

The governor has cited census figures which in 1991 defined middle-class income as $20,000 to $65,000. On ABC's "This Week With David Brinkley," Clinton maintained that he also favored modest tax breaks for Americans with incomes of up to $100,000.

Clinton is advocating an immediate middle-class tax cut of ten percent, which—assuming that it is offset by a compensating tax increase—would have a negligible effect on the national deficit while restoring consumer confidence with what he cleverly calls "consumer cash."

Candidate Clinton is quick to add that the rich, who will bear the expense of this middle-class tax break, will only be paying "their fair share" of taxes—an amount still smaller from a percentage standpoint than they paid in during the Nixon, Ford, and Carter administrations.

The problem with the Clinton plan from the standpoint of public perception, census figures aside, is that inflation has so eroded the purchasing power of family income that those earning $200,000 or more, who would be paying a larger share of taxes, are themselves slipping into the middle class category. In short, critics allege that the tax cut would benefit the middle and lower middle class, while the upper middle class would pay for it.

House Minority Whip Newt Gingrich (R-Ga.) told an interviewer that he "would love for Mr. Clinton to find any economist who, in a recession, says raising anyone's taxes is a good idea." Clinton responded by pointing out that the Republican idea has largely failed in the past "and more likely won't work again." Clinton added that the government could not "just give people with incomes over $200,000 a $12,000 tax cut. That's what we did all through the 1980s," he contends, "and it killed this economy."

Bringing the dead economy back to life would require additional help for the middle class. Expansion of the children's tax credit would, in Clinton's words, "give additional tax relief to families who need it." He makes the point that the overall value of the tax exemption for children has gone dramatically downhill in the post-World War II era, while the cost of raising a family—and the tax burden incumbent upon it—has steadily increased. According to Clinton, today's family of four pays out thirty times as much of their gross income in federal income taxes as their 1940s counterparts.

Clinton says the tax credit expansion would give substantial financial relief to those who, in his words, "work hard and play by the rules." Along with the middle-class tax cut, Clinton estimates that an average American family with two children would be paying as much as $1,300 per year less in federal income taxes.

From whence would the money come to make up the shortfall? Again, Clinton opts for changes in the tax laws which would close what he describes as "tax loopholes for high-income people." Additionally, unspecified cuts might be made in the $200 billion annual government budget.

Clinton has challenged his Democratic and Republican opponents—including the incumbent President—to detail exactly how each plans to reduce the federal budget deficit during a four-year term in office. For the 1992 fiscal year, which ends at the end of September, the deficit is expected to near $350 billion.

Clinton maintains that he cannot promise a balanced budget within a first presidential term. In early January, 1992, on NBC-TV's "Meet the Press," he maintained that balancing the budget would stave off economic disaster for the United States. Nonetheless, the candidate apparently harbored honest-and somewhat refreshing-doubts as to his ability to achieve budget parity within a single four-year term:

Will we get to zero? I certainly hope so. We can't survive with $280 to $300 billion a year in interest payments. It's going to crowd out our ability to build a better future for our working people and for our children.

In his effort to wrestle the deficit under control, Clinton says he is prepared to implement reductions in defense spending, step up control of health care costs, rein in costs connected with failed financial institutions, and add the aforementioned cuts in the costs of government administration—something on the order of 3 percent per year.

Clinton is concerned with the nation's economic performance as it relates to the global balance of power and security. He notes that, in the middle of Ronald Reagan's first term as President, the United States offered its workers higher wages than those paid in any other country on the face of the globe. Today, under George Bush, Clinton believes the country is now in tenth place — and, as he notes, still in decline. He seizes the opportunity to take another shot at the Bush administration when he says:

> *During George Bush's presidency, Germany and Japan have achieved productivity gains three and four times greater than ours, because they educate and train their people better, they invest more in the future, and they organize their economies for global competition—and we don't.*

According the the Clinton agenda, our next president should respond to this growing economic slippage in the world community standing by challenging the nation to compete in the world and win again. Doing so requires that our nation's leaders recognize that, in the post-Cold War era, national security quite literally translates into economic security. As Clinton notes:

> *More of the costs of preserving the military security of Asia and Europe can be shifted immediately to Japan and Germany, releasing billions of dollars that can come home to America and spur U.S. production. Japan and Germany also should be told, in no uncertain terms, that it is time for them, to help shoulder more responsibility for economic growth today by stimulating their economies in order to boost U.S. exports.*

Again Clinton attacks President Bush in claiming that he "has neglected to use America's influence with other advanced countries to insist that, in the modern global economy, they too must do their part to keep world growth going."

For his part, Clinton has acknowledged that his trade proposals would be difficult to implement but insists that once working, they would pay dramatic dividends. Randy Lilleston, with the Arkansas Democrat-Gazette's Washington Bureau, was traveling with Clinton in New Hampshire while President Bush was in Japan meeting with the leaders of several Asian nations in hopes of hammering out a new world order in trade agreements.

In Dover, N.H., Lilleston reported that Clinton sharply criticized Bush's mission to Japan, asking voters who were crowded into a hotel meeting room:

Did you ever think you'd live to see the leader of your country going to another country, hat in hand, saying, "Please don't send your cars to our country anymore. Our people can't help buying them."

During the same campaign speech, Clinton maintained that George Bush was headed to Japan "to see the landlord." Although the remark was apparently meant in jest, it symbolized the growing concern many Americans feel about growing Japanese ownership of this nation's assets.

This particular remark smacks of utter simplicity totally lacking in the practice of world statecraft. What Clinton is saying, however, only echoes what millions of Americans have said for years, that we must stop giving away the proverbial store and pay more attention to our own efforts and difficulties...using the money we would spend elsewhere to address our own problems here at home. According to the Clinton doctrine, America's economic strength must become a "defining element of our national security policy." The nation's economic muscle can be used as both a security blanket and a big stick in dealing with the balance of the global community. This leads observers to conjecture which alternative George Bush opted for, if indeed he opted for either one.

In fairness to President Bush it should be mentioned that, to date, no empowered politician has been able to exercise that sort of control merely through applicaton of the nation's economic strength. Still, the failure of others in no way demands the conclusion that Clinton's ideas are not workable.

The basic cornerstone of Clinton's economic plan requires a President who is unafraid to cut off economic and defense aid to nations who have depended for years upon the United States for both money and security. This move "from a defense to a domestic" economy would, in turn, generate savings to the federal government which could then be directed to encouraging economic development within the United States.

It doesn't take a political scientist to sense the isolationist danger inherent in this broad plan. Here Clinton walks a fine line because he insists that the widening isolationist sentiment "is wrong for the country and sets back everything else we hope to accomplish..." While cuts in defense spending, both at home and on behalf of other nations, would obviously turn the wheels of Clinton's economic recovery program, they must be judiciously made. In his words, "we still must set the level of defense spending based on what we need to protect our interests."

As President, Clinton would halt the production of the controversial B-2 bomber, and make deep cuts in funding for the Strategic Defensive Initiative (Star Wars) program. He believes the United States should respond to the new world order by maintaining a nuclear deterrent and emphasizing intelligence-gathering operations and high technology in a rapid-deployment military organization. This, Clinton maintains, will revamp the United States military machine for the new world political scene.

All of this adds up to a pretty slender tightrope upon which President Clinton would, if he were to follow his own plan, be required to tread. As a candidate, he criticizes President Bush for utilizing his personal relationships with foreign leaders to set a defense agenda, rather than developing his own policy to promote "freedom, democracy, and economic growth."

Clinton's proposed policy, on the other hand, would at the very least let foreign leaders know that the United States has, albeit suddenly, become a bargaining force to be reckoned with. This "get tough" stance echoes the popular public sentiment demanding that this nation force other nations to fend for their own safety and welfare, and to extend to America the same trade opportunities they themselves demand. Critics argue that Clinton, inexperienced in the application of foreign policy, lacks the diplomatic expertise to enforce his plan without irreparable damage to our relationship with global partners. If the critics are correct, the Clinton policy could bode ill for his efforts to steer clear of the isolationist course.

Much of Bill Clinton's economic strategy is aimed at ending the current recession. In "A Plan for America's Future," he notes that:

> *Under George Bush, a smaller share of people who lost their jobs are receiving unemployment benefits—less than 35 percent—than in any previous down turn since the 1930s. The process of restoring economic confidence should have begun six to nine months ago by extending these benefits, but George Bush blocked efforts to do so until November, and even then agreed only reluctantly.*
>
> *We must do more during our country's current economic emergency. Millions of Americans are terrified that if they lose their jobs, they could lose their homes and their health care coverage, too. We need to restore confidence by providing an economic lifeline for middle-class families facing unexpected unemployment. People who work hard and pay taxes deserve a fair break: during the economic emergency, we can provide temporary ways of enabling families to keep up with their health-care premiums and mortgage or rent payments.*

In fairness to President Bush, his refusal to authorize the extension of unemployment benefits was due to his fear of adding to the federal deficit. His critics have alleged that he failed to see the seriousness of the recession and consequently declined to act. Clinton and his fellow Democratic candidates waste no opportunity to attack the "Bush Recession" and resulting economic misery many American families are currently facing.

The Clinton recovery program would allow each of the fifty states to design its own "economic life line plan." While this may be a formidable task for many states, which seem to wrangle endlessly over lesser issues, it nonetheless gives a more region-specific feature to the plan. Clinton notes that:

> For health care coverage, some (states) may choose to help families buy into the Medicaid system; others may provide additional direct payments. For mortgage and rent payments, some may choose to work with private banks; others could expand loan provisions under their existing housing programs. Washington will cover the initial cost of the program and ensure that those who receive help pay it back, once they are working again, through automatic withholding.

Skeptics charge that the Clinton recovery program would only add to the massive federal deficit. But Clinton counters with four specific proposals to give the national economy a proverbial shot in the arm, the theory being that by reviving the nation's sluggish economy, the nation could generate greater tax revenues than it might otherwise see.

Clinton advocates the creation of some 200,000 new federal jobs by "front-loading" the new highway bill so that the money allocated for the first two years is spent in the first year. Again, in a bankrupt Washington, the problem may be coming up with the additional money to spend in a rapid first-year start-up.

Additionally, Clinton maintains that federal regulators should send a clear message to banks "not to call in good loans that are performing, and not to hesitate to make sound loans..." In this way, he says the President can keep thousands of small businesses open and expanding. But without federal guarantees, one might well wonder if the banks themselves—conservative by the very nature of their business—would respond to any sort of governmental plea.

According to Clinton, the government should call on banks to renegotiate loans downward and to decrease the interest rates of sound credit-card customers. In this way, he contends, "the President could help relieve the consumer and business debt burden of millions of families."

Assuming that the nation's banks would heed the call to lower interest rates in the lucrative credit card business, many economists feel that the damage done by easily available consumer credit is irreparable. What they are saying, in essence, is that lowering interest rates would only prod most American credit card holders to go out and charge more, thus miring themselves even more deeply in consumer debt. If one agrees with those theories, Clinton appears to be sending mixed signals.

Clinton explained his reasoning to Arkansas Democrat-Gazette reporter Noel Oman, saying that:

> I think what's happening is that some of the banks are trying to cover their losses in other areas from bad loans and speculation with credit card gains. If the President had been on top of this, I think what he should've done is bring in all the biggest banks in the country and try to jawbone a lower rate for people who pay in a timely fashion.

But Clinton added that, in viewing the situation, he saw the bank's side of the issue as well:

*The one thing is that I do have sympathy with the issuers on
is that a very high percentage of our people are now in
default. You talk to any small merchant and they'll tell you
they're having a larger perrcentage of rejects, but that still
doesn't mean there shouldn't be a lowering of credit card
interest rates for people who pay in a timely fashion. I think
it would be good for the economy, good for the consumers,
good for the small business economy.*

Finally, Clinton is calling for an increase in the ceiling on
mortgage loans eligible for Federal Housing Administration
Insurance. Such an increase, he maintains, needs to be sufficient to cover 95 percent of the median cost of a home in every
metropolitan area. Clinton believes that such a ceiling increase
would enable as many as 500,000 young families to buy their
first homes immediately, thus spurring the sagging construction industry, creating more new jobs, and sending housing
dollars into the economic mainstream.

Clinton maintains that Americans are locked into a "hard-
work, low-wage economy that's going nowhere." He seeks to
transform that modern nightmare into something which will
carry the country forward into "a high-wage, high-growth,
high-opportunity national economy that will carry America
into the 21st century."

To do just that, he has developed a long-term, five-part
strategy which would focus on giving Americans the tools
needed to do their jobs better, rather than demanding that they
develop those tools themselves. In "A Plan for America's Future," Clinton says:

*Our new economic strategy will restore the American Dream
of upward mobility by enabling every person and every business to become more productive. This strategy rewards work,
expands opportunity, and empowers people—so America
can compete and win again.*

In the new world economy, American economic growth will
come not from more federal spending and more federal bu-
reaucrats, but from America's workers learning more and
working smarter, from America's entrepreneurs taking risks
and going after new markets, and from America's companies
designing better products and taking a longer view.

Clinton's five-part strategy would focus, first of all, on the education issue. By altering the methods with which we educate our young people and train our workers, Clinton is convinced that Americans can become "empowered" to be more productive in the workplace. His ideas on revamping the education and training systems were detailed in the preceding chapter.

Secondly, Clinton would be the leader of what he calls "a revolution in government" designed to transform the federal monolith from an obstacle to opportunity into an engine driving the forces of change and progress. Here, Clinton possesses much the same advantage Jimmy Carter had in 1976: as an outsider to Washington politics, he has no vested interest in maintaining the status quo. Carter's failings, curiously enough, were relatively unrelated to this "outsider" status, but, to his inability to deal decisively with substantial foreign policy issues. One might argue that Clinton's educational background would enable him to avoid that same pitfall.

Clinton is clearly taking a lesson from our Japanese competitors when he mentions that the third of his five points would be to encourage American workers and their employers to "reorganize the workplace and the way we do business" in the hopes of increasing productive investment and innovation "throughout the economy." Here, the candidate obviously believes that American business owners can abandon their desire to keep doing things just the way they've always done them. One might assert that, having been governor of Arkansas for a dozen years, Clinton has had a great deal of experience in dealing with just that attitude.

In "A Plan for America's Future," Clinton outlines the changes he sees in the American workplace, saying:

> *Outdated economic arrangements are holding America back, and we need to create new, dynamic, and flexible workplaces where workers at the front line are involved in the decisions that affect their productivity, and entire levels of middle-management can be eliminated. While business and workers have to undertake most of these changes themselves, government can help too.*

Clinton candidly admits that he is not counting on the support of many middle-management employees who are concerned about their job security.

The fourth plank in Clinton's plan for regaining our economic leadership focuses on his "golden rule" of fair trade. He asserts that as President he would stand up for American products and workers by expanding the nation's trade horizons "on just and fair terms." Clinton maintains that this country should allow unrestricted imports from other nations which do not restrict the entry of American products. On the other hand, he believes that countries which restrict American imports should be dealt with according to the proverbial "golden rule"—meaning that American imports to those nations would be restricted as well.

Critics have been quick to point out that Clinton's plan would mean that the United States would be required to generate dozens—if not hundreds—of trade policies for the same item. Each policy would vary, depending upon the other country involved in the trade agreement. "It is a complicated thing," he admitted to Arkansas Democrat-Gazette correspondent

Randy Lilleston, "but we need trade authority for the president to target these areas, very specifically and rapidly." The Clinton reciprocal trade ideas do not apply to agricultural subsidies.

Finally, the Clinton national security policy would, in Clinton's words, "enable us to lead the world we've done so much to make and look out for the interests of our own people at home." This sort of share-the-burden ideology has already been discussed in this chapter, and it certainly addresses the concerns of millions of Americans who see the United States providing defense and aid to foreign nations which don't need, want, or appreciate the help.

Helping those less fortunate in a responsible, responsive way is a fundamental plank in the Clinton platform for America's future. One benefit for the working poor would come about from reforming the Earned Income Tax Credit, ensuring that those who work full-time, all year around, would earn enough to support their families at a level above the poverty line.

Low-income entrepreneurs would receive a shot in the arm via public and private partnerships which would extend small loans and business advice to the poor who possess the drive and initiative to start their own small business.

Clinton has scored a positive point with millions of Americans because of his declaration that the nation's welfare program must "break the cycle of dependency" rather than accelerate it. While, due to the way in which the program is structured, it might not initially save the nation money, it would help to bring to an end the specter of generation after generation subsisting on government handouts. In "A Plan for America's Future," Clinton says:

We've got to break the cycle of dependency and put an end to permanent dependence on welfare as a way of life, by really

*investing in the development of poor people and giving them
the means, the incentives, and the requirement to go to work.
Welfare should be a second chance, not a way of life. We'll
give people on welfare training and education for up to two
years. But after that, if they can work, they'll have to do so.*

The Arkansas version of the Clinton welfare reform plan is
something called "Project Success," a program mandated by
the 1988 Federal Welfare Bill. The program requires welfare
recipients to participate in job training, education, or job placement activities—or run the risk of losing their welfare benefits.
Interestingly enough, for every hundred "Project Success"
participants who get jobs, between 50 and 75 Arkansans have
had their welfare benefits taken away because they will not
comply with the program's guidelines.

Critics allege that the program takes the wrong approach,
citing the fact that guidelines generally require that participants provide their own transportation, which many poor
Arkansans cannot find. Additionally, there are no considerations for child care, and quite often job recipients encounter
difficulty getting benefits such as health insurance. "As soon
as someone gets sick, the family is back on welfare," says Little
Rock advocate Brownie Ledbetter.

Nonetheless, the program seems to be working—not just
in Arkansas, but in other states around the nation. While the
national Aid to Families with Dependent Children has increased nearly 20 percent during the ten months preceding
April, 1991, the Arkansas rate is only ten percent.

"The program works," says Kenny Whitlock, who directs
the bureau of the Department of Human Services which oversees the "Project Success" effort. "The concept works. There
are people getting jobs with this who wouldn't be getting
jobs." As proof, Whitlock cites the fact that nearly three-quar-

ters of "Project Success" participants who left the welfare rolls in 1990 were still off welfare as late as August, 1991. "I'm sold on the concept," he maintained to Arkansas Democrat-Gazette reporter Terry Lemons, adding that the program does "make a difference, and the records reflect that."

Advocating that welfare recipients move from dependence on the government toward gainful employment is but one way in which Clinton is urging personal responsibility as a way of life. A key theme in his campaign is that government helps those who help themselves. Additionally, Clinton insists on more stringent efforts toward child support enforcement, and believes that high school dropouts should forfeit their driver's licenses.

Clinton has also focused attention on the growing debate on national health care. In "A Plan for America's Future," Clinton delivers an exceptionally lofty promise when he says:

In the first year of a Clinton administration, we'll deliver quality, affordable health care to all Americans. If we're going to fundamentally change government, we must devote special attention to dramatically changing the way we deliver health care in this country. We are the only advanced nation in the world that does not provide health care to all its citizens and does not take the lead in controlling health care costs.

Clinton believes that an overhaul of the health care system is essential to the economic competitiveness of the United States. As he points out, there is no need to lessen the quality of health care rendered to Americans; rather, there is a pressing need to restructure the system by which it is delivered. Later in his "Plan," Clinton concludes:

We spend 30 percent more than any other country on health care, and get less for it. Millions of Americans can't change

233

their jobs for fear of losing their health care coverage and not being able to get insurance because of 'pre-existing' health conditions. Thousands of American businesses are losing jobs because health care costs are a 30 percent handicap in the global marketplace.

Clinton's proposed changes in American health care include guaranteeing universal coverage to all citizens, noting that the government will spend something on the order of $800 billion this year on health care while leaving some 34 million people without coverage and millions more inadequately insured. He believes the United States can cover every citizen with the money it is already spending on health care if health care insurance is reformed, spread of excessive technology is halted, massive drug price escalation is stopped, and billing fraud is similarly reduced. According to Clinton, billing fraud alone may account for up to $75 billion of the government's total health care expenditure, leading him to believe that those who both send the bills and pay them should have the opportunity to set guidelines on how much health care should really cost.

In Arkansas, Clinton helped create a program which gives senior citizens the opportunity to take the funds formerly available for nursing home care and spend them on personal care, home health care, transportation to senior centers, or attending adult day care. Consequently, he believes that national responsibility demands long-term care alternatives which will keep the elderly from spending themselves into financial ruin.

As President, Clinton would place medical clinics in the public schools, where children will have access to health care. Additionally, inner city and rural areas would see an influx of primary and preventive health care. Critics allege that the government cannot support such a massive health care effort without an increase in taxes and expenditures. Clinton believes that a reform in the way in which current government health care dollars are spent will allow for federal funding of health care programs without demanding an increase in revenue in order to pay for them.

Clinton's plan to cut military spending could generate savings of $100 billion above the plan endorsed by George Bush. Clinton believes that, given the current global status quo, the United States could successfully cut military spending by a third within the next five years.

While his defense policy does yield substantial savings, Clinton also has some semblance of a plan for those defense workers and Americans in uniform who would be forced to find some other means of employment. He has called for a new advanced research agency to take the collective brilliance of defense industry scientists and engineers into the commercial sector. Another segment of the Clinton plan would allow for reintegration of uniformed military personnel into American society, while calling for new early retirement options, limited reenlistment guidelines, and a slackening of the current recruitment pace.

In closing his fifteen-page "Plan for America's Future," Clinton notes his belief that the economic, defense, health care, and education changes he advocates are necessities rather than options:

> We must do all these things, and something more. The economic challenges we confront today are not just a matter of statistics and numbers. Behind them are real human beings and real human suffering. I have seen the pain in the faces of unemployed workers in New Hampshire, policemen in New York and Texas, computer company executives in California, middle-class people everywhere. They're all showing the

same pain and worry I hear in the voices of my own people in Arkansas, including men and women I grew up with who played by the rules and now see their dreams for the future slipping away.

That's why we're offering a radical new approach to economics. If we offer these hard-working families no hope for the future, no solutions to their problems, no relief for their pain, then fear and insecurity will grow, and the politics of hate and division will spread... our streets will get meaner, our families will be devastated, and our very social fabric —our goodness and tolerance and decency as a people—will be torn apart.

I believe with all my heart that the very future of our country is on the line. That is why these are not just economic proposals. They are the way to save the very soul of our nation.

In the final analysis, Clinton is hoping that Americans realize that their most basic human link is the opposed emotions of hope and suffering. As President, he would face yet again the same battle he has fought for so many years in the unrelenting political empires of Arkansas—he must convince his countrymen that the basic changes he advocates in essential social services are both needed and worth paying for. The most viable testing ground for popular belief in Clinton's programs is, first of all, the Democratic Party's nominating process, and secondly, the November election itself. If he succeeds in earning that support, he will face the most formidable challenge of all-convincing those with whom he shares the reins of government to adopt his vision, pay his price, and fight his battles with him.

As we have seen, Bill Clinton is perhaps the most personable, dynamic politician in the past quarter of a century. If he brings those qualities to Washington, D.C., as President of the United States, he could well succeed in accomplishing the renovations and reforms which have eluded his 41 other predecessors. Hope, like political rhetoric, springs eternal. No matter how many times it has been crushed in our nation's past, there are always grounds for fresh optimism, especially when the bearer of glad tidings knows what he wants to do and has some idea of how to go about doing it.

APPENDIX

★   ★   ★   ★   ★   ★

It's been said that Bill Clinton, looking in his thesaurus one day, came upon the word "covenant" as a synonym for "deal," in this case, used in "New Deal." Hence, his "New Covenant" might best be described as a modern version of Franklin D. Roosevelt's program for radical reform and change. The New Deal, of course, was a spectacular success, putting Depression-era America back to work. While the Depression itself ended in a single day—December 7, 1941—there is much to be said for the methods, the policies, and the results generated by the FDR programs.

Bill Clinton's modern-day "New Deal" is outlined best in a series of three speeches he gave at his old alma mater, Georgetown University. The first speech was delivered on October 23, 1991. The second followed a month later, on November 20. The third and final address was given on December 12. In a word, all three speeches were given in less than two months.

While the addresses themselves do not show us from whence Clinton has come, they do much to show us where Clinton might go, if elected president. I present all three speeches in this book in the hope—shared, I'm sure, by the candidate himself—that each reader will carefully study what Clinton has said, thereby gaining great insight into what he will do. Armed with this information, you may use the brain given to you by our Creator and make your own informed decision. If, prior to casting your ballot, you form your impressions of Bill Clinton based upon his own words, I am certain that he will feel fairly judged.

Jim Moore

The New Covenant: Responsibility and Rebuilding The American Community

Georgetown University, Washington D.C. October 23, 1991

Thank you all for being here today. You are living in revolutionary times. When I was here, America sought to contain communism, not roll it back. Most respected academics held that once a country "went communist" the loss of freedom was permanent and irreversible. Yet in the last three years, we've seen the Berlin Wall come down, Germany reunified, all of Eastern Europe abandon communism, a coup in the Soviet Union fail and the Soviet Union itself disintegrate, liberating the Baltics and other republics. Now the Soviet Foreign Minister is trying to help our Secretary of State make peace in the Middle East. And in the space of one year, Lech Walesa and Vaclav Havel both came to this city to thank America for supporting their quest for freedom. Nelson Mandela walked out of a jail in South Africa he entered before I entered Georgetown in 1964. He now wants a Bill of Rights like ours for his country.

We should be celebrating. All around the world, the American Dream—political freedom, market economics, national independence—is ascendant. Everything your parents and grandparents stood for from World War II on has been rewarded.

Yet we're not celebrating. Why? Because our people fear that while the American Dream reigns supreme abroad, it is dying here at home. We're losing jobs and wasting opportunities. The very fiber of our nation is breaking down.

Families are coming apart; kids are dropping out of school; drugs and crime dominate our streets. And our leaders here in Washington are doing nothing to turn America around. Our political system rotates between being the butt of jokes and the object of scorn. Frustration produces calls for term limits from voters who think they can't vote incumbents out. Resentment produces votes for David Duke—not just from racists, but from voters so desperate for change , they'll support the most anti-establishment message, even from an ex-Klansman who was inspired by Adolf Hitler. We've got to rebuild our political life together before demagogues and racists and those who pander to the worst in us bring this country down.

People once looked to our President and Congress to bring us together, solve problems, and make progress. Now, in the face of massive challenges, our government stands discredited, our people disillusioned. There's a hole in our politics where a sense of common purpose used to be.

The Reagan-Bush years have exalted private gain over public obligations, special interests over the common good, wealth and fame over work and family. The 1980s ushered in a gilded age of greed, selfishness, irresponsibility, excess and neglect.

Savings and loan crooks stole billions in dollars of other people's money. Pentagon contractors and HUD consultants stole from the taxpayers. Many big corporate executives raised their own salaries when their companies were losing money and their workers were losing their jobs. Middle-class families worked longer hours for less money and spent more on health care, housing, education and taxes. Poverty rose. Many inner city streets were taken over by crime and drugs, welfare and despair. Family responsibility became an oxymoron for deadbeat fathers who were more likely to make their car payments than pay their child support.

And government, which should have been setting an example, was even worse. Congress raised its pay and guarded its perks while most Americans were working harder for less money. Two Republican presidents elected on a promise of fiscal responsibility advanced budget policies that more than tripled the national debt. Congress went along with that, too. Taxes were lowered on the wealthiest people whose incomes rose, and raised on middle-class people whose incomes fell.

And through it all, millions of decent, ordinary people who worked hard, played by the rules, and took responsibility for their own actions were falling behind, living a life of struggle without reward or security. For 12 years, the forgotten middle class watched their economic interests ignored and their values run into the ground. In the 1980s, nothing illustrates this more clearly than the fact that charitable giving by middle-class families went up as their incomes went down, while charitable giving by the wealthiest Americans went down as their incomes went up. Responsibility went unrewarded and so did hard work. It's no wonder so many kids growing up on the street think it makes more sense to join a gang and deal drugs than to stay in school and go to work. The fast buck was glorified from Wall Street to Main Street to Mean Street.

To turn America around, we need a new approach founded on our most sacred principles as a nation, with a vision for the future. We need a New Covenant, a solemn agreement between the people and their government, to provide opportunity for everybody, inspire responsibility throughout our society, and restore a sense of community to this great nation. A New Covenant to take government back from the powerful interests and the bureaucracy and give this country back to ordinary people.

More than 200 years, ago our founders outlined our first social compact between government and the people, not just between lords and kings. More than a century ago, Abraham Lincoln gave his life to maintain the Union that compact created. Sixty years ago, Franklin Roosevelt renewed that promise with a New Deal that offered opportunity in return for hard work.

Today we need to forge a New Covenant that will repair the damaged bond between the people and their government and restore our basic values—the notion that our country has a responsibility to help people get ahead. That citizens have not only the right but a responsibility to rise as far and as high as their talents and determination can take them, and that we're all in this together. We must make good on the words of Thomas Jefferson, who said, "A debt of service is due from every man to his country proportional to the bounties which nature and fortune have measured to him."

Make no mistake: This New Covenant means change— change in our party, change in our national leadership and change in our country. Far away from Washington, in your hometowns and mine, people have lost faith in the ability of government to change their lives for the better. Out there, you can hear the quiet, troubled voice of the forgotten middle class, lamenting that government no longer looks out for their interests or honors their values—like individual responsibility, hard work, family, community. They think their government takes more from them than it gives back, and looks the other way when special interests only take from this country and give nothing back. And they're right.

This New Covenant can't be between the politicians and the established interests. It can't be just another back-room deal between the people in power and the people who keep them there. The New Covenant can only be ratified by the people in the 1992 election. That is why I'm running for President.

Some people think it's old-fashioned to talk like this. Some people even think I am naive to suggest that we can restore the American Dream through a covenant between people and their government. But I believe with all my heart after ll years of work as governor, working every day to create opportunity and jobs and improve education and deal with all the problems that we all know so much about—I believe that the only way we can hold this country together, and move boldly forward, into the future, is to do it together with a New Covenant.

Over 25 years ago, Professor Carroll Quigley taught in his Western Civilization class here at Georgetown that the defining idea of our culture in general and our country in particular is "future preference," the idea that the future can be better than the present and that each of us has a personal, moral responsibility to make it so.

I hope they still teach that lesson here, and I hope you believe it because I don't think we can save America without it.

In the weeks to come, I will come back to Georgetown and outline my plans to rebuild our economy, regain our competitive leadership in the world, restore the forgotten middle class, and reclaim the future for the next generation. I will put forth my views on how to promote our national security and foreign policy interests after the Cold War. And I will tell you in clear terms what I believe the President and the Congress owe the people in this New Covenant for change.

But I can tell you, based on my long experience in public life, there will never be a government program for every problem. Much of what holds us together and moves us ahead is the daily assumption of personal responsibility by millions of Americans from all walks of life. I can promise to do a hundred different things for you as President. But none of them will make any difference unless we all do more as citizens. And today, I want to talk about the responsibilities we owe to ourselves, to one another, and to our nation.

It's been 30 years since a Democrat ran for President and asked something of all the American people. I intend to challenge you to do more and to do better.

We must go beyond the competing ideas of the old political establishment: beyond every man for himself on the one hand, and the right to something for nothing on the other.

We need a New Covenant that will challenge all our citizens to be responsible. The New Covenant will say to our corporate leaders at the top of the ladder: We'll promote economic growth and the free market, but we're not going to help you diminish the middle class and weaken the economy. We'll support your efforts to increase profits and jobs through quality products and services, but we're going to hold you responsible to be good corporate citizens, too.

The New Covenant will say to people on welfare: We're going to provide the training and education and health care you need; but if you can work, you've got to go to work, because you can no longer stay on welfare forever.

The New Covenant will say to the hard-working middle class and those who aspire to it: We're going to guarantee you access to a college education, but if you get that help, you've got to give something back to your country.

And the New Covenant will challenge all of us in public service. We have a solemn responsibility to honor the values and promote the interests of the people who elected us, and if we don't, we don't belong in government anymore.

The New Covenant must begin here in Washington. The New Covenant will literally revolutionize government and fundamentally change its relationship to people. People don't want some top-down bureaucracy telling them what to do anymore. That's one reason they tore down the Berlin Wall and threw out the communist regimes in Eastern Europe and Russia. Now, the New Covenant will challenge our government to change its way of doing business, too. The American people need a government that works at a price they can afford.

The Republicans have been in charge of the government for 12 years. They've brought the country to the brink of bankruptcy. Democrats who want the government to do more—and I'm one of them—have a heavy responsibility to show that we're going to spend the taxpayer's money wisely and with discipline.

I want to make government more efficient and more effective by eliminating unnecessary layers of bureaucracy and cutting administrative costs, and by giving people more choices in the services they get, and empowering them to make those choices. That's what we've tried to do in Arkansas—balancing our budget every year, improving services, and treating taxpayers like our customers and our bosses, giving them more choices in public schools, child care centers and services for the elderly.

The New Covenant must challenge Congress to act responsibly. And here again, Democrats must lead the way. Because they want to use our government to help people, Democrats have to put Congress in order. Congress must live by the laws it applies to other workplaces. No more midnight pay raises. Congressional pay shouldn't go up while the pay of working Americans goes down. Let's clamp down on campaign spending and open the airwaves to encourage real political debate instead of paid political assassination. No more bounced checks. No more bad restaurant debts. No more fixed tickets. Service in Congress is privilege enough.

We can't go on like this. We have to honor, reward and reflect the work ethic, not the power grab. Responsibility is for everybody, and it begins here in the nation's Capital.

The New Covenant will also challenge the private sector. The most irresponsible people in the 1980s were those in business who abused their position at the top of the totem pole. This is my message to the business community: As President, I'm going to do everything I can to make it easier for your company to compete in the world, with a better trained workforce, cooperation between labor and management, fair and strong trade policies and incentives to invest in America's economic growth. But I want the jet-setters and the feather-bedders of corporate America to know that if you sell your companies and your workers and your country down the river, you'll get called on the carpet. That's what the President's bully pulpit is for.

All of you who are going into business, it's a noble endeavor. It is the thing that makes this country run. The private sector creates jobs, not the public sector. But you have to know that the people with the responsibility in the private sector should think it's simply not enough to obey the letter of the law and make as much money as you can. It's wrong for executives to do what so many did in the 1980s. The biggest companies raised their pay by four times the percentage their workers' pay went up and three times the percentage their profits went up. It's wrong to drive a company into the ground and have the chief executive bail out with a golden parachute to a cushy life.

The average CEO at a major American corporation is paid about 100 times as much as the average worker. Compare that to two countries doing much better than we are in the world economy. In Germany, it's 23 to 1, and in Japan, which just completed 58 months of untrammeled economic growth, it's 17 to 1. Our government today rewards that excess with a tax break for executive pay, no matter how high it is. That's wrong. If a company wants to overpay its executives and underinvest in the future, it shouldn't get any special treatment from Uncle Sam. If a company wants to transfer jobs abroad and cut the security of working people, it shouldn't get special treatment from the Treasury. In the 1980s, we didn't do enough to help our companies to compete and win in a global economy. We did too much to transfer wealth away from hard-working middle-class people to the rich without good reason. That's got to stop. There should be no more deductibility for irresponsibility.

The New Covenant will also challenge the hard-working middle-class families of America. Their challenge centers around work and education. I know Americans worry about the quality of education in this country and want the best for their children. The Clinton Administration will set high national standards based on international competition for what everybody ought to know, and a national examination system to measure whether they're learning it. It's not enough to put money into schools. We need to challenge the schools to produce, and we've got to insist on results.

I just came from Thomas Jefferson Junior High School here in Washington, and the principal of that school, Vera White, I think, is here with me today. I've been to that school three times in the last five years. That school is in a building that was built when Grant was President. They have the plaster models of the Jefferson Memorial in the school auditorium. But every time I've been in that school, you could eat lunch off every floor in the school. There is a spirit of learning that pervades the atmosphere. Almost everyone in the school comes from an ordinary family in Washington—it's almost 100 percent minority. In several years that school has won the National Math Council's competition, going all the way to the finals for junior high school performance in math. Every time I go there, I'm just overwhelmed by the spirit that exists at Thomas Jefferson Junior High School. The teachers and the principal don't make excuses for the problems that the kids bring to the classroom; they open those kids to a brighter world. We need more of that.

But we also have to recognize that teachers can't do it all. We must challenge all parents and children to believe all children can learn. And here is the biggest challenge of all: Too many American parents raise their kids to believe that how much they learn depends on the IQ that God gave them and how much money their family makes. Yet in the countries we are competing against for the future, children are raised to believe that how much they learn depends on how hard they work, and how much their parents encourage them to learn.

The New Covenant will challenge students of America to stay in school. Students who drop out of school or fail to learn as much as they can are not just letting down themselves and their families. They're failing their communities, because from that point on, chances are they're subtracting from society, not adding to it. In Arkansas, we've tried to enhance responsibility for students by saying that if they drop out for no good reason, they lose the privilege of a driver's license.

The New Covenant means new challenges for every young person. I want to establish a system of voluntary national service for all Americans. In a Clinton Administration, we'll put forth a domestic GI Bill that will say to the middle class as well as low-income people: We want you to go to college, we'll pay for it, it will be the best money we ever spent, but you've got to give something back to your country in return. As President, I'll set up a trust fund out of which any American

can borrow money for a college education, so long as they pay it back either as a small percentage of their income over time or with a couple of years of national service as teachers, police officers, child care workers—doing work our country desperately needs.

And education doesn't stop in school. Adults have a responsibility to keep learning so they can stay ahead of the competition, too. All of us are going to have to work smarter in the years to come. That will require new forms of cooperation in the workplace between management and workers, and a continuing effort to move toward high-performance work organizations.

There's a special challenge in the New Covenant for the young men and women who live in America's most troubled urban neighborhoods. There are children, like those I met in Chicago and Los Angeles, who live in fear of being forced to join a gang or getting shot going to and from school.

Many of these young people believe this country has ignored them for too long, and they're right. Many of them think America unfairly blames them for every wrong in our society—for drugs, crime, poverty, the breakup of the family and the breakdown of the schools—and they're right. They worry that because their face is of a different color, their only choice in life is jail or welfare or a dead-end job, that being a minority in an inner city is a guarantee of failure. But they're wrong—and when I'm President, I'm going to do my best to prove they're wrong.

I know these young people can overcome anything they set their mind to. I believe America needs their strength, their intelligence, and their humanity. And because I believe in them and what they can contribute to our society, they must not be let off the hook. All society can offer them is a chance to develop their God-given abilities. They have to do the rest. Anybody who tells them otherwise is lying—and they know it.

As President, I'll see that they get the same deal as everyone else: They've got to play by the rules, stay off drugs, stay in school, and keep out of the streets. They've got to stop having children if they're not prepared to support them. Governments don't raise children. People do. And for those young people who do get into trouble, we'll give them one chance to avoid prison, by setting up community boot camps for first-time non-violent offenders—where they can learn discipline, get drug treatment if necessary, continue their education, and do useful work for their community. A second chance to be a first-rate citizen.

The New Covenant must be prowork. That means people who work shouldn't be poor. In a Clinton Administration, we'll do everything we can to break the cycle of dependency and help the poor climb out of poverty. First, we need to make work pay by expanding the Earned Income Tax Credit for the working poor, creating savings accounts that make it easier for poor people even on welfare to save. I support my proenterprise grants for those who want to start a small business. At the same time, we need to assure all Americans that they'll have access to health care when they go to work.

The New Covenant can break the cycle of welfare. Welfare should be a second chance, not a way of life. In a Clinton Administration, we're going to put an end to welfare as we know it. I want to erase the stigma of welfare for good by restoring a simple, dignified principle: No one who can work can stay on welfare forever.

We'll still help people who can't help themselves, and those who need education and training and child care. But if people can work, they'll have to do so. We'll give them all the help they need for up to two years. But after that, if they're able to work, they'll have to take a job in the private sector, or start earning their way through community service. That way, we'll restore the covenant that welfare was first meant to be: To give temporary help to those who've fallen on hard times.

If the New Covenant is pro-work, it must also be pro-family. That means we must demand the toughest possible child support enforcement. We need an administration that will give state agencies that collect child support full law enforcement authority, and find new ways of catching deadbeats. In Arkansas, we passed a law this year that says if you owe more than a thousand dollars in child support, we're going to report you to every credit agency in the state. People shouldn't be able to borrow money before they take care of their children.

Finally, the President has the greatest responsibility of all—to bring us together, not drive us apart. For 12 years, this President and his predecessor have divided us against each other—pitting rich against poor, black against white, women against men—creating a country where we no longer recognize that we're all in this together. They have profited by fostering an atmosphere of blame and denial instead of building an ethic of responsibility. They had a chance to bring out the best in us and instead they appealed to the worst in us.

Nothing exemplifies this more clearly than the battle over the Civil Rights Act of 1991. You know from what I've already said today that I can't be for quotas. I'm for responsibility at every turn. That bill is not a quota bill. When the Civil Rights Act was in place from 1964 to 1987, I never had a single employer in my state say, "It's a quota bill." We need rules of workplace fairness for the 70 percent of new entrants in our workforce who will be women and minorities in the decade of the '90s. That's what that bill is for.

Why does the President refuse to let a civil rights bill pass? Because he knows that the people he is dependent on for his electoral majority—white, working-class men and women, mostly men—have had their incomes decline in the 1980s and they may return to their natural home, to someone who offers them real opportunity. And so he is dredging up the same old tactic that the Hard Right has employed in my part of the country, in the South since I was a child. When everything gets tight, and you think you're going to lose those people, you find the most economically insecure white people, and you scare the living daylights out of them.

That is wrong. This President turned away John Danforth, who shepherded Clarence Thomas' nomination through the Senate. John Danforth begged him for a civil rights bill. He said no. He turned away the Business Roundtable, an organization of corporate executives, largely Republican, who said we need a civil rights bill. He said no. And today in the press it's reported that he turned away his own minority leader in the United States Senate, Sen. Bob Dole, who wanted a civil rights bill.

This man does not want a bill. He wants an issue to drive a stake into the heart of America, and it's wrong. And I won't let him get away with it.

I pledge to you that I'm not going to let the Republicans get away with this cynical scam anymore. A New Covenant means it's my responsibility and the responsibility of every American in this country to fight back against the politics of division and bring this country together.

After all, that is what's special about America. We want to be part of a nation that's coming together, not coming apart. We want to be part of a community where people look out for each other, not just for themselves. We want to be a part of a nation that brings out the best in us, not the worst. And we believe that the only limit to what we can do is what our leaders are willing to ask of us and what we are willing to expect of ourselves.

Nearly 60 years ago, in a famous speech to the Commonwealth Club in the final months of his 1932 campaign, Franklin Roosevelt outlined a new compact that gave hope to a nation mired in the Great Depression. The role of government, he said, was to promise every American the right to make a living. The people's role was to do their best to make the most of it. He said, "Faith in America demands that we recognize the new terms of the old social contract. In the strength of great hope we must all shoulder our common load."

That's what our hope is today: A New Covenant to shoulder our common load. When people assume responsibility and shoulder that common load, they acquire a dignity they never knew before. When people go to work, they reestablish connection that they and their children need. When students work harder, they find out they all can learn and do as well as anyone else on earth. When corporate managers put their workers and their long-term profits ahead of their own paychecks, their companies do well, and so do they. When the privilege of serving is enough of a perk for people in Congress, and the President finally assumes responsibility for America's problems, we'll not only stop doing wrong, we'll begin to do what is right to move America forward.

And that is what this election is really all about—forging a New Covenant of change that will honor middle-class values, restore the public trust, create a new sense of community and make America work again. Thank you.

A New Covenant for Economic Change

Georgetown University, Washington D.C. November 20, 1991

Thank you for being here today. A better future for your generation—a better life for all who will work for it—is what this campaign is about.

But I come here today convinced that your future—the very future of our country, the American Dream—is in peril. This country is in trouble. As I've traveled around the country, I've seen too much pain on people's faces, too much fear in people's eyes. We've got to do better.

This month, I visited with a couple from New Hampshire named David and Rita Springs. He's a chemical engineer by training; she's studying to be a lab technician. They told me that a month before his pension was vested, the people who ran his company fired him to cut their payrolls. Then they turned around and sold the company and bailed out with a golden parachute while David Springs and his family got the shaft.

Last week, at a bowling alley in Manchester, I met a fireman who was working two jobs and his wife was working 50 hours a week in a mill. They told me they were worried that even though both of them were working like this and their son was a straight-A student, they still wouldn't be able to afford to send him to college because of the rising cost of college education and because they were too well off to get government help.

At a breakfast in a cafe in New Hampshire, I met a young man whose 12-year-old child had had open-heart surgery, and now no one will hire him because they can't afford his health insurance.

The families I met are from New Hampshire, but they could be from anywhere in America. They're the backbone of this country, the ones who do the work and pay the taxes and send their children off to war. They're a lot like people I've seen in Arkansas for years, living with the real consequences of our national neglect. These are the real victims of the Reagan revolution, the Bush succession, and this awful national recession.

During this administration, the economy has grown more slowly and fewer jobs have been created than in any administration since World War II. People who have jobs are working longer hours for less money; people who don't are looking harder to find less. Middle-class people are paying more for health care, housing, education and taxes, when government services have been cut.

As these hard-working middle-class families look to their President to make good on his promises, his answer to them is: Tough luck. It's your fault. Go buy a house or a car.

Just this week, George Bush said we don't need a plan to end this recession—that if we wait long enough, our problems will go away. Well, he's right about that part: If he doesn't have a plan to turn this country around by November of 1992, we're going to lay George Bush off, put America back to work, and our problems will go away.

We need a President who will take responsibility for getting this country moving again, a President who will provide the leadership to pull us together and challenge our nation to compete in the world and win again.

Ten years ago, America had the highest wages in the world. Now we're tenth, and falling. Last year, Germany and Japan had productivity growth rates three and four times ours because they educate their people better, invest more in their future, and organize their economies for global competition, and we don't.

For 12 years of this Reagan-Bush era, the Republicans have let S&L crooks and self-serving CEOs try to build an economy out of paper and perks instead of people and products. It's the Republican way: Every man for himself and get it while you can. They stacked the odds in favor of their friends at the top and told everybody else to wait for whatever trickled down.

And every step of the way, the Republicans forgot about the very people they had promised to help—the very people who elected them in the first place—the forgotten middle-class

Americans who still live by American values and whose hopes, hearts, and hands, still carry the American Dream.

But Democrats forgot about real people, too.

Democrats in Congress joined the White House in tripling the national debt and raising the deficit to the point of paralysis. Democrats and Republicans in Congress joined the White House on the sidelines, cheering on an S&L boom until it went bust to the tune of $500 billion.

For too many Americans, for too long, it's seemed that Congress and the White House have been more interested in looking out for themselves and for their friends, but not for the country and not for the people who make it great.

And now, after 12 years of Reagan-Bush, the forgotten middle class is discovering that the reward for 12 years of sacrifice and hard work is more sacrifice and more hard times: They've paid higher taxes on lower incomes for service cuts, while the rich got tax cuts, while poverty increased, and the President and Congress got pay raises and health insurance.

We've got to move in a radically different direction. The Republicans' failed experiment in supply-side economics doesn't produce growth. It doesn't create upward mobility. And most important, it doesn't prepare millions and millions of Americans to compete and win in the new world economy.

And we've got to move away from the old Democratic theory that says we can just tax and spend our way out of any problem we face. Expanding government doesn't provide opportunity. And big deficits don't produce sustained economic growth, especially when the borrowed money is spent on yesterday's mistakes, not tomorrow's investments.

Stale theories produce nothing but stalemate. The old economic answers are obsolete. We've seen the limits of Keynesian economics. We've seen the worst of supply-side economics. We need a new approach.

For 12 years, we've had no economic vision, no economic leadership, no national economic strategy. What America needs is a President with a radical new approach to our economic problems that will give new life to the American Dream.

We need a New Covenant for economic change, a new economics that empowers people, rewards work and organizes America to compete and win again. A national economic strategy to liberate and energize the abilities of millions of Americans who are paying more taxes when the government is doing less for them, who are working harder while their wages go down.

The New Covenant isn't liberal or conservative. It's both and it's different. The American people don't care about the idle rhetoric of left and right. They're real people, with real problems, and they think no one in Washington wants to solve their problems or stand up for them.

The goals of our New Covenant for economic change are straightforward:

We need a President who will put economic opportunity in the hands of ordinary people, not rich and powerful special interests;

- A President who will revolutionize government to invest more in the future;
- A President who will encourage the private sector to organize in new ways and cooperate to produce economic growth;
- A President who will challenge and lead America to compete and win in the global economy, not retreat from the world.

That's how we'll turn this country's economy around, recapture America's leadership in the world and build a better future for our children. That's how we'll show the forgotten middle class we really understand their struggle. That's how we'll reduce poverty and rebuild the ladder from poverty to the middle class. And that, my friends, is why I'm running for President of the United States.

Our first responsibility under this New Covenant is to move quickly to put this recession behind us. Last week, I released a plan for what I would do right away to help working people and get the economy moving again. I'd not only extend unemployment benefits, as Congress and the President have finally done, but I'd push through a middle-class tax cut, an accelerated highway bill to create 40,000 to 45,000 new construction jobs over the next six months, and an increase in the ceiling on FHA mortgage guarantees so half a million families could pump up the economy by buying their first home. I do think good credit card customers should receive a break from the 18 to 19 percent rates of banks, which have cut the rates the customers get paid on their deposit accounts. And I'm proud to say that four of the ten banks charging the lowest credit card rates nationwide are in my state.

I would also make sure federal regulators send a clear signal to the financial community not to call in loans that are performing, and not to fear making good loans to local businesses.

But even if we did all those things tomorrow, it wouldn't change the fundamental challenge of the 1990s. We need to get out of this recession, and soon. But we also need a long-term national strategy to create a high-wage, high-growth, high-opportunity economy, not a hard-work, low-wage economy that's sinking when it ought to be rising.

It doesn't have to be that way. I believe we can win again. In the global economy of the 1990s, economic growth won't come from government spending. It will come, instead, from individuals working smarter and learning more, from entrepreneurs taking more risks and going after new markets, and from corporations designing better products and taking a longer view. We're going to reward work, expand opportunity, empower people, and we are going to win again.

There are two reasons why middle-class people today are working harder for less pay. First, their taxes have gone up-but that's only 30 percent of their problem. The other 70 percent is America's loss of economic growth and world economic leadership.

If we're going to turn this country around, we've not only got to liberate ordinary people from unfair taxes, we've got to empower every American with the education and training essential to get ahead.

Let me make this clear: Education is economic development. We can only be a high-wage, high-growth country if we are a high-skills country. In a world in which money and production are mobile, the only way middle-class people can keep good jobs with growing incomes is to be lifetime learners and innovators. Without world-class skills, the middle class will surely continue to decline. With them, middle-class workers will generate more high-wage jobs in America in the '90s.

Empowering everybody begins with preschool for every child who needs it, and fully funding Head Start. It includes a national examination system to push our students to meet world-class standards in core subjects like math and science, and an annual report card for every state, every school district and every school to measure our progress in meeting those standards.

Empowerment means training young people for high-tech jobs, not dead-end ones. Young Americans with only a high school education make 25 percent less today than they would have 15 years ago. In a Clinton Administration, we'll have a national apprenticeship program that will enable high school students who aren't bound for college to enter a course of study, designed by school and local businesses, to teach them valuable skills, with a promise of a real job with growing incomes when they graduate.

Empowerment means challenging our students and every American with a system of voluntary national service. In a Clinton Administration, we will offer a domestic GI Bill that will say to middle-class as well as low-income people: We want you to go to college and we're glad to pay for it, but you've got to give something back to your country in return. As President, I'll ask Congress to establish a trust fund out of which any American can borrow money for a college education, so long as they pay it back either as a small percentage of their income over time or with a couple of years of national service as teachers, police officers, child care workers—doing work our country urgently needs. The fund would be financed with a portion of the peace dividend and by redirecting the student loan program, which is nowhere near as cost-effective as it should be. This program will pay for itself many times over.

But in an era when what you can earn depends largely on what you can learn, education can't stop at the schoolhouse door. From now on, anyone who's willing to work will have a chance to learn. In a Clinton Administration, we'll make adult literacy programs available to all who need it, by working with states to make sure every state has a clear, achievable plan to teach everyone with a job to read, to give them a chance to earn a GED, and wherever possible, to do it where they work. In Arkansas, we had 14,000 people in adult education programs in 1983. Today we have over 50,000. By 1993, we'll have over 70,000. Every state can do the same for a modest cost with a disciplined plan and a flexible delivery system.

And we will ensure that every working American has the opportunity to learn new skills every year. Today, American business spends billions of dollars on training—the equivalent of 1.5 percent of the costs of their payrolls — but 70 percent of it goes to the 10 percent at the top of the ladder. In a Clinton Administration, we'll require employers to offer every worker his or her share of those training dollars, or contribute the equivalent to a national training fund. Workers will get the training they need, and companies will learn that the more you train your workers, the more your profits increase.

We need special efforts to empower the poor to work their way out of poverty. We'll make work pay by expanding the Earned Income Tax Credit for the working poor and by supporting private and public partnerships to give low-income entrepreneurs the tools to start new businesses, through innovative institutions like Shore Bank in Chicago and its rural counterpart, the Southern Development Bancorporation in Arkansas. We've got to break the cycle of dependency and put an end to permanent dependence on welfare as a way of life, by really investing in the development of poor people and giving them the means, the incentives and the requirement to go to work.

Finally, empowering working Americans means letting them keep more of what they earn. Ronald Reagan and George Bush raised taxes on the middle class. I'm going to cut them. In a Clinton Administration, we'll cut income tax rates on the middle class: An average family's tax bill will go down 10 percent, a savings of $350 a year. And the deficit won't go up— instead those earning over $200,000 a year will pay more, though still a smaller percentage of their incomes than they paid in the '70s, not to soak the rich but to return to basic fairness.

Besides empowering citizens, we must lead a revolution in government so it becomes an engine of opportunity again, not an obstacle to it. Voters who went to the polls in this month's elections sent us a clear message: People want more for their money. The experts in Washington think that is a contradiction. But I think the experts are wrong and the people are right.

People want a better deal from government, and they'll get it in a Clinton Administration.

Too many Washington insiders of both parties think the only way to provide more services is to spend more on programs already on the books in education, housing and health care. But if we reinvent government to deliver new services in different ways, eliminate unnecessary layers of management and offer people more choices, we really can give taxpayers more services with fewer bureaucrats for the same or less money. Every successful major corporation in America had to restructure itself to compete in the last decade, to decentralize, become more entrepreneurial, give workers more authority to make decisions and offer customers more choices and better products.

That's what we're trying to do in Arkansas—balancing the budget every year, improving services and treating taxpayers like our customers and our bosses, because they are. Arkansas was the first state to initiate a statewide total quality management program. We've dramatically reduced the number of reports the Department of Education requires of school districts, slashed bureaucratic costs in the Department of Human Services and put the money into direct services that help real people, and speeded up customer services in the Revenue Department. We measure the job placement rate of graduates from vocational-technical programs, and if a program can't show results we shut it down.

So I know it can be done. But let us be clear: Serious restructuring of government for greater productivity is very different from the traditional top-down reorganization plans that have been offered over the last 29 years, including in this campaign. These require a lot of time and energy and generally leave us with more of the same government, not less.

What I am proposing is hard, unglamorous work. It will require us to re-examine every dollar of the taxpayers' money we spend and every minute of time that the government puts in on business. It will require us to enlist the energies of front-line public servants who are often as frustrated as the rest of us with bureaucracy. And if we do it in Arkansas, which has among the lowest taxes in the country, imagine how much more important and productive it will be at the federal level. In a Clinton Administration, we'll make government more effective by holding ourselves to the same standard of productivity growth as business and insisting on three percent across-the-board cuts in the administrative costs of the federal bureaucracy every year.

If we're going to get more for our money, we ought to have a federal budget which invests more in the future and spends less on the present and the past. As President, I'll throw out last year's budget deal, which brought the biggest deficits in American history and the fastest-growing spending since World War II. I'll establish a new three-part federal budget: a past budget for interest payments, a present budget for spending on current consumption, and a future budget for investments in things that will make us richer.

Today the federal government spends only 9 percent of the budget on investing in the future—in education, child health, environmental technology, infrastructure and basic research. We'll double that in a Clinton Administration. We'll begin to finance the future budget by converting resources no longer needed for national defense to the investments needed to rebuild our economic security and by controlling health care costs.

We can bring the deficit down over time, but only if we control spending on current consumption programs by tying overall increases to real revenue increases, not estimates. I propose to limit overall increases in the consumption budget to increases in personal income, so that the federal budget can't go up any faster than the average American's paycheck. Making Congress and the President live by this rule will cut the deficit drastically in five years, in a dramatic budget reform.

Finally, if we're serious about reinventing government, we must reinvent the way we deliver health care in this country. We spend 30 percent more than any other country on health care and do less with it. For many Americans, the rising cost of health care and the loss of it is the number one fear they face on a daily basis. Thousands of American businesses are losing jobs because health care costs are a 30 percent handicap in the global marketplace. Two-thirds of the strikes today are about health care, and no matter how they come out, both sides lose. We are the only nation in the world that doesn't help control health care costs.

We could cover every American with the money we're spending if we had the courage to demand insurance reform and slash health care bureaucracies, and if we followed the lead of other nations in controlling the unnecessary spread of technology, stopping drug prices from going up three times the rate of inflation, and forcing poeple who send bills and the people who pay them to agree on how much health care should cost. We don't need to reduce quality; we need to restructure the system. And no nation has ever done it without a national government that took the lead in controlling costs and providing health care for all.

In the first year of a Clinton Administration, Congress and I will deliver quality, affordable health care for all Americans.

These changes are vital, but American workers and American businesses are going to have to change, too; the private sector is where the jobs are created. Many of the most urgent changes cannot be legally mandated, but we know they're overdue after a decade in which the stock market tripled and average wages went down.

Old economic arrangements are holding America back. It's time for a revolution in the American workplace that will radically raise the status of the American worker and tear down the Berlin Wall between labor and management.

It's been years since the U.S. could outproduce the rest of the world by treating workers like so many cogs in a machine. We need a whole new organization of work, where workers at the front lines make decisions, not just follow orders, and entire levels of bureaucratic middle management become obsolete. And we need a new style of management, where front-line workers and managers have more responsibility to make decisions that improve quality and increase productivity.

Dynamic, flexible, well-trained workers who cooperate with savvy, sensitive managers to make changes every day are the keys to high growth in manufacturing and in the service sector, including government, education and health care, areas where productivity was very weak in the 1980s.

Everyone will have to change, but everyone will get something in return. Workers will gain new prosperity and independence, but they'll have to give up nonproductive work rules and rigid job classifications and be more open to change. Managers will reap more profits but will have to manage for the long run, train all workers and not treat themselves better than their workers are treated. Corporations will reach new heights in productivity, growth and profitability, but CEOs will have to put the long-term interests of their workers, their customers and their companies first.

We should restore the link between pay and performance by encouraging companies to provide for employee ownership, profit sharing for all employees, not just executives. And executives should profit when their companies do. We should all go up or down together. We'll say to America's corporate leaders: No more taking bonuses for yourselves if you don't give bonuses to everybody. And no more golden parachutes if you don't make good severance packages available for your workers.

It's wrong for executives to do what so many did in the '80s. Executives at the biggest companies raised their pay by four times the percentage their workers' pay went up and three times the percentage their profits went up. It's wrong to drive a company into the ground and have the boss bail out with a golden parachute to a cushy life.

The average CEO at a major American corporation is paid 85 times as much as the average worker. And our government today rewards that excess with a tax break for executive pay, no matter how high it is, or whether it reflects increased performance. If a company wants to overpay its executives to perform less well, and underinvest in the future, it shouldn't get any special treatment from Uncle Sam.

If a company wants to transfer jobs abroad and cut the security of the working people, it shouldn't get special treatment from the Treasury. In the 1980s, we didn't do enough to help our companies to compete and win a global economy. We did too much to transfer wealth away from hard-working middle-class people to the rich without good reason and too much to weaken our country with debt that wasn't invested in America. That's got to stop. There should be no more deductibility for irresponsibility.

I believe in business. I believe in the marketplace. I believe that the best jobs program this country will ever have is economic growth. Most new jobs in this country are created by small businesses and entrepreneurs who get little help from the government.

Too often, especially in this government, banks and other investors won't take a chance on good ideas and good people. I want to encourage small business people and entrepreneurs. In a Clinton Administration, we'll offer a tax incentive to those who take risks by starting new businesses and developing new technologies. Instead of offering a capital gains tax cut for the wealthy who will churn stocks on Wall Street anyway, we'll put forth a new enterprise tax cut that rewards those with the patience, the courage and the determination to create new jobs. Those who risk their savings on new businesses that create most of the jobs in the country will receive a 50 percent tax exclusion for gains held more than five years.

And I want to encourage investment here in America in other ways—by making the R&D tax credit permanent, by taking away incentives for companies to shut down their plants in the U.S. and move their jobs overseas, and by offering a targeted investment tax credit to medium- and small-size businesses who'll create new jobs with new plants and equipment.

Finally, we owe American workers, entrepreneurs and industry a pledge that all their hard work will not go down the drain.

We must have a national strategy to compete and win in the global economy. The American people aren't protectionists. Protectionism is just a fancy word for giving up; we want to compete and win. That is why our New Covenant must include a new trade policy that says to Europe, Japan and our other trading partners: We favor an open trading system, but if you won't play by those rules, we'll play by yours. That's why we need a stronger, sharper "Super 301" bill as a means to enforce that policy.

I supported fast-track negotiations with Mexico for a free trade agreement, but our negotiators need to insist upon tough conditions that prevent our trading partners from exploiting their workers or by lowering costs through pollution to gain an advantage. We should seek out similar agreements with all of Latin America, because rich countries will get richer by helping other countries grow into strong trading partners.

We also need a new energy policy to lower the trade deficit, increase productivity, and improve the environment. We must rely less on imported oil and more on cheap and abundant natural gas, and on research and development into renewable energy resources. We must achieve European standards of energy efficiency in factories and office buildings. That will free up billions of dollars to invest in the American economy.

If we want to help U.S. companies keep pace in the world economy, we need to restore America to the forefront, not just in inventing products, but in bringing them to market. Too often, we have won the battle of the patents but lost the war of creating jobs, profits and wealth. American scientists invented the microwave, the VCR, the color TV and the memory chip, and yet today the Koreans, the Japanese and other nations make most of those products.

The research and development arm of the Defense Department did a great job of developing products and taking them to production because we didn't want them produced overseas. We should launch the civilian equivalent—an agency to provide basic research for new and critical technologies and make it easier to move these ideas into the marketplace. And we can pledge right now that for every dollar we reduce the defense budget on research and development, we'll increase the civilian R&D budget by the same amount. We should commit ourselves to a transitional plan for converting from a defense to a domestic economy in a way that creates more high-wage jobs and doesn't destroy our most successful high-wage industrial base, and with it the careers of many thousands of our best scientists, engineers and workers.

We must do all these things and something more. The economic challenges we confront today are not just a matter of statistics and numbers. Behind them are real human beings and real human suffering. I have seen the pain in the faces of unemployed workers in New Hampshire, policemen in New York and Texas, computer company executives in California, middle-class people everywhere. They're all showing the same pain and worry I hear in the voices of my own people in Arkansas, including men and women I grew up with who played by the rules and now see their dreams for the future slipping away.

That's why we're offering a new radical approach to economics: Economics as if people were really important. If we offer these hard-working families no hope for the future, no solutions to their problems, no relief for their pain, then fear and insecurity will grow, and the politics of hate and division will spread. If we do not act to bring this country together in common cause to build a better future, David Duke and his kind will be able to divide and destroy our nation. Our streets will get meaner, our families will be devastated, and our very social fabric—our goodness and tolerance and decency as a people—will be torn apart.

The politics of division, which the Republicans have parlayed into the presidency, will turn on even them. George Bush has forgotten the warning of our greatest Republican President, Abraham Lincoln: A house divided against itself cannot stand. Lincoln gave his life for the American community. The Republicans have squandered his legacy.

I want to be a President who will unite this country. This morning, here at Georgetown, the Robert Kennedy Human Rights Award ceremony was held. Twenty-six years ago, when I was president of my class here, Robert Kennedy accepted our invitation to come to Georgetown to give a speech. In the following year, he gave a very different description of what American politics should be all about. And I would like to read that to you today and ask you how long it's been since you heard an American President say and believe these things:

"Each time a man stands up for an ideal or acts to improve the lot of others or strikes out against injustice, he sends forth a tiny ripple of hope, and crossing each other from a million different centers of energy and daring, those ripples build a current that can sweep down the mightiest walls of oppression and resistance."

That is the spirit I seek to bring to the Presidency. The spirit of renewal of America. I believe with all my heart that the very future of our country is on the line. That is why these are not just economic proposals. They are the way to save the very soul of our nation.

This is not just a campaign. This is a crusade to restore the forgotten middle class, give economic power back to ordinary people, and recapture the American dream. It is a crusade not just for economic renewal but for social and spiritual renewal as well. It is a crusade to build a new economic order of empowerment and opportunity that will preserve our social order and make it possible for our country once again to make the American Dream live at home and to be strong enough to triumph abroad.

A New Covenant for American Security

Georgetown University, Washington D.C. December 12, 1991

I was born nearly half a century ago at the dawn of the Cold War, a time of great change, enormous opportunity and uncertain peril. At a time when Americans wanted nothing more than to come home to resume lives of peace and quiet, our country had to summon the will for a new kind of war—containing an expansionist and hostile Soviet Union which vowed to bury us. We had to find ways to rebuild the economies of Europe and Asia, encourage a worldwide movement toward independence and vindicate our nation's principles in the world against yet another totalitarian challenge to liberal democracy.

Thanks to the unstinting courage and sacrifice of the American people, we were able to win that Cold War. Now we've entered a new era, and we need a new vision and the strength to meet a new set of opportunities and threats. We face the same challenge today that we faced in 1946—to build a world of security, freedom, democracy, free markets and growth at a time of great change.

Anyone running for President right now—Republican or Democrat—is going to have to provide a vision for security in this new era. That is what I hope to do today.

Given the problems we face at home, we do have to take care of our own people and their needs first. We need to remember the central lesson of the collapse of communism and the Soviet Union. We never defeated them on the field of battle. The Soviet Union collapsed from the inside out—from economic, political and spiritual failure.

Make no mistake: Foreign and domestic policy are inseparable in today's world. If we're not strong at home we can't lead the world we've done so much to make. And if we withdraw from the world, it will hurt us economically at home.

We can't allow this false choice between domestic policy and foreign policy to hurt our country and our economy. Our President has devoted his time and energy to foreign concerns and ignored dire problems here at home. As a result, we're drifting in the longest economic slump since World War II, and, in reaction to that, elements in both parties now want America to respond to the collapse of communism and a crippling recession at home by retreating from the world.

I have agreed with President Bush on a number of foreign policy questions. I supported his efforts to kick Saddam Hussein out of Kuwait. I think he did a masterful job in pulling together the victorious multi-lateral coalition. I support his desire to pursue peace talks in the Middle East. I agree with the President that we can't turn our back on NATO. And I supported giving the administration fast-track authority to negotiate a sound and fair free trade agreement with Mexico.

But because the President seems to favor political stability and his personal relations with foreign leaders over a coherent policy of promoting freedom, democracy and economic growth, he often does things I disagree with. For example, his close personal ties with foreign leaders helped forge the coalition against Saddam Hussein, but also led him to side with China's communist rulers after the democratic uprising of students. The President forced Iraq out of Kuwait, but as soon as the war was over, he seemed so concerned with the stability of the area that he was willing to leave the Kurds to an awful fate. He is rightfully seeking peace in the Middle East, but his urge to personally broker a deal has led him to take public positions which may undermine the ability of the Israelis and the Arabs to agree on an enduring peace.

In the aftermath of the Cold War, we need a President who recognizes that in a dynamic new era, our goal is not to resist change, but to shape it. The President must articulate a vision of where we're going. The President and his administration have yet to meet that test—to define the requirements of U.S. national security after the Cold War.

Retreating from the world or discounting its dangers is wrong for the country and sets back everything else we hope to accomplish as Democrats. The defense of freedom and the promotion of democracy around the world aren't merely a reflection of our deepest values; they are vital to our national interests. Global democracy means nations at peace with one another, open to one another's ideas and one another's commerce.

The stakes are high. The collapse of communism is not an isolated event; it's part of a worldwide march toward democracy whose outcome will shape the next century. If individual liberty, political pluralism and free enterprise take root in Latin Americam, Eastern and Central Europe, Africa, Asia, and the former Soviet Union, we can look forward to a grand new era of reduced conflict, mutual understanding and economic growth. For ourselves and for millions of people who seek to live in freedom and prosperity, this revolution must not fail.

And yet, even as the American Dream is inspiring people around the world, America is on the sidelines, a military giant crippled by economic weakness and an uncertain vision.

We face two great foreign policy challenges today. First, we must define a new national security policy that builds on freedom's victory in the Cold War. The communist idea has lost its power, but the fate of the peoples who lived under it and the fate of the world will be in doubt until stable democracies rise from the debris of the Soviet empire.

And second, we must forge a new economic policy to serve ordinary Americans by launching a new era of global growth. We must tear down the wall in our thinking between domestic and foreign policy.

We need a coherent strategy that enables us to lead the world we have done so much to make, and that supports our urgent efforts to take care of our own here at home. We cannot do one without the other.

We need a New Covenant for American security after the Cold War, a set of rights and responsibilities that will challenge the American people, American leaders and America's allies to work together to build a safer, more prosperous, more democratic world.

The strategy of the American engagement I propose is based on four key assumptions about the requirements of our security in this new era:

- First, the collapse of communism does not mean the end of danger. A new set of threats in an even less stable world will force us, even as we restructure our defenses, to keep our guard up.
- Second, America must regain its economic strength to maintain our position of global leadership. While military power will continue to be vital to our national security, its utility is declining relative to economic power. We cannot afford to go on spending too much on firepower and too little on brainpower.
- Third, the irresistible power of ideas rules in the Information Age. Television, cassette tapes and the fax machine helped ideas to pierce the Berlin Wall and bring it down.
- Finally, our definition of security must include common threats to all people. On the environment and other global issues, our very survival depends upon the United States taking the lead.

Guided by these assumptions, we must pursue three clear objectives. First, we must restructure our military forces for a new era. Second, we must work with our allies to encourage the spread and consolidation of democracy abroad. And third, we must re-establish America's economic leadership at home and in the world.

When Americans elect a President, they select a Commander-in-Chief. They want someone they can trust to act when our country's interests are threatened. To protect our interests and our values, sometimes we have to stand and fight. That is why, as President, I pledge to maintain military forces strong enough to deter and when necessary to defeat any threat to our essential interests.

Today's defense debate centers too narrowly on the size of the military budget. But the real questions are, what threats do we face, what forces do we need to counter them, and how must we change?

We can and must substantially reduce our military forces and spending, because the Soviet threat is decreasing and our allies are able to and should shoulder more of the defense burden. But we still must set the level of our defense spending based on what we need to protect our interests. First let's provide for a strong defense. Then we can talk about defense savings.

At the outset of this discussion, I want to make one thing clear: The world is still rapidly changing. The world we look out on today is not the same world we will see tomorrow. We need to be ready to adjust our defense projections to meet threats that could be either heightened or reduced down the road.

Our defense needs were clearer during the Cold War, when it was widely accepted that we needed enough forces to deter a Soviet nuclear attack, to defend against a Soviet-led conventional offensive in Europe and to protect other American interests, especially in Northeast Asia and the Persian Gulf. The collapse of the Soviet Union shattered that consensus, leaving us without a clear benchmark for determining the size or mix of our armed forces.

However, a new consensus is emerging on the nature of post-Cold War security. It assumes that the gravest threats we are most likely to face in the years ahead include:

- First, the spread of deprivation and disorder in the former Soviet Union, which could lead to armed conflict among the republics or the rise of a fervently nationalistic and aggressive regime in Russia still in possession of long-range nuclear weapons.

- Second, the spread of weapons of mass destruction, nuclear, chemical and biological, as well as the means for delivering them.
- Third, enduring tensions in various regions, especially the Korean peninsula and the Middle East and the attendant risks of terrorist attacks on Americans traveling or working overseas.
- And finally, the growing intensity of ethnic rivalry and separatist violence within national borders, such as we have seen in Yugoslavia, India and elsewhere, that could spill beyond those borders.

To deal with these new threats, we need to replace our Cold War military structure with a smaller, more flexible mix of capabilities, including:

- *Nuclear deterrence.* We can dramatically reduce our nuclear arsenals through negotiations and other reciprocal actions. But as an irreducible minimum, we must retain a survivable nuclear force to deter any conceivable threat.
- *Rapid Deployment.* We need a force capable of projecting power quickly when and where it's needed. This means the Army must develop a more mobile mix of mechanized and armored forces. The Air Force should emphasize tactical air power and airlift, and the Navy and Marine Corps must maintain sufficient carrier and amphibious forces, as well as more sealift. We also need strong special operations forces to deal with terrorist threats.
- *Technology.* The Gulf War proved that the superior training of our soldiers, tactical air power, advanced communica-

tions, space-based surveillance, and smart weaponry produced a shorter war with fewer American casualties. We
must maintain our technological edge.
- •*Better Intelligence.* In an era of unpredictable threats, our
intelligence agencies must shift from military bean counting to a more sophisticated understanding of political, economic and cultural conditions that can spark conflicts.

To achieve these capabilities, I would restructure our forces
in the following ways:

First, now that the nuclear arms race finally has reversed
course, it's time for a prudent slowdown in strategic modern-
ization. We should stop production of the B-2 bomber. That
alone could save $20 billion by 1997.

Since Ronald Reagan unveiled his "Star Wars" proposal in
1983, America has spent $26 billion in futile pursuit of a fool-
proof defense against nuclear attack. Democrats in Congress
have recommended a much more realistic and attainable goal:
defending against very limited or accidental launches of ballis-
tic missiles. This allows us to proceed with R&D on missile
defense within the framework of the ABM treaty—a prudent
step as more and more countries acquire missile technology.

At the same time, we must do more to stop the threat of
weapons of mass destruction from spreading. We need to
clamp down on countries and companies that sell these technologies, punish violators and work urgently with all countries for tough, enforceable international non-proliferation
agreements.

Although the President's plan does reduce our conventional force structure, I believe we can go farther without un-
dermining our core capabilities. We can meet our responsibilities in Europe with less than the 150,000 troops now proposed
by the President, especially as the Soviet republics withdraw
their forces from the Red Army. We can defend the sea lanes

and project force with 10 carriers rather than 12. We should continue to keep some U.S. forces in Northeast Asia as long as North Korea presents a threat to our South Korean ally.

To upgrade our conventional forces, we need to develop greater air and sea lift capacity, including production of the C-17 transport aircraft. But we should end or reduce programs intended to meet the Soviet threat. Our conventional programs, like the new Air Force fighter and the Army's new armored systems, should be redesigned to meet regional threats.

The administration has called for a 21 percent cut in military spending through 1995, based on the assumption, now obsolete, that the Soviet Union would remain intact. With the dwindling Soviet threat, we can cut defense spending by over a third by 1997.

Based on calculations by the Congressional Budget office, my plan would bring cumulative savings of about $100 billion beyond the current Bush plan. If favorable political and military trends continue, and we make progress on arms control, we may be able to scale down defense spending still more by the end of the decade. However, we should not commit ourselves now to specific deeper cuts ten years from now. The world is changing quickly, and we must retain our ability to react to potential threats.

Also, we must not forget about the real people whose lives will be turned upside down when defense is cut deeply. The government should look out for its defense workers and the communities they live in. We should insist on advanced notification and help communities plan for a transition from a defense to a domestic economy. Thirty-one percent of our graduate engineers work for the defense industry. They and other highly skilled workers and technicians are a vital national resource at a time when our technological edge in a world economy must be sharper than ever before. I have called for a new advanced research agency—a civilian DARPA (Defense Advanced Research Agency)—that could help capture for commercial work the brilliance of scientists and engineers who have accomplished wonders on the battlefield.

Likewise, those who have served the nation in uniform cannot be dumped on the job market. We've got to enlist them to help meet our many needs at home. By shifting people from active duty to the National Guard and reserves, offering early retirement options, limiting re-enlistment and slowing the pace of recruitment, we can build down our forces in a gradual way that doesn't abandon people of proven commitment and competence.

Our people in uniform are among the most highly skilled in the areas we need most. We need to transfer those human resources into our work force and even into our schools, perhaps in part by using reserve centers and closed bases for community-based education and training programs.

The defense policy I have outlined keeps America strong and still yields substantial savings. The American people have earned this peace dividend through forty years of unrelenting vigilance and sacrifice and an investment of trillions of dollars. And they are entitled to have the dividend reinvested in their future.

Finally, America needs to reach a new agreement with our allies for sharing the costs and risks of maintaining peace. While Desert Storm set a useful precedent for cost-sharing, our forces still did most of the fighting and dying. We need to shift that burden to a wider coalition of nations of which America will be a part. In the Persian Gulf, in Namibia, in Cambodia and elsewhere in recent years, the United Nations has begun to play the role that Franklin Roosevelt and Harry Truman envisioned for it. We must take the lead now in making their vision real—by expanding the Security Council and making Germany and Japan permanent members; by continuing to press for greater efficiency in U.N. administration, and by exploring ways to institutionalize the U.N.'s success in mobilizing international participation in Desert Storm.

One proposal worth exploring calls for a U.N. Rapid Deployment Force that could be used for purposes beyond traditional peacekeeping, such as standing guard at the borders of countries threatened by aggression; preventing attacks on civilians; providing humanitarian relief, and combating terrorism and drug trafficking.

In Europe, new security arrangements will evolve over the next decade. While insisting on a fairer sharing of the common defense burden, we must not turn our back on NATO. Until a more effective security system emerges, we must give our allies no reason to doubt our constancy.

As we restructure our military forces, we must reinforce the powerful global movement toward democracy.

U.S. foreign policy cannot be divorced from the moral principles most Americans share. We cannot disregard how other governments treat their own people, whether their domestic institutions are democratic or repressive, whether they help encourage or check illegal conduct beyond their borders. This does not mean we should deal only with democracies or that we should try to remake the world in our image. But recent experience in Panama to Iran to Iraq shows the dangers of forging strategic relationships with despotic regimes.

It should matter to us how others govern themselves. Democracies don't go to war with each other. The French and British have nuclear weapons, but we don't fear annihilation at their hands. Democracies don't sponsor terrorist acts against each other. They are more likely to be reliable trading partners, protect the global environment and abide by international law.

Over time, democracy is a stabilizing force. It provides non-violent means for resolving disputes. Democracies do a better job of protecting ethnic, religious and other minorities. And elections can help resolve fratricidal civil wars.

Yet President Bush too often has hesitated when democratic forces needed our support in challenging the status quo. I believe the President erred when he secretly rushed envoys to resume cordial relations with China barely a month after the massacre in Tiananmen Square; when he spurned Yeltsin before the Moscow coup; when he poured cold water on the Baltic and Ukrainian aspirations for self-determination and independence, and when he initially refused to help the Kurds.

The administration continues to coddle China, despite its continuing crackdown on democratic reforms, its brutal subjugation of Tibet, its irresponsible exports of nuclear and missile technology, its support for the homicidal Khmer Rouge in Cambodia, and its abusive trade practices. Such forbearance on our part might have made sense during the Cold War, when China was a counterweight to Soviet power. But it makes no sense to play the China card now, when our opponents have thrown in their hand.

In the Middle East, the administration deserves credit for bringing Israel and its Arab antagonists to the negotiating table. Yet I believe the President is wrong to use public pressure tactics against Israel. In the process, he has raised Arab expectations that he'll deliver Israeli concessions and fed Israeli fears that its interests will be sacrificed to an American-imposed solution.

We must remember that even if the Arab-Israeli dispute were resolved tomorrow, there would still be ample causes of conflict in the Middle East: Ancient tribal, ethnic and religious hatreds; control of oil and water; the bitterness of the have-nots toward those who have; the lack of democratic institutions to hold leaders accountable to their people and restrain their actions abroad, and the territorial ambitions of Iraq and Syria. We have paid a terrible price for the administration's earlier policies of deference to Saddam Hussein. Today, we must deal with Hafez Assad in Syria, but we must not overlook his tyrannical rule and domination of Lebanon.

We need a broader policy toward the Middle East that seeks to limit the flow of arms into the region, as well as the materials needed to develop and deliver weapons of mass destruction; promotes democracy and human rights, and preserves our strategic relationship with the one democracy in the region: Israel.

And in Africa as well, we must align America with the rising tide of democracy. The administration has claimed credit for the historic opening to democracy now being negotiated in South Africa, when in fact it resisted the sanctions policy that helped make this hopeful moment possible.

Today, we should concentrate our attention on doing what we can to help end the violence that has ravaged the South African townships, by supporting with our aid the local structures that seek to mediate these disputes and by insisting that the South African government show the same zeal in prosecuting the perpetrators of the violence as it did in the past when pursuing the leaders of the anti-apartheid movement. The administration and our states and cities should only relax our remaining sanctions as it becomes clearer that the day of democracy and guaranteed individual rights is at hand. And when that day does dawn, we must be prepared to extend our assistance to make sure that democracy, once gained, is not lost there.

An American foreign policy of engagement for democracy will unite our interests and values. Here's what we should do:

First, we need to respond more forcefully to one of the greatest security challenges of our time, to help the people of the former Soviet empire demilitarize their societies and build free political and economic institutions. Congress has passed $500 million to help the Soviets destroy nuclear weapons, and for humanitarian aid. We can do better. As Sen. Sam Nunn and Rep. Les Aspin have argued, we should shift money from marginal military programs to this key investment in our future security. We can radically reduce the threat of nuclear destruction that has dogged us for decades by investing a fraction of what would otherwise have to be spent to counter that threat. And, together with our G-7 partners, we can supply the Soviet republics with the food and medical aid they need to survive their first winter of freedom in 74 years. We should do all that we can to coordinate aid efforts with our allies, and to provide the best technical assistance we can to distribute that food and aid.

No national security issue is more urgent than the question of who will control the nuclear weapons and technology of the former Soviet empire. Those weapons pose a threat to the security of every American, to our allies, and to the republics themselves.

I know it may be bad politics to be for any aid program. But we owe it to the people who defeated communism, the people who defeated the coup. And we owe it to ourselves. A small amount spent stabilizing the emerging democracies in the former Soviet empire today will reduce by much more the money we may have to commit to our defense in the future. And it will lead to the creation of lucrative new markets which mean new American jobs. Having won the Cold War, we must not now lose the peace.

We should recognize Ukraine's independence, as well as that of other republics who make that decision democratically. But we should link U.S. and western non-humanitarian aid to agreements by the republics to abide by all arms agreements negotiated by Soviet authorities, demonstrate responsibility with regard to nuclear weapons, demilitarize their economies, respect minority rights, and proceed with market and political reforms.

We should use our diplomatic and economic leverage to increase the material incentives to democratize and raise the costs for those who won't. We have every right to condition our foreign aid and debt relief policies on demonstrable progress toward democracy and market reforms. In extreme cases, such as that of China, we should condition favorable trade terms on political liberalization and responsible international conduct.

We need to support evolving institutional structures favorable to countries struggling with the transition to democracy and markets, such as the new European Bank for Reconstruction and Development, whose mission is to rebuild the societies of Central and Eastern Europe. We are right to encourage the European Community to open its doors to these societies, perhaps by creating an affiliate status that carries some but not all of the privileges of membership.

We should encourage private American investment in the former Soviet empire. The Soviet republics, after all, are rich in human and natural resources. One day, they and Eastern Europe could be lucrative markets for us.

We should regard increased funding for democratic assistance as a legitimate part of our national security budget. We should support groups, like the National Endowment for Democracy, which work openly rather than covertly to promote domestic pluralism and free markets abroad. I would encourage both the Agency for International Development and the U.S. Information Agency to channel more of their resources to promoting democracy. And just as Radio Free Europe and the Voice of America helped bring the truth to the people of those societies, we should create a Radio Free Asia to carry news and hope to China and elsewhere.

Finally, just as President Kennedy launched the Peace Corps 30 years ago, we should create a Democracy Corps today that will send thousands of talented American volunteers to countries that need their legal, financial and political expertise.

Our second major strategic challenge is to help lead the world into a new era of global growth. Any governor who's tried to create jobs over the last decade knows that experience in international economics is essential and that success in the global economy must be at the core of national security in the 1990s.

Without growth abroad, our own economy cannot thrive. U.S. exports of goods and services will be over a half trillion dollars in 1991—and 10 percent of our economy. Without global growth, healthy international competition turns all too readily to economic warfare. Without growth and economic progress, there can be no true economic justice among or within nations.

I believe the negotiations on an open trading system in the GATT (General Agreement of Tariffs and Trade are of extraordinary importance. And I support the negotiation of a North American Free Trade Agreement, so long as it's fair to American farmers and workers, protects the environment, and observes decent labor standards.

Freer trade abroad means more jobs at home. Every $1 billion in U.S. exports generates 20,000 to 30,000 more jobs. We must find ways to help developing nations finally overcome their debt crisis, which has lessened their capacity to buy American goods and probably cost us 1.5 million American jobs.

We must be strong at home to lead and maintain global growth. Our weakness at home has caused even our economic competitors to worry about our stubborn refusal to establish a national economic strategy that will regain our economic leadership and restore opportunity for the middle class.

How can we lead when we have gone from being the world's largest creditor country to the world's largest debtor nation—now owing the world $405 billion? When we depend on foreigners for $100 billion a year of financing, we're not the masters of our own destiny.

I spoke in my last lecture about how we must rebuild our nation's economic greatness, for the job of restoring America's competitive edge truly begins at home. I have offered a program to build the most well-educated and well-trained work force in the world and put our national budget to work on programs that make America richer, not more indebted.

Our economic strength must become a central defining element of our national security policy. We must organize to compete and win in the global economy. We need a commitment from American business and labor to work together to make world-class products. We must be prepared to exchange some short-term benefits—whether in the quarterly profit statement or in archaic work rules—for long-term success.

The private sector must maintain the initiative, but government has an indispensable role. A recent Department of Commerce report is a wake-up call that we are falling behind our major competitors in Europe and Japan on emerging technologies that will define the high-paying jobs of the future—like advanced materials, biotechnology, superconductors and computer-integrated manufacturing.

I have mentioned a civilian advanced research projects agency to work closely with the private sector, so that its priorities are not set by government alone. We have hundreds of national laboratories with extraordinary talent that have put the United States at the forefront of military technology. We need to reorient their mission, working with private companies and universities to advance technologies that will make our lives better and create tomorrow's jobs.

Not enough of our companies engage in export—just 15 percent of our companies account for 85 percent of our exports. We have to meet our competitors' efforts to help small-and medium-sized businesses identify and gain foreign markets.

And most important, government must assure that international competition is fair by insisting to our European, Japanese and other trading partners that if they won't play by the rules of an open trading system, then we will not play by theirs.

We have no more important bilateral relationships than our alliance with Japan, a relationship that has matured from one of dependency in the 1950s to one of partnership today. Our relationship is based on ties of democracy, but as we cooperate, we also compete. And the maturity of our relationship allows American Presidents, as I will, to insist on fair play. As we put our own economic house in order, Japan must open the doors of its economic house, or our partnership will be imperiled with consequences for all the world.

Now we must understand, as we never have before, that our national security is largely economic. The success of our engagement in the world depends not on the headlines it brings to Washington politicians, but on the benefits it brings to hard-working middle-class Americans. Our "foreign" policies are not really foreign at all.

When greenhouse gas emissions from developed nations warm the atmosphere and CFCs eat away at the ozone layer, our beaches and farmlands and people are threatened. When drugs flood into our country from South America and Asia, our cities suffer and our children are put at risk. When a Libyan terrorist can go to an airport in Europe and check a bomb in a suitcase that kills hundreds of people, our freedom is diminished and our people live in fear.

So let us no longer define national security in the narrow military terms of the Cold War. We can no longer afford to have foreign and domestic policies. We must devise and pursue national policies that serve the needs of our people by uniting us at home and restoring America's greatness in the world. To lead abroad, a President of the United States must first lead at home.

Half a century ago, this country emerged victorious from an all-consuming war into a new era of great challenge. It was a time of change, a time for new thinking, a time for working together to build a free and prosperous world, a time for putting that war behind us. In the aftermath of that war, President Harry Truman and his successors forged a bipartisan consensus in America that brought security and prosperity for 20 years.

Today we need a President, a public, and a policy that are not caught up in the wars of the past—not World War II, not Vietnam, not the Cold War. What we need to elect in 1992 is not the last President of the 20th century but the first President of the 21st century.

This spring, when the troops came home from the Persian Gulf, we had over 100,000 people at a welcome-home parade in Little Rock. Veterans came from all across the state—not just those who had just returned from the Gulf, but men and women who had served in World War II, Korea and Vietnam. I'll never forget how moved I was as I watched them march down the street to our cheers and saw the Vietnam veterans finally being given the honor they deserved all along. The divisions we have lived with for the last two decades seemed to fade away amid the common outburst of triumph and gratitude.

That is the spirit we need as we move into this new era. As President Lincoln told Congress in another time of new challenge, in 1862:

"The dogmas of the quiet past are inadequate to the stormy present. The occasion is piled high with difficulty, and we must rise to the occasion. As our case is new, so we must think anew, and act anew. We must disenthrall ourselves, and then we shall save our country. Fellow citizens, we cannot escape history."

Thank you very much.